STO

ROBERT
ME

NEW WORK OPPORTUNITIES FOR OLDER AMERICANS

PRENTICE HALL
Englewood Cliffs, New Jersey 07632

J

Prentice-Hall International (UK) Limited, *London*
Prentice-Hall of Australia Pty. Limited, *Sydney*
Prentice-Hall Canada, Inc., *Toronto*
Prentice-Hall Hispanoamericana, S.A., *Mexico*
Prentice-Hall of India Private Limited, *New Delhi*
Prentice-Hall of Japan, Inc., *Tokyo*
Simon & Schuster Asia Pte. Ltd., *Singapore*
Editora Prentice-Hall do Brasil, Ltda., *Rio de Janeiro*

©1993 *by*
PRENTICE-HALL, Inc.
Englewood Cliffs, NJ

10 9 8 7 6 5 4 3 2 1

Library of Congress Cataloging-in-Publication Data

Menchin, Robert S.
    New work opportunities for older Americans /
Robert S. Menchin.
        p. cm.
    Includes index.
    ISBN 0-13-370016-X
    1. Aged—Employment—United States. 2. Age and
employment—United States. 3. Reirees—Employment
—United States. 4. Aged volunteers—United States.
I. Title.
HD6280.M376 1993   93-4455
331.3'98'0973—dc20   CIP

ISBN 0-13-370016-X

PRENTICE HALL
Career and Personal Development
Englewood Cliffs, NJ 07632

Simon & Schuster, A Paramount Communications Company

Printed in the United States of America

For Marylin, Jonathan and Scott

ACKNOWLEDGMENT

A book of this kind is produced through interaction with lots of people. When they learned the subject of the book, they came forward with great enthusiasm to tell me about their experiences and involvement with work at a later age. I benefited from the cooperation of professionals with credentials that measured a full inch after their name and others whose only credentials were gray hair, some well-earned wrinkles, and a paycheck.

It is important that I acknowledge the help of the many organizations researching and disseminating information and promoting work opportunities for older Americans. They include:

> *The Commonwealth Fund* and its "Americans over 55 at Work" program. The goal of this program is to increase the number of older Americans in paid employment by expanding the employment opportunities for such workers throughout the economy.

The American Association of Retired Persons. The many useful services that AARP provides its 32 million (!) members include its Worker Equity Initiative and the AARP Volunteer Talent Bank.

The National Council on the Aging. Two units of the NCOA, The National Association of Older Worker Employment Services and The National Center for Voluntary Leadership in Aging, have been particularly active in helping older Americans find work.

Operation ABLE, a not-for-profit agency whose mission is to provide employment opportunities for older adults. It is the model for similar organizations in Arkansas, Nebraska, and Vermont and in metropolitan areas throughout the nation.

My thanks too, to some very special people:

Mike Snell, The Michael Snell Literary Agency

Dan Lacey, editor of "Workplace Trends Newsletter," author of "The Paycheck Disruption," and several other books on work-related issues

David M. Mitchell, associate area representative for Worker Equity, American Association of Retired Persons (AARP)

John Allen, JD, Allen-Warren Inc.

Leonard J. Hansen, mature-market consultant

Lawrence Kamisher, Lawrence Executive Search

Carallee Kern, executive director, National Association for the Cottage Industry

Paul LaPorte, U.S. Department of Labor, Bureau of Labor Statistics

John Mazor, senior communication specialist, American Pilots Association

Kenneth Edwards, Your Own Business Inc.

James E. Eden, Marriott Corporation

Wilbert F. Solomon, chief, Division of Older Worker Programs, U.S. Department of Labor

Joe Vangsness, computer consultant

Ken Plonski, Del Webb Corporation

David Savageau, Place Rated Partnership

Margaret E. Mahoney, president, The Commonwealth Fund

Mark Fagin, director, Center for Economic Development and Business Research, Jacksonville, Alabama

My thanks to them, to my son Jonathan for his help in editing the book, and to Marylin and Scott for being there.

TABLE OF CONTENTS

INTRODUCTION

Common wisdom would have us believe that people in their teens and twenties are "all mixed up" and floundering while mature adults have it all together. In truth, the young are not the only ones who feel lost. I find many of my contemporaries, in their mid-fifties and older, confused and searching. They feel unproductive and left behind and are looking for ways to structure their days and establish goals for their later years.

Every day, men and women who scrimped and saved for retirement find that it's not all it was cracked up to be. They have been sold a bill of goods by people with a vested interest in "golden acres" and all that it represents—people who sell golf equipment, market retirement developments, and promote luxury cruises to "the mature market." Despite the luxuries and the senior playgrounds called "retirement developments," many older men and women still feel that something central to their life is missing. So often the satisfaction that mature adults are seeking can be found in work, but having worked so hard to afford the absence of work, they cling to the idea of endless leisure as paradise, wondering why it doesn't make them happy. The posed smiles of seniors in the retirement-village brochure cannot match the satisfaction and dignity of a job well done.

Although many of my retired contemporaries are happy with their lives of leisure and new-found freedom, a substantial number—at least one in four—*want to work*. Mature men and women thrive when they are able to combine productive activity with an easier, post-retirement lifestyle, but too often they remain idle simply because they are unaware of the many new and emerging work opportunities available to them. In the current economic slump, with unemployment reaching record highs, they are discouraged from looking for work because they believe that their age disqualifies them and that there is no job for them out there.

If you are one of "them," this book can help correct that false assumption and alert you to the growing need for your skills, experience, and mature judgment. The first chapter explains why and how you now have a second chance. Chapter Two talks money—in view of the Social Security penalties on earned income over a certain amount, does it pay to work? Chapter Three probes the psychological and social reasons for working. It says that work can be the most important element in achieving satisfaction in the later years. And that, when health and circumstances allow, older men and women should pursue work, whether the income from work is needed or not.

The fourth and fifth chapters provide specific examples of new work opportunities for you and for other mature individuals who treasure their independence and want to keep working.

Chapter Six tells you how to use the law to fight back whenever and wherever age discrimination rears its ugly head. Chapters Seven and Eight provide job-hunting strategies specifically for mature men and women, while Chapter Nine focuses on work opportunities for the older woman. More and more Americans have chosen the entrepreneurial route to success, and Chapter Ten discusses the pros and cons of business ownership in the later years. Chapter Eleven covers volunteer work opportunities A to Z in the United States and abroad.

Your most powerful allies in your search for work are the government and private organizations and support groups that help older individuals find their niche in the workplace. The twelfth and final chapter contains an annotated roster of the largest and most effective of these organizations.

A skills shortage in vital areas of our economy threatens America's ability to compete in global markets. Although the shift from heavy industry and agriculture to an information and services society has increased the need for a more highly skilled, technically adept work force, our educational system has not caught up with the shifts. It doesn't provide new workers with the technical skills to fill today's jobs. With the loss of skilled, experienced workers to early retirement, the problem takes on even greater urgency.

We can alleviate the "skills drain" by improving the education and training of new entrants and making it more relevant to the needs of the work place and by allowing more skilled immigrants into the country. But another solution to the shortage of skilled labor has been largely ignored. It is a solution close at hand and carries benefits to the nation and a large number of its people: put the skill, experience, and energy of our older men and women to work.

The large number of Americans age 55 and over represents a valuable, but underutilized resource. Three major groups share the blame:

1. Employers who have bought the myths about older workers being unproductive and costly.

2. Social Security, which has built disincentives to work into the system. Seniors forfeit retirement benefits on earnings over a certain amount and pay taxes that together add up to marginal tax rates of 50 percent and higher.

3. Finally, and most significant, older adults themselves must share the blame. They have allowed themselves to be seduced into retirement, early and otherwise, and have resigned themselves to the "over the hill" status that society has assigned to them.

I started to write this book because I believe strongly in the benefits of work in the later years. This opinion, which formed the premise of the book was, frankly, based on personal preference. As I went about delving into the subject and talking to older Americans and professionals on aging, my opinion was not only confirmed, it was strengthened. I found myself a strong advocate, and the book became a mission.

Everything I read, everybody that I talked to, validated my belief in the importance of work to the physical and mental health of older men and women. To my intuition and personal attitude on the matter, they added tangible evidence and examples based on personal experience. They urged me to tell employers who haven't yet gotten the message why it makes good business sense to recruit, hire, and retain older workers and to tell older workers about the benefits of work in the later years.

Sigmund Freud explained the positive correlation between work and mental health when he wrote, "No other technique for the conduct of life attaches the individual so firmly to reality as laying emphasis on work; for his work at least gives him a secure place in a portion of reality, in the human community."

There are basic human needs that only work can provide, whether that work is salaried employment, self-employment, small-business ownership, or unpaid volunteer service. The important thing is the work itself.

The stories and comments of the real people mentioned in this book inspire and instruct. In order to maintain their privacy some of the names have been changed, but their voices carry the ring of truth.

At what age does one become an "older worker"?

In my previous book, *The Mature Market*, I wrote about an organization called "The 35+ Committee," a New York–based organization that conducts demographic media research on the radio-listening patterns of different segments of the population. Radio listeners are typically very young. For this group, radio listeners *35 and over represent the mature market!*

The Department of Labor classifies individuals as "older workers" when they reach their fortieth birthday. A highly respected self-help group for unemployed professionals confirms this boundary by calling itself "Forty Plus."

So, at age 40 one becomes an "older worker"? Not quite.

Title V of the Older Americans Act makes job opportunities available to persons 55 and older, thus redefining "old."

Social Security benefits become available to early retirees at age 62, but in order to collect the full base amount of benefits you have to be 65. Even so, if your earnings from work exceed a certain amount you have to give back a significant part of your earnings. Until age 70. From 70 on you can earn any amount from work and keep it all.

This runs a 35-year span of older-American categories, from ages 35 to 70, making it difficult, if not impossible, to focus on a single image of "old."

To people in their twenties and thirties, 50 is "old." To a man celebrating his eightieth birthday, 50 is "young." In

Disneyland, 55 is "old." A few miles to the south, in St. Petersburg, Florida, 65 is "young." Bernard Baruch summed up the relativity of age when he said "To me, old age is 15 years older than I am."

This book was started when the country was in the throes of a quick Desert Storm victory and when economists were talking labor shortages. It was completed during a period of economic difficulty and high unemployment. The overriding issue in the 1992 election was clearly stated: Jobs. Jobs. Jobs.

If young and middle-aged people were unable to find work, what chance was there for the men and women in their mid-fifties and older? No wonder so many "discouraged" older workers simply stopped looking. Much of the discouragement of older adults results from a lack of knowledge about new and emerging work opportunities particularly suited to their wants and needs at this stage of their lives. This book is just one of a large number of initiatives designed to raise the awareness level of older adults and to tell them that this is a good time for older job seekers. Despite the recession and the job drought, there are numerous opportunities, options, and alternatives for work-seeking men and women in all the stages of their mature years and with different reasons for seeking work.

- Men and women making a midlife change in career
- Early retirees
- Older retirees
- Laid-off, otherwise unemployed workers age 55 and older
- Mature homemakers and housewives who haven't worked outside the home before—or who worked earlier in life and want to return to work after many years

The great differences in attitude toward work within the mature population is no different from the attitude about work among the young and middle-aged. Some "thank God it's Friday," and others look forward to Monday morning. This book carries a message to older adults who want to work, or need to work, or both: You survived the Great Depression of the thirties and lived through World War II. You witnessed the birth of nuclear warfare and nuclear energy and wars in Korea and Vietnam. You were here when television and the computer age began. You saw the beginning and are still here at the end of the Cold War and the death of Communism. During your life they put a man on the moon. Having lived through the most dynamic years of crisis and change in history, you've learned to adapt and survive.

You are the kind of employee that good companies want. You have every reason to look forward to Monday morning.

Robert S. Menchin
Chicago, Illinois

It is one of life's laws
that as soon as one door closes,
another one opens
but too often we look
at the closed door
and disregard the open one.

■ ■ ■

—Andre Gide (1869–1951)

This book is about open doors.

CHAPTER ONE

SECOND CHANCE

Retired is being tired twice, I've thought,
First tired of working,
Then tired of not.

— Richard Armour

Retiring after 25 years as a bank loan officer in San Diego, my friend Frank Lewis looked forward to finally indulging his great love of sailing. But sailing every day, day in and day out, soon began to pall. It was certainly not what he expected. When I asked him what he missed most by not working he said, "I miss the weekends."

One year and one month after the retirement party and the gold watch, Frank did what so many other older Americans want to do—he retired from retirement. Fed up with the boredom and tedium of full-time leisure, he took up a new challenge in a new field and in a new place. He's now teaching elementary school in a Seattle suburb, looking forward to sailing on the weekends and enjoying it more than ever.

Sailing, fishing, gardening, golf, and other greatly anticipated pleasures can be a drag as a full-time occupation. Frank's story, one of many, is echoed by men and women across the country who found retirement a false paradise and are seeking ways to get back to work.

Some move to a new line of work and find the change rejuvenating; others want to stay in their own field but with a different work schedule. Nine-to-fivers shift to part-time, skilled technicians take up job-sharing, professionals use computers and networking technology to work at home, Northerners find work in the Sunbelt, salaried workers become self-employed free lancers, and executives hang out their shingles as consultants. Freed from dependence on the weekly paycheck, many older men and women start a small business. Others, financially secure and with less need for income, are drawn to public service and volunteer work. The possibilities are limited only by your imagination.

In the eighties, while many of us were middle-aged and working at our career jobs in our so-called prime working years, the economic upheavals of corporate restructuring, leveraged buyouts, divestiture and downsizing changed the outlook for job seekers. In a single decade almost ten million manufacturing jobs were wiped out and more than three million managers were laid off. This continued into the nineties, with high-wage full-time jobs disappearing in record numbers. The labor shortage of the early eighties turned into a job drought in the early nineties. Although this made it tougher to find work, changes in the work place and new "Information Age" technology have created opportunities that enabled older Americans to combine work and leisure in ways that were not possible before. Rather than hiring full-time employees with fixed salaries and benefits, companies developed large contingency forces of part-timers, independent contractors, free lancers, and other flexible-hours workers—an arrangement that fits nicely with the lifestyle and work preference of many mature men and women.

The Conference Board, a New York-based research organization, estimates that there are 35 million such contingency workers, and the number is expected to grow.

SUN CITY

At 5:30 A.M. every weekday morning, Sylvia Glover, a resident of Del Webb's Sun City in Tucson, wakes up. She dresses in a business suit, just as she did for 12 years when she was the school librarian in Bloomfield Hills, Michigan.

She walks from her house in the adults' community where she lives, passing a hubbub of activity already underway at the Social Center: woodworking groups, swimming lessons, and the mixed chorus warming up. Along the way she waves to her happily retired neighbors on the golf course and the bocci courts. A quarter of an hour later she arrives at work. Now eight months past her sixty-first birthday, Sylvia spends 40 hours a week, 52 weeks a year as a PBX operator at the bustling Sun City sales office. Her explanation is simple enough: "I don't play golf. I don't play bridge. I just love to work."

Sylvia, who holds a bachelor's degree in English education and a master's degree in library sciences, worked for *Arizona Highways* magazine for 3½ years and is now a permanent full-time employee at Sun City, Tucson. She says, "I'm not in the career mode anymore, but I still enjoy working."

Sylvia Glover is one of a large and growing number of mature adults who are changing their expectations and their view of retirement. People are living longer, and the generation of men and women in their mid-fifties-and-older are healthier, more active, and more capable of productivity than in any earlier period in our history.

Contrary to general perception, retirement is not an abrupt event, and the end of career employment does not automatically lead to immediate work stoppage. Typically, older workers leave the work force gradually as they go from career employment to one or more post-career "bridge" jobs or to self-employment before they stop work completely. Bridge jobs and self-employment are usually referred to as "post-retirement work," and people who hold such work are considered "semiretired." Neither is an accurate label since retirement means stopping work completely and many older men and women continue long and hard at other work after they leave their career employment.

Nearly 6 in 10 workers leave career employment before age 60, 71 percent do so by age 62, the first age of eligibility for Social Security benefits. Fewer than 10 percent remain in career positions until the traditional retirement age of 65. A study of post-career work experience of recent generations of older Americans shows the most recent retirees engaging in more post-career work.

Generally, workers shift to some form of bridge employment for many years before full and final retirement. According to the Employee Benefit Research Institute, more than one third of workers continue to work for 10 years or more after leaving their career employment.

Labor force participation rates for men in the United States at ages 60–64 (2.6 million) are significantly higher than they are in Italy, France, or West Germany. For females at ages 60–64 U.S. labor participation rates are higher than in any other developed country, except Japan and Sweden. Although the U.S. population's retirement pattern is about average for the developed world, a large number of older Americans are at work. In 1991 there were 125 million Americans in the labor force. Of these, 11.7 million were 55 to 64 years of age and 3.5 million were 65 and over. Some mature adults, particularly those whose career positions end when they are relatively young, move into other work. A substantial number move into some form of reduced work commitment—a job with less stress or responsibility and fewer hours of work.

According to a study by the Employee Benefit Research Institute, "Partial retirement is rare among persons under age 62, increases rapidly between ages 62 and age 67, and then gradually declines. At the peak age (66–67), one-fifth of all workers are partially retired, and at least 45 percent of all workers partially retire at some point in their working lives."

Percentage of Workers Partially Retired at Given Ages

	60–61	62–63	64–65	66–67	68–69	70–71
All workers	7.8%	13.0%	18.2%	20.3%	18.6%	16.4%
Males	7.0	12.6	18.2	21.1	19.4	17.7
Females	10.9	14.7	18.0	17.2	16.0	12.2

(Source: Based on data in "Bridge Jobs and Partial Retirement," *Journal of Labor Economics*, which uses data from a U.S. Department of Health and Human Services survey.)

Americans are more likely to work after age 65 than are older people in other developed countries—with the exception of the Japanese. Japan's labor-force participation after age 65 is unusually high. Nearly half of the men and one sixth of the women are still working. Is the large number of older persons in that country's work force and Japan's remarkable production record merely coincidental, or is it telling us something significant about the value of older men and women in the workplace?

Why you want to work

Income is the reason most older adults and retirees give for wanting to work. For many, work is a financial necessity. For others, who receive Social Security and possibly pensions and income from savings and investments, the money is a kind of bonus. It allows them to live better.

Although working is particularly important for those under 62 who are not yet eligible for Social Security benefits and Medicare health insurance, money is a major consideration in the to-work-or-not-to-work decision of most older adults. Declining interest rates have reduced the income of seniors living on the yield from their savings accounts and CDs. At the same time, inflation, while slowed in recent years, continues to chip away at the amount of groceries a dollar can buy. The soaring cost of health care hits seniors harder than any other age group, and income from employment makes it easier to keep up with the high cost of getting old.

Employment income can lift your retirement lifestyle from "just getting by" to "living well." Even if you are well-to-do, you can't help but appreciate the cushion that income from work provides. A paycheck means that you don't have to take a bite out of your nest egg every time you make a purchase. It means you don't have to worry about money and can afford the extras that make life a little nicer.

The worst of work nowadays
is what happens to people
when they cease work.

■ ■ ■

—G.K. Chesterton

Many Americans will spend nearly as many years in retirement as they spend in the work force. In choosing to work after retirement, individuals generally base their decision on some combination of needs and wants, balancing financial realities with personal interests. After a lifetime of productive labor, retirement means freedom—freedom, at last—to spend your time as your wish. But freedom without the money to afford the good things of life is more like house arrest. Work provides the money to enjoy the periods of leisure to their fullest. And something more: Work in the later years provides a second chance for involvement in the mainstream of American life.

Expected Number of Years After Retirement*

Expected Retirement Age	For an Individual	For Couple Same Age
55	28 years	34 years
60	24 years	30 years
65	20 years	25 years
70	16 years	21 years
75	12 years	16 years

* Based on Internal Revenue Service life-expectancy tables.

Older adults work during their later years for the money and for other reasons. I am convinced that it is the "other reasons" that keep men and women on the job or running their own small businesses well into their later years. The nonfinancial benefits of work come in many forms: *Identity; Prestige; Self-esteem; Mental stimulation; Involvement and interaction with others.* And with different priorities for different people.

You don't have to be a workaholic to miss productive employment. In his book *The Sky's The Limit* Dr. Wayne Dyer says that everyone needs to be productive: "The feeling of being useful, of creatively making a difference, of pursuing some task and carrying it out to completion is crucial. These are basic needs."

A job is often the central organizing factor in your life. Over the years it has provided you with a structure, a daily routine. Complete retirement changes the patterns of a lifetime.

Employment Status of Americans 55-and-Over

Working Full Time	9.9 million
Working Part Time	4.4
Not Working	
Of which, those not wanting to work	26.4 million
Those unable to work	6.3
Those willing and able to work	5.4

—The Commonwealth Fund

THE SEEKERS

Among the mature adults who want to work are:

■ The laid off and unemployed victims of cutbacks and "downsizing" and former employees of shut-down factories, closed-up offices, and failed retail establishments

- Women who want to enter or return to the work force after many years as housewife and mother
- And retirees who miss the work and want the income

Many retirees, unhappy with retirement and eager to return to work, have been discouraged from rejoining the labor force because of the tough competition for available jobs. We have good news for you. The work place is changing, and attitudes toward older workers are becoming more realistic. As employers continue to "downsize," they have filled the gap by creating the kinds of "bridge jobs" that most older adults want—part-time jobs, "temp"jobs, seasonal work, and home-based jobs. Older workers willing to adapt to the new demands of today's work place will find numerous work opportunities.

THIRD AGE ADULTS

Historically, Americans have been viewed as moving through two active periods of life before retirement. The first is youth and adolescence, which ends at maturity when the young man or woman graduates from high school or college. The second is the age of work, which ends with retirement, a time for leisure, comfort, and rest. Many older adults refuse to accept this demarcation. They are part of the Third Age movement, a French term created in June 1973 as Les Universités du Troisieme Age. The Third Age, as defined by the French university, describes retirement as the time to reach out for personal fulfillment, take up new skills, and seek out new cultural horizons.

This concept is echoed in Richard Bolles' classic book *The Three Boxes of Life*. Bolles contends that these three boxed-in periods—getting an education, going to work to earn a living, and living in retirement—is at best limiting and at worst damaging. He says that a balanced, dynamic, and productive life should include a lifelong flow that incorporates all three elements concurrently.

Whether you consider yourself a member of the Third Age or an adventurer ready to break out of Bolles' boxes of life, returning to work after being formally retired from long-term career employment enables you to start an active, new stage of life.

You join million of other older Americans seeking new jobs, starting new businesses, and finding new ways to serve as a volunteer in your community.

10 Reasons Why People Retire Early

1. Can afford to do so
2. Hate their job
3. Cash incentives and "sweetened" retirement benefits
4. Pressure from employer and other workers
5. Layoffs, plant closings, company "downsizing"
6. Reached career plateau, and promotion opportunities cease
7. Poor health
8. Seek work with shorter hours
9. Other plans for use of time (travel, starting a business, greater involvement in hobbies and recreation, caregiving, etc.)
10. Interests and preference of spouse

Malcolm Morrison, the director of the Office of Vocational Rehabilitation at the Social Security Administration and an expert on retirement and age discrimination in employment, says that today's early retirement pattern does not preclude productive roles later in life. "On the contrary," he writes in an article in the *Journal of the American Academy of Arts and Sciences*, "the opportunity to 'retire' relatively early from a long-term job creates a choice for mature persons about whether and how to continue productive social participation. Although many barriers still exist—particularly the lack of cultural norms and defined roles for post-retirement life—early 'retirement' may actually stimulate *more* productive activity in older age."

EARLY RETIREMENT

The arbitrary age 65 is used by the Social Security Administration as the age at which it pays full benefits. The government's decision to pay full Social Security benefits at age 65 derives from the forced retirement age determined by German Chancellor Otto von Bismarck in 1889. The good Chancellor could be so generous with Germany's social welfare system because few people lived long enough then to collect their government pension.

The decision to declare 65 the retirement age was made at a time when life expectancy was 41.7 years for males and 43.5 years for females. *If a new calculation were made today, using a similar logic, then retirement from work would start somewhere between age 95 and 100.* Retirement at age 65 is founded on outdated assumptions that link the ability to work to a specific age. In a paper on the employment of older adults, the American Medical Association has argued for moving up the mandatory retirement age because of the lengthened life span. The AMA takes the position that increased life expectancy is of little value to a vital worker if, at an arbitrary age, he or she is denied the right to work and produce.

Retirement, as a condition available to the general population, is a relatively new phenomenon. Earlier in this century, pensions were for the favored few, and before 1938 Social Security did not exist. The idea of "early retirement" is newer still. A prosperous post-World War II economy and strong labor forces enabled people in their fifties and early sixties to leave their jobs while relatively young and live off the fruits of their productive earlier years. "Sweetened" early retirement incentives grew as companies that wanted to economize and reduce their payrolls made special offers to encourage older workers to retire.

There is no fixed retirement age that everyone would agree to. Some want to retire early, some want to stay longer, and some want to work forever, their health and family situation permitting. To some people early retirement means doing all the things they never had time for before. To others it means being forced into a life of boredom and money worries. And to others it means a different job and possibly a new career. A significant number of older men and women would like to quit working, but cannot afford to because they don't have a pension to count on and their savings fall short of their needs.

The trend, however, is to early retirement—a mixed blessing. For John, early retirement is a heaven-sent means of escape from a job he hates; for Jane, it means being put out to pasture much too early and before she is ready. These days a firing isn't a firing, it's "outplacement." Since "mandatory retirement" sounds heartless, euphemisms are invented. One gentleman I spoke to told me that his company gave him notice that he had been "involuntarily leisured." (The damage is the same, but it does sound more compassionate, doesn't it?)

In recent years, the early retirement trend has grown stronger, especially among men. According to a study by the University of Southern California, on the average American men retire between the ages of 61 and 62 and 33 percent of them go back to work. As expected, the percentage of older persons in the work force was higher in 1948 than in 1988.

	1948	*1988*
Males age 65+ in the labor force	50%	16%
Females age 65+ in the labor force	9%	7%

Many companies offer older workers generous payouts if they accept early retirement. Usually presented as "voluntary," early retirement offers are often accompanied by subtle pressures to leave gracefully. Companies say they encourage early retirement in order to open up positions for younger employees. Left unsaid is the fact that many companies moved higher-paid older workers out so that they can bring in cheaper, younger workers. Some corporations aggressively pushing early retirement may become defendants in age-discrimination suits as courts try to find the line that separates voluntary from involuntary retirement. (Did they jump or were they pushed?) Companies are also starting to question the economic advantage of dumping valued employees. As early retirement becomes more prevalent, the company's costs in severance pay, pensions, health and life insurance, and training replacements may outweigh its benefits.

Although many companies have lowered their labor costs by offering early retirement, badly administered early retirement programs have caused lawsuits from older workers who were illegally forced out of their positions. Early retirement may also backfire on the company that loses competent and experiénced employees and then has problems replacing their skills. Employers have underrated the strengths that older workers bring to the job, including the contributions they can make in the introduction and adaptation of new technologies. In many cases, instead of pushing early retirement, firms can benefit by redesigning jobs and training older workers—measures that will become increasingly important with the rapid aging of the labor force in the years ahead.

While many employees in their fifties and early sixties prefer to move on and do something different, a large number of men and women are not ready for retirement. For many individuals leaving the work force when they are still vigorous and anticipating many more years of life, early retirement can be traumatic. But the trend is toward early retirement. The average retirement age becomes younger each year. In addition, longevity has expanded the number of years and the proportion of people's lives spent in retirement. Aside from the need to finance the additional years of life, early retirement can cause great psychological pain for men and women who are encouraged to give up their role as productive members of the community and are put out to pasture before their time. In his book *Economic Crisis, Work, Leisure Time* Xavier Gaullier says:

Old age policy has become employment policy. It is the economic decision-makers who determine that you are old, and at an increasingly early age.

You are old at an ever-younger age, and for reasons related to employment and having no relation to your state of health or your intellectual capacities.

The result, in the opinion of Gaullier, is to create a new class of individuals who consider themselves not employed, unemployed, or retired, and who definitely do not yet identify with older pensioners.

Some long-term employees reluctantly choose early retirement, a decision they want to retract. According to James E. Challenger, president of outpatient specialists, Challenger, Gray & Christmas, "People who are discharged are often hasty in their choice of early retirement instead of implementing a program to seek new employment. Some may decide that they will not subject themselves to the possibility of being discharged again. At that point, early retirement can seem to be an attractive alternative. However, about one out of three decide retirement is not for them within the first six months."

Aside from the cash incentives offered by the employer, there are three main reasons why individuals choose early retirement. . .

1. The individual may have a working spouse to provide the extra income needed in retirement.

2. He or she may be reluctant to relocate. Most people want to avoid moving to a new area, preferring to remain where they are now living.

3. They may want to realize a long-held objective of not having to work again. Challenger says, "It's the attitude most subject to rapid change once the person has retired."

Challenger said that persons who were once in his firm's outplacement program call and ask, "Do you remember me? I took early retirement rather than searching for a job. I realize now that it was a mistake. Now what?" The firm welcomes the person back to the program and offers counsel on available alternatives after retirement turns sour.

Before deciding to retire
from your job, stay home a week
and watch daytime television.

■ ■ ■

—Anonymous

REVERSE RETIREMENT

Typically, mature individuals reduce their commitment to work as they age. Some retire completely from career jobs while others make a more gradual transition involving some form of bridge employment before leaving the labor force.

A substantial number of older workers return to work after first retiring or partially retiring. One quarter of all workers reverse full retirement and go back to work. At the same time, 26 percent of partial retirees reverse this status and go back to work full time. In its newsletter, The Employee Benefit Research Institute takes note of the large number of retirement reversals and suggests that "these groups often make retirement decisions without sufficient information about what retirement is like or that their incomes unexpectedly become insufficient later in life."

A DIVERSITY OF INTERESTS

The job seekers in the 55-plus population are more diverse than those in any other age segment. They represent all ethnic and racial groups. They include professionals, white-collar, blue-collar, service, and farm workers.

The over-55 population available for work includes displaced workers and retirees—both the "young-old" not quite ready to retire and the mature retirees who want to get back to work. Women who spent many years as housewives and raising children are now seeking ways to join the working mainstream of American life.

For some people, work is their life and their identity; for others it is a source of financial independence and the money that makes leisure time more enjoyable. Your own decisions about work in your later years can be made only with an understanding of your particular needs, interests, and competence and how they mesh with the demands of today's job market.

WHERE DO YOU FIT IN?

Although a strong correlation exists between age and work status, age alone should not determine your place in the scheme of things. We all know individuals in their fifties who are ambivalent about work and resistant to change; and we know people in their seventies, who welcome challenge and embrace work with youthful zest.

Here's an overview of the unemployed 55-plus population. Where do you fit in? Remember, this is merely a rough guide with overlap and individual differences within each group.

Mature Workers in Their Mid-Fifties to Age 62

In this age segment people fall into two subgroups—midlife career changers and displaced workers.

Mid-life career changers are men and women often plateaued or burned out in their jobs. Despite their relative youth and need to work, they believe that the economy or conditions within their field jeopardize their chances. They need new challenges, an opportunity for advancement, and if they can get it, a larger paycheck.

In this category they are probably seeking full-time work with benefits. They want to maintain their health insurance and build up their Social Security benefits and their pension credits.

Displaced older workers under age 62 usually have recent work experience. These laid-off and unemployed workers may be facing difficult economic conditions in their part of the country. They must maintain health insurance, build Social Security credits, and find work at companies that provide worker pensions. Since they are too young to receive Social Security and are probably not receiving a pension, full-time work with employee benefits is a financial necessity. According to the U.S. Department of Labor Bureau of Labor Statistics, the annual earnings of full-time wage and salary workers (based on median usual weekly earnings, first-quarter 1992 averages) was:

MEN,	55 years and over	$29,068
	55 to 65	29,588
	65 years and over	22,412
WOMEN,	55 years and over	19,344
	55 to 65	19,552
	65 years and over	17,888

In searching for full-time employment, they may be limiting their options by a reluctance to relocate to greener pastures and/or a strong identification with their former position and job title. Also, their skills may be obsolete or their work experience may be a mismatch with available jobs.

Between ages 55 and 62, both midlife job changers and displaced workers are—perhaps for the first time in their lives—coming face to face with age as a factor in their chances for employment.

Under Age 62 and Retired

They are still too young for Social Security but they may be receiving pension benefits as part of an early retirement incentive package that includes health insurance. Those without a pension and company-paid health benefits may find that the nest egg doesn't provide the income they need.

Aside from feeling the financial pressures, many in this situation are unhappy with retirement and want to get back to work. Their work objectives range from full-time work to a part-time job and a flexible work schedule.

Here again, age bias—real or imagined—rears its ugly head, and strong identification with a former position and job title may limit other possibilities. At this relatively young age self-employment and starting or buying a business are options worth consideration.

Retirees 62 to 69

Social Security benefits may lessen the motivation to work, but as the sole source of income it falls far short of financial independence. In addition, the need for structure in their lives is a strong incentive to work.

Many people in this age group believe that employers are not interested in them, that their skills are obsolete, and that they cannot fit in with a younger work force. They may have a health condition that limits, but does not preclude, work.

For this group, the greatest obstacle to finding work is inertia and resistance to change and to learning new skills. In addition, they are unaware of the wide range of job opportunities open to them, and they lack job-hunting skills. In this situation, they may need special education and training to update old skills or acquire new ones. They need to sharpen their job-hunting skills and investigate new and emerging work opportunities.

I hate the word retirement.

■ ■ ■

—Johnny Carson, leaving
the *Tonight* show after 30 years.

Retirees 70 and Over

Retirees in this age group receive full Social Security no matter how much they earn. Since there are no disincentives to increasing income from work, many older retirees acquire renewed interest in financial compensation. The social and psychological benefits of work are still an important factor for retirees 70 and over. Many people in their late seventies and eighties work out of necessity, but some do so by choice. It makes them feel useful and needed. And they are.

Typically, in this category their interest is in part-time work, flexible hours, work-at-home arrangements, and volunteer work. In this category their concerns may include obsolete skills, the absence of recent work experience, health limitations, and their inability to interact with younger workers.

Mature Women

Women entering or reentering the job market after a hiatus of many years as housewives and homemakers face the double hurdle of sex discrimination and age bias. But the real problem—the major barrier—is the lack of marketable skills.

They should define their experience and abilities in business terms, and translate their homemaker skills to the needs of the job market. They need to acquire additional skills to keep pace with changing needs and to learn to market themselves in a competitive world.

The large and ever-growing number of older women at work today tells you that it can be done.

IMPOSED EARLY RETIREMENT

A poignant example of the emotional hardship that can result from imposed early retirement comes from the Middle East. In Israel a group of older men dressed and left their homes early in the morning pretending to go to work every day rather than "disgrace" themselves by telling their families that they were prematurely retired. In the United States as well, retirement has lowered self-esteem and shattered the morale of many older adults. More serious consequences include the rising suicide rate of white males beginning at age 65 and the higher mortality rates among retirees than workers.

The effect of early retirement on the retirement-dependency ratio—the ratio of retirees to workers—carries the potential for conflict between the generations. Currently, there are 20 retirees to every 100 workers. By the year 2025, there will be 40 retirees to every 100 workers. Will the working population of the future be willing to support this large and growing number of retirees?

A number of changes can help to cut down the dependency load. Among them:

- Raise the eligibility age for Social Security. (This has already been done.)

- Raise the eligibility age for private pensions. (Currently, employers are actually lowering the eligibility age rather than raising it. Knowledgeable observers believe that this could change.)

- Provide greater incentives to full-time and part-time employment for older people. This is the area that shows the most promise in cutting down the dependency ratio—and relates directly to the basic premise of this book.

About three fourths of working people age 55 and over prefer to continue working. (Incentives that would keep older workers on the job—as expressed by the workers themselves—are listed on Page 23.)

One highly effective incentive would be to cut the Social Security "earnings penalty." Many legislators believe that this is inevitable, and it may already have occurred by the time you read these words.

Incentive to Work

▪ ▪ ▪

What would keep you working past retirement age—and how does it compare with the incentives that other seniors want to remain at work past retirement age?

A Gallup Poll published in AARP's *Working Age* gives the incentive preference for employees age 40 and over. Here are the results of the poll, broken down between men and women:

	Percent of Women*	Percent of Men*
Flextime	50	39
Part-time work	44	38
Increased Social Security benefits	41	29
Temporary employment	41	31
Phased retirement	38	34
Job redesign	38	33
Increased pension benefits	37	27
Sabbaticals or extended vacations	33	31
Job sharing	33	29
Compressed work week	33	29
Job reassignment	30	27
Job training	23	13

* Percent of employees rating the factor a major consideration in delaying retirement

WHAT THE POLLS SAY

Workers age 50 and over vary as to when they plan to retire. According to the Gallup Poll, 9 percent plan to retire before age 62, 37 percent haven't decided. More than 19 percent said they will never retire!

Surprisingly, the poll shows that interest in retirement decreases as age increases. While 29 percent of those age 50 to 59 said they would rather retire, only 6 percent of those 70 and over want to retire. Also, individuals with more education are less likely to want to retire.

When the folks interviewed for the poll were asked, "What would keep you at work?" 36 percent said the chance to keep a current job; 18 percent said part-time work at the same job. Preference for keeping a current job increases with age, from 35 percent of those under 60 to 57 percent of those 70 and over. Of the 61 percent in the survey who were retired, 53 percent said they would rather be working and 7 percent said they would work part time.

Once again, the poll reveals great diversity of attitude toward work among older Americans. In addition to education, health and financial status play an important part in shaping attitudes.

We come away from an avalanche of statistics with one important fact. Three fourths of working people age 55 and over prefer to continue working. Anything that inhibits their ability—your ability!—to keep working also limits your opportunities and adds to this country's terrible waste of human resources. According to a survey commissioned by The Commonwealth Fund, a severe labor shortage in crucial areas will occur within the next 10 years. Your services and those of other mature individuals may be the only answer to this country's labor squeeze. It may seem strange talking about a "labor squeeze" during periods of high unemployment, but even in the worst of times, there is movement. People get promotions and transfers. People get into disagreements with the boss and get fired. People move to a new area, leaving a job opening behind. Currently, a bidding war is in progress among many small nations for Soviet scientists fleeing the Soviet Union's dissolution. Page after page of want ads beg for nurses. Productive salespeople are always in demand. The need for experience and skill—the very attributes older workers bring to the job—remains unabated.

Many don't even try

Of the one in four retirees who would rather be working, some do something about it and actually find work. Many don't even try. Listen to their reasons:

"I can't compete with a 40 year old. Besides, I won't fit in with younger people."

"I'm not sure I want to take on the responsibility of a full-time job at this age."

"They just don't hire people my age."

"What's the point—I'd lose my Social Security benefits."

"I don't have a college degree."

"I wouldn't know how to start looking."

Sound familiar? Despite the many mature workers, many older adults suffer the same insecurities. An "awareness" gap about available work opportunities keeps them unhappy and unemployed. By accepting yesterday's myths about older people in the work place, they have become co-conspirators in their own devaluation.

Noted psychologist B. F. Skinner advised older men and women against being too quick to turn things over to another generation. To do that, he warns, "is to lose one's position in the world and destroy important social reinforcers. Parents who turn their fortunes over to their children and then complain that they are neglected are a classic example, and it is possible for aging scholars to do something of the same. To bring one's work to an end in the expectation that one will be satisfied with well deserved kudos is to find oneself out of date. The world moves forward."

Embracing Change

Despite the diversity of the situations described here, the shared experiences of more than half a century of life shape our priorities and our plans for the future. With the materialism and highly charged rat race of the post-World War II years behind us, we are more interested in the quality of life than in conspicuous consumption. With age we become less competitive and more sanguine. We want to collect "experiences" rather than things.

Work is a basic experience of life—it is too important and too valuable to be forfeited to the young.

Because we have lived through a period of the greatest change in world history, we have learned to cope with change. The change that seems so monumental to our children and grandchildren is merely, as Yogi Berra says, "'Deja vu' all over again." We see patterns and themes in the changes and we hope that we come away wiser and more mature. The decades of change have made us tougher and smarter. We're survivors.

CHAPTER TWO

DOES IT PAY TO WORK?

> From birth to age 18,
> a girl needs good parents,
> from 18 to 35 she needs good looks,
> from 35 to 55 a good personality
> and from 55 on she needs cash.
>
> —Sophie Tucker

People are living longer now than ever before and spending more of their lives outside the labor force. The length of time spent in retirement has more than doubled in the last century and some people may spend as much as one-third of their life in retirement. And sadly, every year older adults leave work without the money needed to provide for the added years in retirement.

Studies made in the early 1970s concluded that retirees needed from 40 to 60 percent of their preretirement income in order to maintain their standard of living. A more recent study conducted in 1990 concludes that you'll need far more—probably 75 to 80 percent of the amount you made when you retired. If you don't want to compromise your standard of living you must take steps to increase your income. And money alone becomes a good enough reason to work.

A study by researchers at the Georgia State University Center for Risk Management and Insurance Research and the Atlanta office of the Alexander & Alexander Consulting Group provides the following estimate of the money needed for retirement (based on the income of a married couple with no dependents). The retiree is assumed to be age 65 with Social Security benefits and the spouse age 62 at the time of retirement.

Funds Needed for Retirement

Preretirement Income	Income Needed in Retirement	Percent of Preretirement Income
$15,000	$13,444	90 percent
20,000	17,032	85
25,000	20,436	82
30,000	23,756	79
40,000	30,717	77
50,000	36,659	73
60,000	42,830	71
70,000	48,866	70
80,000	54,459	68
90,000	59,000	66

The figures in the first and second columns are pretax amounts. The difference reflects reduced costs after retirement, including lower overall taxes.

LIFE WITHOUT A PAYCHECK

As you can see by the preceding chart, an individual with $25,000 in job income would need $20,436 in retirement income—or 82 percent of preretirement income—to maintain his or her standard of living. An individual with $40,000 in job income would need $30,717—or 79 percent of preretirement income. (These replacement ratios measure financial need at the point of retirement. They do not reflect the impact of inflation. For a more realistic estimate of post-retirement needs one should project replacement ratios 10 to 20 years into the future.)

Older adults already retired or contemplating retirement ask themselves:

How can I maintain the standard of living that I had before retirement?

Where is the additional income I need going to come from?

Will I run out of money while I still have plenty of life to live?

The four major sources of retirement income are Social Security, private pensions, income from savings and investments . . . and income from work. *Work provides income for roughly half of retired couples and 16 percent of retired single people.*

HOW LONG WILL $100,000 LAST?

The fear of running out of money while still healthy and with plenty of life left to live hangs over most of the retired population. How long your nest egg will last depends on how much you withdraw each year and the return you get on the money that remains invested. John Allen of Allen-Warren, Inc. has assembled a series of tables that show how long $100,000 of invested capital will last if you make withdrawals that go up each year to cover inflation.

This chart, reprinted with his permission, shows what happens when you make withdrawals (that go up 4 percent a year to cover inflation) on the first of the year.

Withdrawal Starting at	Years Money Will Last Invested at the Following Yields			
	4%	6%	8%	10%
$ 2,000	50	151	forever	forever
5,000	20	25	36	forever
10,000	10	11	12	14
15,000	7	7	8	8

If the rate of return from your savings and investment is 6 percent, and you withdraw $5,000 per year, your $100,000 nest egg will last 25 years. If rate of return from your savings and investments is 10 percent, and you withdraw $5,000 per year, your $100,000 nest egg will last forever and never be depleted because your money is earning more each year than you are withdrawing.

18 Money Reasons Why Older Adults Work

1. My current income is not enough to live on.
2. I need the income from work to maintain the standard of living I had before retirement.

3. I want to raise my standard of living and afford the things I couldn't afford before.

4. To keep up with inflation.

5. To obtain health insurance and other benefits.

6. To compensate for reduced company retiree health benefits.

7. I want the income from work for a specific personal purpose (travel, buy a new home, buy a new car or a better car, etc.).

8. With the income from work I won't have to dip into principal for living expenses.

9. Education of child—or children.

10. Income needed to contribute to the living expenses of children or a dependent relative.

11. My income from work will allow my spouse to retire.

12. My paycheck is a confirmation of my usefulness and the value of my services.

13. To accumulate enough money to start or buy a business.

14. I need the income to make up for the reduced rate of return on savings and investments.

15. To safeguard family's financial security.

16. To provide financial assistance to younger generation. (The Commonwealth Fund reports that 9.3 million older Americans provide a sizable part of the income of their children or grandchildren.)

17. To contribute to the needs of a surviving spouse, dependent child, or relative.

18. To build an estate and provide a larger bequest for heirs.

SOCIAL SECURITY

Most retirees depend on Social Security benefits and the return on savings to maintain their standard of living. Social Security was never designed to cover all your income needs in retirement. It was designed to replace *part* of the earnings you were receiving before retirement and to supplement the income you have from other sources, such as the return on savings and investments. But new data released by the Subcommittee on Retirement Income and Employment of the House Select Committee on Aging, show that half of all retirees during the last part of the 1980s went into retirement with less than $10,000 in savings (not counting a house and a car). Compare the kind of returns one could reasonably expect on such modest savings with the money needed to live comfortably in the later years and the need for supplemental income becomes apparent.

Social Security benefits, the core of most retirement budgets and a key factor in an older adult's decision to work or not to work, account for 44 percent of the total income for individuals 65 and over.

The average monthly Social Security benefits in 1993, after cost of living adjustment, was $653 for all retired workers and $1,106 for a senior couple, both receiving benefits. But Social Security giveth (a check that you can count on every month) and Social Security taketh away (when you earn over a certain amount from work).

The size of your monthly Social Security retirement check depends on how much money you earned before retiring and the age at which you started collecting your benefits. Your benefit amount is based on your earnings average over most of your working career. Higher lifetime earnings result in higher benefits. If you have some years of no earnings or low earnings, your benefit amount may be lower than if you had worked steadily.

The size of your Social Security check is also affected by your age at the time you start receiving benefits. If you start your retirement benefits at age 62—the earliest possible retirement age—your benefit will be lower than if you waited until a later age.

Many people prefer to continue working as long as possible. Aside from the paycheck itself, there are other financial incentives to remaining on the payroll: Your eventual Social Security benefits will be higher if you retire later. If you work until 70, you will receive full benefits, regardless of how much you earn. And, if you continue to work past age 65, you are entitled to a special bonus—known as delayed retirement credit—for each year of work performed.

The usual retirement age for people retiring now is age 65. Your local Social Security office calls this "full retirement age," and the benefit amount that is payable is considered the full retirement benefit. Longer life expectancies have increased the full retirement age in gradual steps until it reaches age 67. The table below will help you find your full retirement age.

Age to Receive Full Social Security Benefits

Year of Birth	Full Retirement Age
1937 or earlier	65
1938	65 and 2 months
1939	65 and 4 months
1940	65 and 6 months
1941	65 and 8 months
1942	65 and 10 months
1943–1954	66

(continued on next page)

(continued)

Year of Birth	Full Retirement Age
1955	66 and 2 months
1956	66 and 4 months
1957	66 and 6 months
1958	66 and 8 months
1959	66 and 10 months
1960 and later	67

You can start your Social Security retirement benefits as early as age 62, but your check will be less than your full retirement benefits. If you take early retirement, your benefits will be reduced based on the number of months you will receive checks before you reach full retirement age.

If your full retirement age is 65, the reduction for starting your Social Security at age 62 is 20 percent . . .

At age 63, it is 13⅓ percent.

At age 64, it is 6⅔ percent.

There is a financial advantage to retiring on a reduced benefit after 62 but before 65—you will have collected several thousand dollars before you reach 65. If you wait until 65 to start collecting full benefits, it will take a number of years to catch up to the total benefits already received.

Delayed Retirement

Many people prefer to continue working as long as possible. Aside from the paycheck itself, there are other financial incentives to remaining on the payroll: You'll be adding a year of high earnings to your Social Security record for each year you stay at your job. If you work until 70 you will receive full benefits no matter how much you earn. And, if you continue to work past age 65, you are entitled to a special "bonus"—known as a delayed retirement credit—for each year of work performed.

Delayed retirement increases will be added in automatically from the time you reach your full retirement age until you start taking your benefits, or you reach age 70. The percentage increase depends on your date of birth. Use the table below to determine the increase you will receive for delayed retirement.

Increases for Delayed Retirement

Year of Birth	Yearly Percentage Increase
1916 or earlier	1 %
1917–1924	3 %
1925–1926	3.5%
1927–1928	4 %
1929–1930	4.5%
1931–1932	5 %
1933–1934	5.5%
1935–1936	6 %
1937–1938	6.5%
1939–1940	7 %
1941–1942	7.5%
1943 or later	8 %

You don't have to retire to get Medicare hospital insurance at 65. But you do need to contact your local Social Security office about three months before your 65th birthday in order to sign up for Medicare. In some circumstances, medical insurance costs more if you delay applying for it.

CHOOSING YOUR RETIREMENT DATE

If you decide to start your Social Security retirement benefits after age 62, it is a good idea to contact your local Social Security office in advance to find out which month is best to claim benefits. Your choice of a retirement month could mean additional benefits. For example, it may be to your advantage to have your Social Security benefits start in January, even if you plan to retire later in the year. Under the rules at the time this is being written, many people can receive the most benefits possible with an application that is effective in January.

As you can see, the rules are complicated. That's why it's important that you discuss your plans with a Social Security claims representative in the year *before* the year you plan to retire.

When I was young
I thought that money
was the most important thing in life;
now that I am old I know it is.

■ ■ ■

—Oscar Wilde

THE FINANCIAL IMPACT OF EARNINGS
AFTER RETIREMENT

To compensate for the reduction in family income, Social Security beneficiaries often turn to additional earnings from a job or self-employment. Whether they are motivated by the money or psycho/social needs, or by some combination of both, their desire to work reverberates through my conversations with men and women in their late fifties and sixties. At the same time another factor, the punitive effect of earnings from work on their Social Security benefits, sends a counter message: "Why should I work when I have to give back Social Security benefits on the money I earn? It doesn't pay to work."

Social Security cash benefits were created to prevent dependency by providing workers with continuing income when their usual income from work is cut off. If you earn too much money working after retirement your Social Security benefits can be reduced or even eliminated.

How much is too much? The amount that you may earn and still collect full benefits depends on which of the three specific age groups you belong to. There are different guidelines for those eligible for Social Security under 65, for those 65 and over, and for those age 70 and over. In 1993:

> *Under 65* the amount you can earn without losing your benefits is $7,680. If your earnings exceed that amount, $1 in benefits will be deducted for each $2 you earn above $7,680.

> *From age 65 to 70* you may earn up to $10,560 without losing any Social Security benefits for the year. If you earn more, $1 in benefits is deducted for each $3 earned above $10,560.

> *After age 70* your Social Security retirement benefits are not in any way affected by your earnings.

What are wages? Wages may include bonuses, commissions, fees, vacation pay or pay in lieu of vacation, cash tips of $20 or more a month, severance pay, and certain noncash compensation such as meals or living quarters.

If you expect to earn more than the annual limit, you must contact your Social Security office promptly to give them an estimate of your earnings for the year. If you later find that your earnings will be higher or lower than you estimated, you'll need to contact Social Security again to change your estimate.

Also, you're required to report your earnings to Social Security by April 15 of the year following any year you earned above the limit and received some Social Security benefits. This report is in addition to your Federal income tax return. There is a substantial penalty for not filing an annual report of earnings on time.

If you overestimated your earnings, which means that Social Security withheld more of your benefits than required, they will pay you any money you are due. If, on the other hand, you underestimated your earnings, you will have to repay some of the benefits you received.

In the year that you reach age 70, you need to report your earnings only for months before the month you turn 70. Self-employed recipients can prorate their net earnings from self-employment to figure the amount to count for the months before they turned 70. Earnings in or after the month you reach age 70 won't affect your Social Security benefits.

SPECIAL MONTHLY RULE

A special rule applies to your earnings for your first year of retirement. Under this rule, you can receive a full Social

Security check for any month you are "retired," regardless of your yearly earnings.

To be eligible for a Social Security check for a particular month, your earnings must be under a monthly limit. They count your wages in the month you earn the money—not the month you are paid.

The monthly limits for 1993 are:

- Age 65 through 69—$880
- Under age 65—$640

When earnings for a particular month exceed the monthly limits, the yearly limits apply. The $1-for-$2 and $1-for-$3 rules cannot be applied to selected months. This means that you could lose a whole month's Social Security benefit if your earnings exceeded the monthly limit by even one dollar.

If you are self-employed, you can receive a Social Security benefit for any month you do not do "substantial" work in your business. Work of more than 45 hours per month is generally considered substantial. Less than 15 hours is not. Work between 15 and 45 hours is usually considered substantial if you are involved in management or a highly skilled occupation.

WHAT INCOME DOESN'T AFFECT YOUR SOCIAL SECURITY BENEFITS?

The following types of income do not count toward the earnings limits:

- Investment income
- Interest

- Social Security, Veterans, or other government benefits
- Annuities
- Capital gains
- Gifts or inheritances
- Rental income (unless you are a real estate dealer or you both rent a farm to someone and take an active role in the production or the management of production of farm commodities)
- Income from trust funds
- Sick pay after the sixth full month you last worked or were paid after your employment ended
- Moving expenses
- Travel expenses
- Jury duty pay

A PERSONAL OBSERVATION

Budget-cutters in both the legislative and executive branch of government would like to blame Social Security for the massive national deficit. They accuse the lazy "greedy geezers" of exerting their political power to maintain Social Security benefit levels and annual cost of living adjustments. And then, when we as older Americans demand the right to continue to work so that we can remain independent, social forces build barriers against older adults working later in life. Limitations on earnings from work is just one example of the penalties society creates to prevent our independence.

THE TAXMAN COMETH

Your senior status does not protect you from the long arm of the IRS. The dollars you earn from working are taxed but only 50 percent of Social Security benefits are subject to income tax for retired individuals whose annual income exceeds $25,000 and couples whose income exceeds $32,000. As this is being written raising that percentage to 85 is being discussed in Congress and is under consideration at the Clinton White House. You need to consider the possibility that your earnings from work will push you into a higher tax bracket.

Before seeking or accepting work you should know how your earnings will affect your total financial picture. Working, even as a free lancer or in a home-based business, could affect your financial status; it will certainly complicate your tax returns. You need to discuss the matter with a knowledgeable accountant, a qualified tax return preparer or a staffer at your local IRS office. IRS publications No. 17 and 567, free for the asking, cover this matter in detail.

WORK-RELATED EXPENSES

While you're weighing the impact of earnings from work on your financial status, figure into the equation the work-related expenses that may be relevant to you:

> *Transportation.* Unless your job is within walking distance from your home, you will have to drive to work or use public transportation. In either case, the cost of transportation is a valid consideration.

Outside meals. The brown-bag lunch that you fix yourself may be healthier and more nutritious than the meal you buy on the outside, but you may not want or be able to bring your own. So count the difference between the meals you'd fix yourself if you were home and the outside meals that you'll be eating on the job. It may not seem like much but it all adds up.

Clothing. The casual, leisure clothes that you wear around the house or out for a walk may not be appropriate in a working environment. For men it may mean a suit instead of a sport coat; for women, a business outfit instead of jeans and a sweater. Where that's the case, the cost of new clothes should be considered. And don't forget the additional cost of professional laundering and dry cleaning.

Household help. You may need to pay outside help to do some of the household chores that you would be doing yourself if you were not working. The house still needs cleaning, and the lawn still needs mowing.

So—DOES IT PAY TO WORK?

Considering the disincentives built into the system, how much it will cost you in lost Social Security benefits and additional taxes, plus whatever work-related expenses are involved, does it pay to work?

In my many conversations on the subject with working seniors who continue to work despite penalties and taxes, the answer seems to be a resounding "Yes!"

Whether your "Yes" is as certain and as enthusiastic depends on many factors, some financial and others involving the work and what work means to you.

Some older Americans work to survive, others to thrive. And then, there is that large number of older Americans somewhere between surviving and thriving who work for the supplemental income *and* because they want the work itself.

Even for people with substantial employment income from work, the mental- and physical-health benefits of work far outweigh any reduced net increase in income.

RIDING THE INTEREST-RATE ROLLER COASTER

Only your earnings from employment or self-employment count in determining the size of your Social Security check. Income from savings, investments, pensions, or insurance does not count. In recent years however, it has become more difficult to live on the return from savings and investments. Back in the 1980s, when Al Ross, a retired haberdasher living in Boca Raton, Florida, was getting as much as 16 percent interest on his savings account, his $150,000 nest egg provided him with almost $1200 of income a month. Al said, "My wife and I needed every bit of it plus my Social Security benefits to maintain our lifestyle and pay for a few trips up north to visit the kids." When interest rates started dropping Al shopped around for the highest yield he could get, and most of his savings went into bank Certificates of Deposit. When the yields on CDs dropped below 5 percent Al's income from savings dropped to $625 a month. "At that point,"

Al said, "I could either dip into my principal—which is something none of us wants to do—or I could cut back, move to a less expensive apartment, and give up travel."

Al Ross is one of the seniors who the AARP estimates own 54 percent of all interest-bearing money market and CD accounts. The typical older American has 30 percent of his or her net worth tied up in interest-bearing assets. According to Economic Analysis Associates, a research firm in Stowe, Vermont, people 65 and over lose $14 billion in income for every one-percentage-point drop in short-term rates.

Although falling interest rates may lift the national economy, they can devastate the finances of retirees who depend on the return from their savings and investments to supplement their Social Security benefits. At the beginning of 1992 interest rates dropped to their lowest level in 27 years and nobody really knows how low they can go. The decline in interest rates was prompted by the Federal Reserve's efforts to bring the country out of recession. But if you're an older American living on a fixed income, the declining yields on your savings and investments has had the opposite effect. Declining yields have dashed the hopes of many older Americans for a comfortable retirement free of money worries.

Some investment vehicles carry the potential for higher earnings but few retirees can afford to take the risk inherent in stocks and mutual funds. As one retired schoolteacher told me, "At our age we have to be cautious. We are afraid to put our money in the stock market and in the riskier things like junk bonds."

Declining interest rates, inflation, and a justifiable fear of stock market risks have left many retirees in a serious financial dilemma. For them—and possibly for you—the most logical solution to the problem is work. Income from work can provide the money to make up for falling interest rates and inadequate savings. And work gives them some-

thing more: a second chance for involvement in the mainstream of American life.

Work spares us
three great evils:
boredom, vice and need.

■ ■ ■

—Voltaire

CONCERN NUMBER 1

Americans 65 and over depend on Medicare to cover basic
medical care and it does indeed lift some of the burden of
medical costs at a time when they are most likely to be
substantial. Unfortunately, Medicare does not protect seniors
completely from the soaring costs of health care.

Older Americans are spending more than twice as much
on health care, even after adjusting for inflation, as they were
before the government established Medicare.

According to a report by Families USA, an advocacy
group for older adults, the skyrocketing costs of services not
covered by Medicare, as well as premiums, deductibles, and
co-payments under the Federal health insurance program
have pushed the average older family's out-of-pocket costs
from $1,961 to $3,305 in 1991. (In dollars not adjusted for
inflation, these costs were $347 in 1961.)

The Wall Street Journal quotes Ron Pollack, executive
director of Families USA: "Medicare has helped our parents
and grandparents, but despite Medicare, older Americans
are today being squeezed much harder by health costs than
during John F. Kennedy's time."

Why have older persons' out-of-pocket health expenditures risen despite Medicare? Several reasons. Medicare doesn't pay for most prescription drugs or eye and dental care. Medicare has gone from charging no premiums to charging $320 a year (1993). And the cost of private health insurance that many Medicare beneficiaries purchase to pay for expenses that Medicare doesn't cover (sometimes referred to as "Medigap" insurance) has more than doubled since 1961. Seniors spending on nursing-home care, the biggest chunk of their overall health care insurance, has quadrupled in the past 30 years, and long term health care insurance has risen accordingly.

Out-of-Pocket Health-Care Costs for Families Headed by Someone Age 65 or Older, in 1991 Dollars

	1961	*1972*	*1991*
TOTAL	$ 1,589	$ 1,854	$ 3,305
Direct	1,265	1,331	2,332
Hospital	228	175	90
Physician	316	184	408
Nursing home	287	582	1,194
Other	454	390	640
Insurance premiums	304	523	973
Private	304	309	653
Medicare		214	320

Source: Families USA

INFLATION

The loss of income due to lower return on savings and investments is cushioned by lower inflation. So goes the argument of those who minimize the effect of low interest rates on the income of retirees. They say a mere 3.1 percent increase in the Consumer Price Index in 1991, as opposed to 10.3 percent ten years earlier, makes the financial loss caused by lower interest rates easier to bear. But older individuals don't get the full benefits from lessened inflation because their spending doesn't reflect the components of the Consumer Price Index. Older Americans spend a higher percentage of their incomes on health care—and health care is the one expense that continues to soar. (See table on page 48.) Consequently, they are being squeezed from both sides, trapped between lower income from savings and investments and rising prices in a major expense area.

Social Security benefits are linked to the U.S. Consumer Price Index; the amount of the monthly check is tied to increases in the cost of living. This offers little protection. The yearly cost-of-living increase in the Social Security check (3 percent in 1993) is based on the cost of living for the overall population. It certainly does not reflect the cost of living for older Americans.

The goods and services you must have as an older adult have been rising in price three times faster than the Consumer Price Index. When the U.S. inflation rate is at 5 percent, the cost of retirement can rise 15 percent or more a year. The cost of medical care—a major expenditure for older Americans—jumps 20 to 25 percent per year. And those who believe that their taxes will go way down when they retire are in for a rude awakening: State and local taxes, including property taxes, are rising 15 to 20 percent in many areas.

Percent increase in consumer price index (CPI)

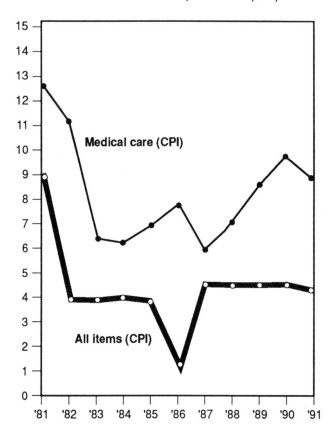

Source: *U.S. Department of Labor*

Out-of-control medical care costs. Lower returns on savings and investments. Higher taxes and inflation. Consequently, many older men and women who thought they could live comfortably on the income from Social Security and their savings find that the total falls short of their needs.

For them—for you—income from work can make the difference.

How Inflation Shrinks Your Nest Egg

The dollar you put away for retirement is not the dollar you will take out. This chart will give you some idea of how much today's dollar will be worth in the years ahead at inflation rates from 4 to 10 percent.

Annual Inflation Rate (in cents)							
Years Ahead	*4%*	*5%*	*6%*	*7%*	*8%*	*9%*	*10%*
1	96	95	94	94	93	92	91
2	93	91	89	87	86	84	83
3	89	86	84	82	79	77	75
4	86	82	79	76	74	71	68
5	82	78	75	71	68	65	62
6	79	75	71	67	63	60	56
7	76	71	67	62	58	55	51
8	73	68	63	58	54	50	47
9	70	65	59	54	50	46	42
10	68	61	56	51	46	42	39
15	56	48	42	36	32	28	24
20	46	38	31	26	22	18	15

Figures rounded to the nearest cent.

Social Security earnings limitations and taxes shouldn't keep you from pursuing work. You can accept a job at any salary level knowing that with the combination of benefits and earnings you'll still be ahead.

Through careful management of hours and income many older workers manage to stay within Social Security limitations and don't have to sacrifice any benefits. Since taxes and penalties erode your outside earnings, it is essential that you figure out how it will affect your Social Security benefits and your tax status before you accept employment.

C H A P T E R   T H R E E

NOT BY BREAD ALONE

A perpetual holiday is a good working definition of hell.

—George Bernard Shaw

My friend Jack Goodson is having the time of his life. Free from responsibilities and the alarm clock, Jack's retirement is like a never-ending cruise in the Caribbean. He swims, works out, naps every afternoon, spends his evenings building model ships, and is constantly busy with a large coterie of friends.

For Bob Donovan, retirement is something else. He misses his job as controller of a machine tool company and everything that the job meant to him: identity, status, people, and the sense of involvement that made him jump out of bed every morning. He is driving himself and his wife crazy.

From "happily retired" to "old, unemployed, and miserable." Depending on your finances and your temperament, retirement can be your blessing or your hell. Some look

51

forward to and choose retirement, others are pushed into it. To those who chose retirement and are enjoying themselves, you deserve every minute of it—have a ball!

For those who miss work—either right away or after being retired a while—all kinds of possibilities are available. Given the number and variety of work opportunities for older adults, those who complain about being put out to pasture haven't got a leg to stand on. Your "retirement" may have separated you from a comfortable rut, but it hasn't affected your ability—or your right—to work if that's what you want to do.

Back to Work

In 1985 Bill Watson of Council Bluffs, Iowa, won $4.1 million in the Iowa lottery. He did what most people would expect him to do. He quit his job as a firefighter and settled down to enjoy a leisurely life with a guaranteed income of $150,000 a year until the year 2005.

After a few years of retirement Bill discovered that Easy Street was a dull place to live. He missed the firehouse. In 1992 he went back to work as a Council Bluffs firefighter. His reason was quite simple: "It's an exciting job."

The idea that a lottery-winning millionaire would return to work because he missed the job was considered so novel that it was covered on the wire services and appeared in newspapers, radio, and TV across the country. But Bill Watson's decision did not seem strange at all to millions of retired Americans who understood his dilemma.

"Retirement is not a blessing for most seniors. It's either an emotional or a financial rip-off. They're tired of living in a dependent relationship with bureaucracy and society."

These remarks, made at a senior center in Santa Rosa, California, are echoed in senior centers and retirement communities coast to coast by mature people who would rather be working.

In his book *Work in America*, J. O'Toole identifies the psychological value of work:

1. Work contributes to self-esteem; through mastering a task, one builds a sense of pride in one's self.

2. Work is also the most significant source of personal identity; we identify who we are through our jobs.

3. Work is a prime way for individuals to impose order, control, or structure on their world.

Self-esteem. Personal identity. Structure. For these and other life-affirming benefits, a large number of older Americans, many of whom have no financial urgency to do so, get back into the game. One quarter of all workers reverse full retirement; they increase the commitment to work after first retiring. The Talmud elevates work as one of man's most worthwhile pursuits. Freud considered the love of work as the mark of an emotionally healthy individual. One psychiatrist who counsels older people tells me that work is their "search for dignity." She considers older adult employment the "most important source of involvement in daily life."

Recent studies give a rough approximation of the retired population's attitude toward retirement: About one half want to be retired, one quarter are not able to work because of health or family situations, and about 13 million retired men and women want to work.

What are the 13 million retired men and women who would rather be working doing about it?

If you are an unemployed mature individual who would rather be working, what are you doing about it?

Trouble in the Promised Land

The long-awaited pleasures of full-time leisure have proven to be a disappointment to many people. In retirement something was lost; and something very crucial to their physical and mental well being was missing from their lives. The job was more than a paycheck. It provided a social setting, a gathering of colleagues to whom you could talk about trivia or about very intimate matters. Fellow workers were there for a congenial conversation when you felt like talking and provided a built-in support system in times of difficulty. The job gave them a sense of belonging and acceptance.

Many who looked forward to the leisure and freedom of retirement found that the paradise they were expecting was more like purgatory. In retirement they found themselves empty, rudderless, and marginal. For most of their lives they equated what they were with what they were doing and how much money they made. Now they were doing nothing and earning nothing. Endless golf, gardening, and travel was no substitute for the self-esteem, identity, and structure that work provided. Once again, we turn to George Burns, who says, "To wake up in the morning and have nothing to do but play golf or bridge would not be enjoyable. To work and then have a couple of hours free to play golf or bridge is a pleasure."

Arthur Lewis, a recent retiree and an unhappy camper, says he misses his friends and colleagues at the work place: "I guess you could say that the people on the job were my surrogate family. I even miss the people I didn't like—they gave me something to bitch about. They were part of my environment and kept me young."

For millions of older men and women separation from work means a loss of identity, a giant step backward. Retirement removes the individual from the arena in which he or she was able to demonstrate competence and initiative. Hobbies, travel, and increased family involvement do not provide the gratification they got from work. Total leisure leaves the individual without a reason to anticipate tomorrow.

A recent retiree told me he didn't realize how much work helped to organize his days: "It was someplace that I had to be at a certain time in order to get certain things done. A place I could hang my hat."

Distinguished psychologist Dr. Richard Mowsesian believes that what you do is what you are. He says, "Without work and a clearly defined work ethic to sustain them, older citizens suffer the indignity of becoming nonpersons."

In his book, *Work in America*, J. O'Toole echoes the sentiment. He states: " . . . to be denied work is to be denied far more than the things that paid work buys; it is to be denied the ability to define and respect one's self."

Percentage of Civilian Noninstitutional Population in the Labor Force, by Age and Sex: 1950 and 1990

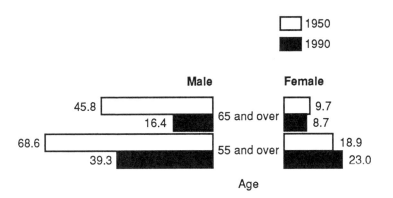

Source: U.S. Bureau of Labor Statistics, Data for 1990, Employment and Earnings, Vol. 38, No. 1, January 1991

There is a strong link between employment and life satisfaction. Specialists in the problems of aging find a large number of unhappily retired older adults who suffer depression, loneliness, and a sense of isolation from the real world. For many mature adults, the end of work is the start of physical and mental decline.

With retirement, many older men and women forfeit the sense of accomplishment that comes with bringing home a regular paycheck. Their voices echo in senior centers and retirement developments across the nation. A storekeeper: "I was happier when I was working." An accountant: "I was able to save a lot of businesses from going under. I knew what I was doing was worthwhile. I don't have that feeling about what I'm doing at this point." An advertising executive: "I knew how to do things no one else in the agency could do. I was kind of indispensable, and I miss that." A social worker: "I need to be needed."

One of the most interesting replies I received when I asked retirees what they missed most came from a pipe-smoking shuffleboard player. He said, "I miss the Xerox." Sometimes it's as simple as that.

LONELINESS AND BOREDOM

Social networks—the friends and friendships so important to happiness—change as people age. Fewer work-related friendships develop as seniors sink deeper and deeper into retirement. One recently retired housing developer told me that since he left work and most of his friends have moved South he has few opportunities to make new friends who share the interests that occupied most of his life. "The people around here," he said, "they don't know anything about construction. They bore me silly."

What the retired need
. . . isn't leisure, it's occupation.
Two weeks is about the ideal
length of time to retire.

■ ■ ■

—Alex Comfort, *A Good Age*

As I look around, I see more older Americans done in by boredom and the lack of mental stimulation than by heart disease and Alzheimer's.

Gerontologists and specialists on aging confirm my observation and offer numerous examples of the ways in which boredom affects the mental and physical health of older people and hastens aging. Jules Willing quotes a newly retired gentleman who found himself sitting on the porch and staring into space: "I began to realize that without having to earn a living, raise a family, manage a household, I'd actually have to find things to think about. . . . What an astonishing revelation that was!"

Physical and Mental Health

Some older men and women find that their health has improved when they retire from a hard and unpleasant job they hate. Others, however, find that their health begins to deteriorate when they leave a fulfilling job. (It is interesting to note that Japanese workers work more and longer than workers in any other developed nation and are estimated as the healthiest in the world, with the highest life expectancy.)

In her book *The Aging Employee,* Rose Coser cites evidence from sociologist Zena Blau that the loss of a job can cause people to become "old." Dr. Blau found that it is neither age nor physical change so much as the loss of an occupation that "leads people to alter their age-identity and accept old age." Among those she studied, fewer of those employed and in their sixties thought of themselves as old. The retired in their sixties felt old nearly as often as did employed people 70 and older.

Retirees suffer from depression at a rate higher than any other segment of the population. Depression among older Americans is considered by physicians and psychologists as "a major health problem" and the cause of an increase of personal and family deterioration. Society's answer to the problem is to build more mental hospitals and nursing homes and funnel greater amounts of financial aid for treatment of older people. Older adults in increasing numbers are being treated by psychiatrists and therapists to repair the damage caused by too much leisure. The medical profession now has an arsenal of pills—trazodone, bupriopion, and fluoxetine—to ease the depression and unhappiness of seniors. And yet, many doctors agree that very often work is the best medicine.

THE TRAUMA OF RETIREMENT

According to the National Center for Career Life Planning, of the 40 major shocks that can batter you from infancy to old age, the shock of mandatory retirement ranks ninth, a trauma just behind deaths of members of your family and divorce. Psychologist Ira J. Tanner is quoted as saying that what frequently happens during the first four months after retirement "is that there is a likelihood of heart attacks and strokes—all related to the trauma."

Mental-health professionals now generally concede that in many fields and for many people, retirement is taken too early. They find convincing evidence of a causal relationship between enforced idleness and deteriorating health. Life satisfaction is lower among older people who are not working but are able and willing to work. When healthy, active people not ready for full-time leisure are forced to leave the work force, the transition becomes a major crisis in their life. Sometimes, because of pride, older workers use ill health as an excuse for retirement when actually they never had a choice. They would rather be seen as sick than declared "useless" by their employer.

Besides the personal damage to the individual, the way we discard older workers regardless of their capacities is counter to the national interest. This country needs its most highly trained and skilled workers in order to compete in global markets. As time goes by, and the number of healthy, vital older people increases, the issue of mandatory retirement—at any age—will become the subject of intensive study and discussion. There's good reason to examine the rules and redefine the concept of retirement.

THEY'RE NOT DOING YOU ANY FAVORS

The gold watch and the farewell party are all part of the ritual to lull the individual into the sunset. For the unprepared, for individuals whose work has been the heart and soul of their lives, total retirement is a hard blow.

In his book *The Reality of Retirement,* Jules Z. Willing reports that "a high proportion of retirees has a hospital stay in the first year of retirement; some studies report a 90 percent chance of hospitalization in the first years. The causes vary widely, but almost always there is some sort of health crisis. I believe that this crisis is related in some way and is a physical response to an otherwise unanswered alarm signal that is clamoring in the nervous system."

Withdrawal from active involvement with the world at large often leads to an increased preoccupation with personal aches and pains. It's a process that feeds on itself. With the absence of intellectual stimulation, real aches and pains become more pronounced, and imagined aches and pains become real. Soon the preoccupation with self dominates your days. In her studies on the positive impact of an active mind on the physical and mental health of older persons, Dr. Ellen Langer, professor of psychology at Harvard University, finds that not only can there be remission of various ailments, but life expectancy for nursing-home patients can be increased if greater intellectual demands are made of them.

Going back to work after a heart attack could speed emotional recovery. In a study made by Drs. Kathryn Rost and Richard Smith of the University of Arkansas at Little Rock, about half the people who survive a first heart attack suffer depression that can be long-lasting and debilitating even though they have fully recovered physically. Among 90 heart-attack patients who promptly went back to work, emotional distress decreased significantly within four months and continued to decrease thereafter. Of 53 patients who chose not to go back to their jobs, emotional distress increased over the same period. The researchers found that " . . . resumption of employment substantially enhanced their psychological well-being."

GOOD INTENTIONS

Are the companies and the government being good to us by encouraging early retirement and providing financial benefits that reduce the need to work? Yes, if the result is a dignified maturity and freedom from want. But if the result is a lot of bored and depressed older adults who require more mental hospitals and access to psychiatrists and other therapists, maybe they are too good to us. Maybe they are doing us more harm than good. Maybe these older adults—and you—should be looking at the root cause of this unhappiness. While you may not be in a position to correct society's "good intentions" in its treatment of the older generation, you can do something about your own situation. You can take the initiative in whatever it takes to keep yourself physically and mentally active. For many Americans that means work—and the independence, dignity, and involvement in society that comes with it.

It's Not the Money. I Work Past Retirement Age Because . . .

I need to be active and productive.

My work keeps me physically and mentally healthy.

It keeps me young.

Retirement is a crashing bore—I need the physical activity and mental stimulation that my work provides.

Work gives me a reason to get up in the morning and out of the house.

Work gives structure to my day and a sense of order to my life.

When I go to bed at night, I feel that I've accomplished something.

I need to contribute to society, not just take.

I enjoy leisure more when it's part of my life and not all of my life.

I am very good at what I do, and I like doing what I'm good at.

I want to make new friends; work gives me contact with people of all ages.

When people ask me what I do, I don't like telling people that I'm retired. I want to be seen as a working, productive person.

I'm convinced that work is good for my health—and that my health will deteriorate if I don't work.

Surrounded by retirees, being gainfully employed gives me status and prestige.

A few hours separation from my spouse while we're working improves our relationship. Exchanging our experiences at work makes our conversations more interesting.

Work provides the challenge I need in my life.

I like work—always have.

While some men and women are lured into a "paradise" called retirement and wind up going to shrinks and popping anti-depressant medication, others are keeping themselves stimulated and alert naturally by getting to work and meeting whatever challenges the job throws at them.

If work were a pill, it would be the most frequently prescribed medication for the depression of older adults.

THE BLESSINGS OF LONG
LIFE—AND THE CONSEQUENCES

Although we have Social Security, IRAs, and other savings programs to allow people to provide for the financial needs of their later years, there is no complementary preparation for the psychological and emotional needs of 15 to 25 later-life years spent without work.

A rise in the suicide rate and substance abuse by increased drug dependence through unnecessary medication and excessive use of alcohol by older Americans has become a serious concern. While much of this is the consequence of aging and declining health, enough of it is related to retirement blues to encourage a new evaluation of retirement.

A Denver physician tells of other consequences of idleness and too much leisure: "Alcohol too often becomes an easy way to pass a boring part of the day. Someone who, during his or her working years, would never have thought of drinking during the day now finds it easy to go to the refrigerator for a beer or take a bottle off the alcohol shelf. The results: I have seen people who were perfectly healthy before 65 develop severe liver damage between the ages of 65 and 70."

INVOLUNTARILY LEISURED

Being forced to retire before you are ready is an unhappy experience. It is particularly so for the men and women who maintain their status through their position. The trauma of being forced to move from a well-defined and stable role to retirement, a more ambiguous state, can be devastating.

There has generally been little preparation for the sudden shift from goal-oriented activity to idle days and nights.

A retiree living in Sarasota, Florida, writes: "When I took early retirement to get away from northern winters and a job filled with pressures and tensions, I made the mistake of thinking that my future would be all fishing, golfing, and beach-walking. I retired completely unprepared for the abrupt change of pace.

"When the fishing, golf, and beach-walking turned into boring pastimes, I overdosed on alcohol, TV, and idleness. Relations with my wife, who was active in church and volunteer work, became increasingly strained."

Eventually he joined his wife in her volunteer projects. He is busy again and now "I'm beginning to feel I'm doing something worthwhile. The pleasure has returned to the fishing and golfing and the TV set has become a friend again. Once again, I look on them as rewards for the work I'm doing."

What was his biggest mistake? Could it have been avoided? Another Sarasota resident answered the question for me: "My mistake was making such a complete break between work and retirement. I should have prepared myself better for the slowdown, developing some work-like interests that I could carry over into retirement, or perhaps lining up a part-time job or a volunteer project before I rushed into—nothingness."

For healthy and active men and women, retirement is nothing more than enforced leisure. The advertisements and brochures of financial services promoting saving for retirement and real-estate developers selling land in paradise paint a rosy picture. They do not talk about the negative aspects of retirement developments—the boredom and monotony of idleness and the limitations of living with and relating only to older people. As a result, thousands of vital and active people have turned childlike in a playground for seniors.

One doesn't have to be a "workaholic" to miss work. Physically and mentally healthy older people seek a balance in their life by pursuing work. They know that leisure and recreation are more enjoyable when they are part of a lifestyle that includes work.

Among industrialized nations, Japan has the highest proportion of men aged 60 and over participating in the labor force. Why are Japanese men so eager to work? In a survey by the Japanese Ministry of Labor over half of the working 60- to 69-year-old men said they worked for noneconomic reasons. "Working is conducive to improved health" was mentioned by 25 percent of the 60 to 64 age group and 22 percent of the 65 to 69 group. Responding to current and anticipated labor shortages, most Japanese enterprises have a formal policy to assist older workers to remain healthy and productive through job adjustment, reduction of working hours, or changes in work operation and physical environment.

W isdom too often never comes,
and so one ought not to reject it
merely because it comes late.

■ ■ ■

—Justice Felix Frankfurter

ESCAPE FROM TOGETHERNESS

One of the things that you may have looked forward to in retirement was the chance to spend more time with your spouse. It is ironic that for many couples years of wedded bliss can turn into a nightmare of too much togetherness. One

65-year-old homemaker called her husband's retirement, "A lot less money and a lot more husband."

A comment heard with increasing frequency in the beauty salons of Florida and Arizona is: "I married him for better or for worse. But not for lunch."

At poolside in Sun City West I overheard: "We sleep together. We eat together. We play golf together. We go to the movies together. We're never out of each other's sight. I need space and I need to spend some time by myself and with other people." Did she say that or did he? It doesn't matter. Either partner could have said it with equal fervor.

Recovering Our Losses

An independent and dignified old age should be available to everyone, not just the privileged few. The cold truth, however, is that for most people retirement means a radical change of status. To make the later years into something other than a series of constant losses—loss of youth, loss of friends, loss of income, loss of power and status—you have to take decisive action. Planning and serious effort will enable you to win back some of the things you lost. Work, for example.

While the intent is noble, current trends toward earlier retirement make you and thousands like you a spectator in the bleachers of our society—unpaid, unproductive, and uninvolved—while you are still vigorous and capable. They're not doing you any favors. Very often an ulterior motive lies behind these good intentions. Some corporations push early retirement because they mistakenly believe that younger people are more productive. Some want to replace higher-paid older people with lower-paid younger people. Some are trying to avoid the cost of health benefits for older people. Unions may not be acting in the interest of older people by negotiating early retirement but they are also interested in opening up jobs for younger union members.

Denying older people work—and work options appropriate to their skills—robs them of their independence and forces them to depend on the generosity of government and relatives. The cruelest aspect of society's attitude toward older persons is the vulnerability of older persons and their acceptance of the stereotype. It makes them accomplices in their own devaluation. When we find retirees describing themselves primarily in terms of who they were, rather than who they are now, we sense the damage that too much retirement too soon has done.

Medical professionals and gerontologists advise older men and women to continue to work for as long as possible. In the National Institute of Health's 11-year investigation of the variables that contribute to longevity, they found that the degree to which a person derives satisfaction from his or her work is the greatest single factor affecting longevity. This should be all the motivation you need to find not just a job but the right job for you.

Given the advice of medical specialists and the experience of many men and women, we might be justified in echoing the message on the cigarette package: *"Warning: Retirement may be detrimental to your health."*

YOUR RIGHT TO WORK

Your rights as an older American include the right to contribute to the social order in a way that is consistent with your capabilities. Successful aging requires fighting off the stereotyped limitations of age. Fight the inclination to let go, to spend your days and nights watching television. Don't retire *from* something, retire *to* something. You delay aging with work—productive work with clearly defined goals. Work to earn money, maintain your independence, avoid boredom, stay involved, feel useful, stay abreast of changing times, forget your worries, maintain your independence, mix with people of all ages, heighten the enjoyment of the hours off work, keep mentally alert, and learn new skills.

Work is the key to how people define themselves. For ourselves, and for society at large, we have to rethink our concept of work and retirement. When you reach out to reestablish yourself in the work place, you are defying the stereotype and swimming against the tide. But that's part of the fun. You open up the possibility of good things happening when you choose to work late.

Older Americans at Work:
14 Emerging Trends

1. Older adults today are healthier, more active, and longer living than any preceding generation of older Americans.

2. The trend to early retirement will create a pool of young-old workers not yet ready for full-time leisure and seeking work.

3. Increasingly, restless and bored retirees will choose to return to work as "temps," part timers, and free lancers.

4. The need to provide income for more years of life—plus inflation and lower yields on savings—will motivate more people to work in their later years.

5. Growing recognition by employers of the value of older workers will create more jobs for mature men and women and increase their participation in the work force.

6. Flexible hours, job sharing, and other innovative work arrangements will attract older workers seeking a post-retirement lifestyle.

7. More seniors will seek work as Social Security limitations on earned income are eased.

8. Vigorous enforcement of federal and local laws prohibiting age discrimination will protect older workers' right to equal opportunity.

9. More private and government programs will emerge to provide occupational-skills training and enable older adults to compete in the job market.

10. Advanced technology (telephone communication, FAX machines, and computer modems) will allow more older Americans to work at home.

11. Entrepreneurship will grow as a work option in the later years as more mature individuals start new businesses or buy existing businesses and franchises.

12. A growing awareness of emerging job opportunities and the help available to them from support groups, job clubs, and other organizations will encourage older adults to seek work.

13. As older Americans increase in number and gain greater political clout, their interests in work are more likely to be served.

14. Retirement will be redefined as work is interspersed with periods of leisure, retraining, and self-renewal spread over a lifetime.

TRUE GRIT

In increasing numbers, men and women are remaining active and productive well into their later years. Some come into their own in old age, in ways that eluded them when they were younger. In her book *By Youth Possessed, The Denial of Age in America,* Victoria Secunda tells us why they deserve our admiration and respect: "People who live full and productive lives beyond the age of sixty-five are to be admired not only because of the vigor and creativity of their lives but, more important, because they are able to do so in spite of cultural generalities made about them.

"Lacking social reinforcement for their individuality and growth, one can only describe their age indifference as true grit."

Today's older generation is the first to enjoy the benefits of the longevity revolution. Many are making great strides in their careers and record numbers are forging new careers. Lydia Bronte, a research fellow at the Phelps Stokes Institute in New York, recently completed a five-year study of the work lives of 150 people age 65 to 102. Her conclusions are reported in a recent issue of *Newsweek:* "Many people are as active as they've ever been during those years . . . The single most important thing was that they found work that they loved." Some of Bronte's subjects switched jobs many times over in their lives. Some found their true calling only in their later years.

History is crowded with examples of "true grit" in the later years. Picasso, Casals, Churchill, de Gaulle, and many other celebrated "overachievers" have demonstrated the creative potential of maturity. George Bernard Shaw was writing at 91. Michelangelo designed churches at 88. Claude Monet began his *Water Lilies* series at age 76, completing it at age 86. At 88, Frank Lloyd Wright designed the Marin County Civic Center. Grandma Moses, a farmer-lady, took up painting at age 76 when arthritis forced her to give up needlepoint. One of America's greatest primitive painters, she continued to paint for 25 years. George Burns and Bob Hope in their eighties and nineties continue to entertain millions.

When he was 96, and still playing the cello, Pablo Casals observed, "Aging is a relative matter. If you continue to work and absorb the beauty of the world around you, you find that age does not necessarily mean getting old."

Former U.S. secretaries of state are among those older Americans challenging the stereotype. As this is being written Cyrus Vance, 75, is headed for South Africa in response to a call from the UN to moderate a volatile dispute in that country and Henry Kissinger, 69, runs an international consulting firm in New York. Some of the entertainment industry idols we grew up with are still active in their later years: Dick Clark, Paul Newman, and Charles Bronson are in their sixties, Dinah Shore, Robert Mitchum, and Gregory Peck are in their seventies.

Several books are devoted to the achievements of famous people in their later years: *The Crown of Life* by Hugo Munsterberg, *The Book of Ages* by Desmond Morris, *Going Strong* by Pat York, *The Ulyssean Adult* by John A.B. McLeish, and *Tolstoy's Bicycle* by Jeremy Baker, the last of which takes its title from the fact that Tolstoy learned to ride a bicycle at age 67.

Older men and women who have made major contributions in all fields are a model and an inspiration to all of us. But high achievement in the later years is not the exclusive province of geniuses and extraordinary people. Equally worthy of our admiration are the millions of people who don't have famous names. Unheralded and often unnoticed, older men and women throughout the world are "involved" in society, each in his or her own way. Whether they are carving great sculptures or driving a school bus or waiting on tables, they are challenging the stereotype. They are in the game at a time when they were supposed to have retired or have been retired.

Following are some of the better-know later bloomers from age 60 to 90 and beyond.

At age 60, Alexei Kosygin became Prime Minister of the Soviet Union; Cervantes began to write *Don Quixote*; Victor Hugo wrote *Les Miserables;* Izaac Walton wrote *The Compleat Angler;* Alfred Stieglitz, the photographer, married artist Georgia O'Keeffe and created some of his greatest photographs; French monk Dom Perignon made his first batch of champagne; Irving Berlin wrote the music for *Easter Parade;* Katharine Hepburn starred on Broadway in *Coco.*

At age 61, Nikita Krushchev headed the Soviet Union; John Adams, Andrew Jackson, and Gerald Ford assumed the U.S. presidency; Oliver Wendell Holmes became a Supreme Court Justice; Sir Edward Coke became the first-ever Lord Chief Justice of England; Albert Einstein became a U.S. citizen; Count Zeppelin retired from the army and launched the first dirigible; and P. T. Barnum produced his first circus.

At age 62, Louis Pasteur created the first injection against rabies; David Ben-Gurion became the first Prime Minister of Israel; FDR won his fourth term as President; Charles Darwin published his masterwork on evolution, *The Descent of Man;* Linus Pauling won his second Nobel prize; Spanish artist Goya painted his masterpiece, *The Disaster of War;* Joseph Albers painted *Homage to the Square;* and Ibsen wrote his greatest play, *Hedda Gabler.*

At age 63, Harold Macmillan became Prime Minister of Great Britain; Nikita Krushchev became Premier of the USSR; John Quincy Adams, a former president of the United States, was elected a member of the House of Representatives; Disraeli became Prime Minister of England for the first time; Anaïs Nin published the first volume of her diaries; Archibald MacLeish won the Pulitzer prize for his play *JB;* Stanislavsky wrote *An Actor Prepares;* Charlie Chaplin wrote the screenplay and music, and produced, directed, and starred in *Limelight*; Richard Wagner had his masterpiece, *The Ring,* performed for the first time; and Casanova continued his endless love affairs and wrote his infamous memoirs.

At age 64, Harry S. Truman and George Bush were elected President of the United States; former president William Howard Taft became Chief Justice of the Supreme Court; François Mitterand became President of France; J. P. Morgan formed U.S. Steel; Ferdinand de Lesseps directed the completion of his brainchild, the Suez Canal; Alfred Hitchcock directed *The Birds*; Oscar Hammerstein wrote the lyrics for *The Sound of Music;* explorer Richard Burton published his erotic *Thousand and One Nights;* and Voltaire wrote *Candide.*

At age 65, Douglas MacArthur became the ruler and "Shogun" of Japan during its occupation; Winston Churchill became Prime Minister for the first time; Joseph Haydn composed the Austrian national anthem; Dame Nellie Melba performed *La Boheme* at Covent Garden; Alfred North Whitehead published his four major works; Boris Pasternak completed *Dr. Zhivago;* George Cukor directed *My Fair Lady;* and "Bear" Bryant ran the "Crimson Tide" as football coach at the University of Alabama.

At age 66, Colonel Harlan Sanders started the Kentucky Fried Chicken fast-food chain; Michelangelo painted his masterpiece, *Last Judgment,* on the altar of the Sistine Chapel; Frank Lloyd Wright designed "Falling Water," the Pennsylvania house built over a waterfall; Ginger Rogers performed on a nightclub tour of North America; and Kenneth Clark wrote *Civilization.*

At age 67, Sigmund Freud wrote *The Ego and the Id*; Barbara Tuchman wrote *A Distant Mirror;* Michael Faraday converted the force of gravity directly into electricity; architect and sculptor Bernini completed the *Piassa di San Pietro;* Joseph Strauss saw the completion of his greatest structure, the Golden Gate Bridge in San Francisco; H. G. Wells wrote *The Shape of Things to Come;* George Bernard Shaw wrote *St. Joan;* Josephine Baker made her comeback on the Broadway stage—and Tolstoy had his first bicycle lesson.

At age 68, William H. Harrison became President of the United States; Charles de Gaulle was elected President of France; Clarence Darrow defended John Scopes in the "monkey trial"; Lillian Carter (the future president's mother) joined the Peace Corps, working as a nurse at a clinic in India; Mies van der Rohe designed the Seagram Building in New York City; Henry Moore completed his sculpture *Reclining Figure*; Mrs. Patrick Campbell started her film career; Lillian Hellman wrote *Pentimento;* Cecil B. DeMille directed *Samson and Delilah;* and Judge John Sirica presided at the Watergate trials.

At age 69, Ronald Reagan was elected the fortieth President of the United States; Zenko Suzuki took office as Prime Minister of Japan; Gunnar Myrdal wrote *Asian Drama: an Enquiry into the Poverty of Nations;* Margaret Mead wrote *Culture and Commitment;* Noah Webster published his dictionary; Mormon leader Brigham Young became a father for the fifty-sixth time; Copernicus wrote *De revolutionibus orbium coelestium,* the book considered the starting point of modern astronomy; Buckminster Fuller designed the largest-ever geodesic dome for Expo '67 in Montreal; Stravinsky composed "The Rake's Progress"; Sophocles wrote *Oedipus Rex;* and New York Yankees manager Casey Stengel led the team to an American-League pennant.

At age 70, Golda Meir became Prime Minister of Israel; Benjamin Disraeli returned to office as Prime Minister of Great Britain; Carl Gustav Jung wrote *The Psychology of Transference;* Robert Broom proved that mammals had evolved from reptiles in his discoveries at the bone caves in the Transvaal; noted Cornish artist Alfred Wallis began his first painting; Toscanini conducted the first-ever performance of the new NBC Symphony Orchestra; Somerset Maugham wrote *The Razor's Edge*; Maurice Chevalier was featured in *Gigi;* Rex Harrison entered into his sixth marriage; and Hilda Johnstone represented Great Britain in the 1971 Olympics equestrian dressage competition.

At age 71, Winston Churchill delivered his momentous "Iron Curtain" speech; Gilbert Stuart painted his famous portrait of John Adams; George Herbert Mead wrote *Mind, Self and Society;* Philip Johnson designed the Chippendale skyscraper for AT&T; John Houseman received his first Academy Award for *The Paper Chase*; Bette Davis won an Emmy award for her performance in *Strangers;* Coco Chanel became a major force in the fashion world; and Glynn Wolfe married Donna Maria Hessee, his twenty-fourth marriage.

At age 72, Jomo Kenyatta became Prime Minister of Kenya; Bertrand Russell wrote *A History of Western Philosophy*; Rodin completed his famous Nijinsky statues; Susan B. Anthony was elected president of the American Women's Suffrage Society; Mies van der Rohe attended the opening of his greatest architectural achievement, the Seagram Building in New York City; Robert Graves published his controversial translation of the *Rubaiyat* of Omar Khayyam; French novelist Collette wrote *Gigi;* Karl Wallenda, the circus tightrope walker, walked on a high wire strung between the top floor of the Eden Roc and the Fontainebleau hotel in Miami.

At age 73, Konrad Adenauer became Chancellor of Germany; Freud wrote *Civilization and Its Discontents;* Peter Roget completed his *Thesaurus;* Picasso completed some of his greatest works and continued to paint until age 90; Verdi composed "Othello"; novelist Harriet Doerr won the National Book Award for her first book; Graham Greene wrote *The Human Factor;* Judge Learned Hand wrote his landmark decision on the Alcoa antitrust suit; Madame Tussaud opened her wax museum in London; and Walt Stack completed the International Triathlon, a 2.4-mile ocean swim, a 112-mile bicycle race, and a full-length marathon run.

At age 74, Daniel Malan became Prime Minister of South Africa; Frank Lloyd Wright started his first drawings for the Guggenheim Museum in New York City; Henry Moore completed his sculpture "Sheep Piece"; Franz Liszt gave piano concerts in Luxembourg; Isaac Bashevis Singer won the Nobel Prize for literature; John Wingfield ran the marathon; and Felix Grucci won the 1979 Monte Carlo annual international fireworks competition.

At age 75, Chaim Weizmann was elected President of Israel; Disraeli resigned as British Prime Minister and wrote a best-selling novel; Alexander Calder designed the exterior for the Braniff Airlines' DC-8; pianist Claudio Arrau gave 110 concerts, performing new works; Vladimir Horowitz performed in concert with the New York Philharmonic Orchestra; Cecil B. DeMille produced and directed *The Ten Commandments;* Frank Sinatra performed at his birthday party; Busby Berkeley revived *No, No, Nanette* on Broadway; and Charles Stolfus took up roller skating and invented a new kind of skate with polyurethane wheels.

At age 76, Winston Churchill became Prime Minister for the second time; William Gladstone became British Prime Minister for the third time; Grandma Moses started to paint because her arthritic fingers could no longer embroider; Antonia da Ponte designed the Rialto bridge in Venice; Maggie Kuhn celebrated the tenth anniversary of the "Gray Panthers," an organization dedicated to combating ageism; Mies van der Rohe designed the New National Gallery in Berlin; Edward Steichen published *The Family of Man*; and Pablo Picasso completed 44 variations on the painting *Las Meninas.*

At age 77, Mahatma Gandhi won independence for India; John XXIII was elected Pope and brought a new regime to the Catholic Church; Eleanor Roosevelt was appointed U.S. delegate to the UN; Claude Monet began work on *Water Lilies*, a complete room of paintings; Clara Barton, founder of the American Red Cross, served in the Spanish-American War in Cuba; Richard Strauss composed *Capriccio,* one of his five operas; Barbara Cartland wrote her two hundred and fifty-fourth romance novel; Mae West appeared in the movie *Myra Breckenridge;* and Luis Bunuel produced and directed *That Obscure Object of Desire.*

At age 78, Field Marshal von Hindenburg was selected President of Germany; Giovanni Giolitti became Prime Minister of Italy for the fifth time; Ayatollah Khomeini took over the government of Iran after the fall of the Shah; Erich Fromm wrote *To Have or To Be*; Matisse designed the Chapel of the Rosary in Vence, France; H. G. Wells received a D.Sc. from London University for his doctoral thesis; conductor Sir Thomas Beecham set off on a world tour with his orchestra; Edward Hopper painted *Second Story Sunlight;* and Justice

Oliver Wendell Holmes rendered his famous decision on free speech.

At age 79, George Cayley conducted the first successful glider flight; John Dewey wrote *Experience and Education*; Sir Christopher Wren designed St. Paul's Cathedral in London; Verdi composed *Falstaff*; Dame Edith Evans won the New York Critics Award for her performance in *The Whisperers;* Andrés Segovia fathered a child; and Gloria Swanson married for the sixth time.

At age 80, Marshal Yeh Chien-ying became Chairman of China's National People's Congress; Konrad Adenauer in West Germany, Marshall Tito in Yugoslavia, and General Franco in Spain continued to head their governments; Dr. Armand Hammer negotiated a giant chemical fertilizer deal between the West and Comecon; Buckminster Fuller published his masterwork *Synergetics*; Marc Chagall created the sets and costumes for the Metropolitan Opera production of Mozart's *The Magic Flute;* Grandma Moses held the first "one woman" showing of her work; Pablo Casals married his pupil; George Burns won the Academy Award for his performance in *The Sunshine Boys;* Boris Karloff starred in *Targets*; and Justice Tanney rendered the decision in the Dred Scott case.

At age 81, Benjamin Franklin was elected as a delegate to the U.S. Constitutional Convention; Morarji Desai became Prime Minister of India; Goethe wrote *Faust*; Mies van der Rohe designed the Museum of Modern Art in Berlin; Amos Alonzo Stagg was elected "College Coach of the Year"; James Cagney appeared in *Ragtime*; and Nellie Brown won her first swimming race at the Washington, D.C., Masters swimming club.

At age 82, William Gladstone became Prime Minister of Great Britain for the fourth time; Winston Churchill published the first of his four-volume work on the *History of the English-Speaking People*; Congressman Claude Pepper led the charge to defend Social Security benefits; Lewis Mumford wrote two new books; Matisse painted *Papiers-decoupes*; William Kane continued to win prizes as a a rodeo performer; and George Burns enjoyed his greatest success playing God in *Oh God*.

At age 83, Sir William Gladstone began his last term as Prime Minister of Great Britain; Eamon De Valera was reelected President of Ireland; Russian revolutionary Alexander Kerensky wrote *Russia and History's Turning Point*; Barbara McClintock won the Nobel Prize for research in genetics; Charlie Chaplin received an Academy Award for *Limelight;* and Mabel Hunter sang in concert at the Kennedy Center in Washington.

At age 84, President Tito of Yugoslavia visited China and the USSR; Marshal Petain became President of the puppet Vichy government; Pablo Casals gave a cello recital at the White House; and W. Somerset Maugham wrote *Points of View.*

At age 85, Jung wrote *Man and His Symbols*; Toscanini conducted the NBC Symphony Orchestra in Beethoven's *Ninth Symphony;* Carl Sandburg published a new volume of poetry; and ragtime pianist Eubie Blake recorded an album for Columbia Records.

At age 86, Field Marshal von Hindenburg continued as President of Germany; Francis Rous received the Nobel prize; Robert Frost recited his poem *The Gift Outright* at the inauguration of JFK; James Michener's latest novel *Mexico* makes the best-seller list.

At age 87, Theodore Green was elected to another term as a U.S. Senator from Rhode Island; Bernard Berenson completed his autobiographical trilogy; Bob Hope entertained

American troops during the Desert Shield operation; George Burns performed for the Queen and Prince Philip.

At age 88, Michelangelo completed his *Rondanini Pieta*; and Konrad Adenaur started writing his memoirs.

At age 89, Havergal Brian wrote one of his ten symphonies; Artur Rubinstein gave a recital at London's Wigmore Hall; Frank Lloyd Wright completed the famous Guggenheim Museum; Albert Schweitzer was at work at his hospital in West Africa; and Mary Baker Eddy continued to lead the Christian Science movement.

At age 90, Will Durant and his 77-year-old wife Ariel completed *The Story of Civilization*; Pablo Picasso continued to add drawings and engravings to his 20,000 works and celebrated his birthday by releasing 90 doves; Pablo Casals was staging cello recitals; and Leopold Stokowski recorded 20 albums after age 90.

AGE WORKS— HERE

I can't get old; I'm working.
I was old when I was 21 and out of work.

—George Burns

Once you're free of the confines of 9-to-5 work in a central-
ized work location, a whole new world of employment options opens up for you. You can work part time all year, or
full time part of the year. You can free lance or work as an
independent contractor. You can be paid by the hour, by the
piece, by the sale, or by the project. This new flexibility speaks
directly to the interests of older men and women. It says
"Freedom." It says "Variety." It says, "The kind of job you
want is out there for you."

The shift from heavy industry and agriculture to high
tech and services has created important changes in the kind
of workers that are needed. In the new work environment,
brains are more important than brawn, and experience, sea-

soned judgment, and stability take on greater importance. In such a labor market you enjoy a competitive edge.

Now more than ever before older workers compete successfully for available jobs because many younger workers simply do not have the skills necessary to meet the needs of today's employers. They lack such basics as writing, math, problem solving, and communication. In many urban schools the dropout rate is near 50 percent, and it is estimated that about 70 million adults in the United States are functionally illiterate.

For business, deficiency in basic skills is just one of the problems. Another is finding qualified employees who are flexible and willing to work part time and other nontraditional working hours.

Many Older Americans Who Want To Work Remain Idle. 7 Reasons Why . . .

1. The awareness gap. A large number of older men and women are unaware of the many job opportunities open to them.
2. Indecision and inertia. To work or not to work? I'll think about it tomorrow.
3. Employers' bias and stereotyping of older workers as unproductive and unmotivated.
4. Obsolete skills. Many older Americans have failed to keep up with the demands of a changing job market.
5. Mature people with an attitude: "They owe me a job."
6. Appearance. Many older job seekers do not take the time and effort to look neat, trim, and well-groomed. A sloppy appearance reflects attitude.

7. Misunderstanding of Social Security limitations on earnings from work. In 1993, only seniors making more than $10,560 for the year from work had to forfeit some of their earnings. Even with earnings limitations, for most seniors it pays to work.

According to Dan Lacey, editor and publisher of *Workplace Trends*, nearly one third of the American work force is now classified as *contingent*—"meaning they aren't conventional paycheck employees of the companies that provide their income. They work for outside contractors, work at home, or work part time . . ."

In the basic skills such as reading and writing, older adults are superior to many younger workers, and not only are seniors willing to take part-time work and flexible working schedules, they actually prefer such arrangements. On both counts—competence and flexibility—older Americans provide the contingent work force that industry is seeking.

According to Jane Schnitzler, branch manager of Right Temporaries Inc., a temporary help company, the demand for part time and temporary help runs counter to general employment trends. When companies are cutting back and "downsizing" during rough times, they count on the contingent work force of part-timers and temporary workers to fill in the gap. Paul Rupert, associate director on New Ways to Work, a San Francisco research group, also questions the notion that flexibility goes out the window during hard times. He says, "In this recession more than in previous ones, flexibility can be used to help cushion the effects of the downturn."

Part-time work seems the logical bridge between full-time work and retirement. Part-time work offers older workers the best of both worlds; it can provide income and the psychological and social benefits of work and, at the same time, allow plenty of time for leisure and recreation. For many seniors, working part time also eliminates any concern about Social Security limitations on earnings. The Employee Benefit Research Institute reports that almost 30 percent of the workers age 55 and over are employed part time—about 10 percentage points higher than the average for all adult workers. The Small Business Administration reports that more than two thirds of workers 65 and over are employed part time.

Businesses with peak hours or seasons—shopping centers, supermarkets, restaurants, department stores, hotel and travel services, for example, use part-timers as extra help. Fields with intermittent shortages of qualified workers, such as nurses, secretaries, paralegals, and lab technicians count on part-time help to fill in the gaps.

The need for competent part-time workers is growing as companies seek greater flexibility in their work force. According to a new survey by Hay/Higgins Co., employee-benefits consultants, 14 percent of the companies surveyed offered telecommuting options and 40 percent had flexible-hours policies, up from 35 percent in 1987.

It is apparent that the high cost of providing health benefits is behind the shift many companies are making from full-time to part-time schedules. Small firms are less likely to offer fringe benefits than larger firms are, and part-time jobs are much less likely to offer fringe benefits than full-time jobs are. Many older workers willingly accept part-time jobs with few fringe benefits because they are already covered by Social Security (Medicare) or private pension benefits from previous jobs. The Small Business Administration reports that in 1988, 83 percent of workers between ages 65 and 69 were covered by some form of private health insurance; 82 percent were covered by Medicare. While health insurance benefits are a strong work incentive from ages 55 to 64, it is not much of a factor after age 65, when Medicare becomes available. The older job applicant who can say to a potential employer, "I don't need your health-care insurance—I'm already covered," enjoys a decided advantage in today's job market.

Annual earnings of part-time and salary workers 25 years of age and older (based on the Bureau of Labor Statistics 1992 median usual weekly earnings) was $8,008. The bureau does not calculate part-time earnings for adults 55 and over, but considering the nature of the work, part-time earnings for older adults is probably similar, and possibly a little higher.

GOING FOR THE GRAY

In 1989, after an extensive search of many cities, retail giant Sears Roebuck selected Mobile, Alabama, for its new facility. According to Sears executive Jim Rohrer, they selected Mobile because it had an existing pool of potential employees who wanted part-time work only. The search focused on three categories, retirees, homemakers, and students. In a recent telephone conversation, Mr. Rohrer said: "Of these three categories: it was the retirees who worked out best for us. We want people who have had life experience. If I was hiring someone from my family—my son, my wife, or my mother—I would hire my mother because she has had the most life experience and I am convinced that she would do the best job of all.

"*If your purpose is to supply superior customer service then you have to hire someone who understands what superior customer service means.* And that's our older generation. That's our folks—we love these workers."

The company's other site selections were based on the same criteria: a pool of potential part-time employees, particularly older adults.

Sears is just one of the many companies that actively pursue older workers. Sears wants people with life experience who prefer to work part-time. Other companies need older workers' special skills, greater stability, and ability to relate to mature customers.

For these and other practical reasons, employers seeking help are turning to the tried and true—the older adult. Employers are actively recruiting mature people and changing company policies, adjusting work hours, and redesigning the work process to accommodate older workers.

TARGETING OLDER ADULTS FOR JOB OPENINGS

Targeting men and women in their mid-fifties and older for full- or part-time work enables cost-conscious companies to tap the skills of older workers. The positions offered range widely, from engineers and scientists at Lockheed to tellers and customer-relations personnel at Western Savings and Loan in Arizona.

Ongoing programs at McDonald's and Days Inn are designed to bring in older workers as part-timers for food service or reservation clerk positions. Jobs offered under these programs are often low level and low paying and therefore may not appeal to skilled seniors with better options, but many older job seekers find them just what they are looking for. Both McDonald's and Days Inn go all out to make older workers welcome and to redesign and restructure job assignments to fit the older workers' needs. A wiry and energetic gray-haired woman working as a reservations clerk at Days Inn told me, "It's nice to work where you are wanted and appreciated."

In addition to McDonald's and Days Inn, many other companies are targeting older men and women in their hiring. Among the companies in active pursuit of senior job seekers are:

Texas Refinery Corporation employs as sales representatives 500 part-time workers who are 60 years of age and older.

Georgia Power Company seeks individuals 65 and older to weatherize the homes of their mature customers 60 and older.

Continental Illinois Bank & Trust puts retirees to work in clerical assignments one to two days per week.

State Mutual Life Assurance Company of America gives its own retirees first option on part-time jobs as they become available.

Hastings College of the Law (University of California) hires retired professors from other law schools on a full-time basis. The professors retain their pensions from other institutions while drawing a salary and full benefits from Hastings. In a recent year, 13 of 48 faculty members were over age 65.

F.W. Dodge Company allows retirees to work collecting data on completed building permits.

Atlantic-Richfield hires retirees with critical skills as geologists, geophysicists, and systems analysts. The re-hired workers receive full benefits and increased pension levels through their additional employment.

Western Savings & Loan employs retirees as tellers and in customer-relations positions.

ACCOMMODATING OLDER WORKERS

At one company an employee approaching his fifty-eighth year moves to a job that requires less heavy lifting. At another a female manager in her early sixties becomes a trainer. Elsewhere, an executive becomes a special-projects technical adviser. All involve job redesign and job reassignment. In each case, while the job may be less physically or mentally demanding, it remains interesting and allows the older employee to maintain a high performance level.

Many older workers are also caretakers for others and may be overwhelmed by both a demanding full-time job and responsibilities to an elderly relative. To accommodate older workers, many companies have introduced dependent care, flexible hours, long-term care insurance, and other programs designed to retain seasoned workers and allow them to work to their abilities.

Stouffer Foods is a model of job reassignment for older workers. The company's frozen-food plant has two product assembly lines: a fast-paced retail line involves small retail packages, and a slower-paced institutional line involves more precise handling of packages for cafeterias and hospitals. Mature workers who are unable to maintain the speed required on the retail line are typically shifted to the slower-paced line, where they can maintain quality control and productivity.

Several Japanese companies have mandatory reassignment policies. Japan's five largest steel firms have, under union contracts, installed programs in which administrators at a specific age—typically 55—resign their position to become "techincal specialists" or to assume nonsupervisory duties. Nissan Motor Company, for example, reassigns assembly-line workers in their late forties to less demanding work as forge or press operators.

Although many U.S. employers recognize the advantage of redesigning jobs to accommodate older workers, not as many companies adopt the practice as could profitably do so. They contend that most older workers want to move to higher-paying jobs with more responsibility rather than less demanding jobs. However, as the labor force grows older and more employees grasp the opportunity to continue working well into their later years, and as employers learn to tailor job redesign and reassignment to suit their individual businesses, the practice will become more prevalent.

Companies in the forefront of this practice include:

Xerox Corporation. The company provides a voluntary reassignment option for hourly workers. Employees 55 and older with 15 years of service (or 50 and over with 20 years of service) may bid on jobs with lower stress and pay levels. About 10 to 15 percent of eligible employees have utilized the option.

Control Data Corporation. Retirees who previously held positions in midlevel management or in technical fields are hired as "business advisers." Hired as independent consultants, they are paid through short-term contracts, and salaries are integrated with pensions. A "flexiplace" policy, originally created to allow disabled employees to work at home, extends the practice to older workers involved in text editing and other computer-related assignments.

General Dynamic (Convair Division). The company takes into consideration employees' physical abilities and limitations in making job assignments and transfer decisions. As jobs become too physically demanding, an employee may make a reassignment request. Such requests are typically honored.

Builders Emporium. The company accommodates older workers by hiring a night crew of younger workers to lift boxes and restock shelves. Older workers handle administrative tasks and sales.

Intertek Services Corporation. Retirees from other companies are sought as independent contractors for the company's clients. Their assignments involve preaward surveys, manufacturing, assembly, and special-processes monitoring, expediting, and troubleshooting.

Employment Status of Americans 55+ (in millions)

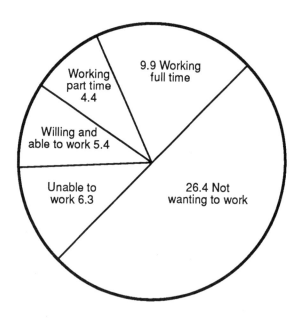

Source: Data from Louis Harris and Associates national survey for The Commonwealth Fund, *Americans Over 55 At Work Program, 1992.*

ABILITY IS AGELESS

In increasing numbers, companies have come to recognize the skill, knowledge, and expertise of older workers and have initiated programs to hold and to hire mature adults. Some 77 exhibitors bought booth space at Operation ABLE's Twelfth Annual Job Fair for Workers Past 45 held in Chicago in November 1991. Among the exhibitors at the Fair to recruit older workers were giant corporations (Canon, Tellabs, Commonwealth Edison), financial services (Harris Bank, Household Mortgage Services, Northern Trust), health-care services (Blue Cross/Blue Shield, Northwestern Hospital, Children's Memorial Hospital), and government agencies (IRS, Illinois Department of Employment Security, U.S. Office of Personnel Management). According to an ABLE spokesman, "All of the 77 exhibitors at the Fair had jobs to offer older workers." *This, despite the fact that the Fair was held when the nation was in a recession and unemployment figures were climbing.*

Similar job fairs for mature job seekers are held in many cities, including Boston, Chicago, and New York, where a recent Ability Is Ageless Fair drew more than 4,000 job seekers and more than a hundred companies recruiting job applications from older workers. Even in hard times when companies are cutting back, things need to get done and jobs change hands. It is estimated that 20 percent of the jobs in the United States change hands every year. Savvy businesspeople have discovered the value of mature adults as a contingent work force.

For certain companies, holding and hiring older workers is seen as a way of attracting older consumers to their products and services, meeting affirmative-action standards, and spreading the work ethic among younger work forces by utilizing older workers as role models. Since employers expect their work force to be older in the near future and want to gain experience in employing retirement-age individuals, farsighted companies hold and hire older workers. The roster of those honored at Operation ABLE's 1992 Distinguished Service Awards offers an overview of some of the older Americans at work today and what their employers' think of them:

William Patterson, 72, engineering assistant, East Bank Club of Chicago. "In the ten years Bill has been with us he has never been late. Besides being loyal and friendly, he never complains and is willing to take on any task no matter how difficult."

Loretta Sargent, 78, crew, McDonald's Corporation. "Loretta answered our want ad in the newspaper 'just for fun' and was told that the work might be too hard for her. Well, fourteen years later she's still keeping up the fast pace, and liking it!"

Patricia Hromadka, 62, premium accounting, CSA Fraternal Life Insurance. "Patricia is caring, considerate and will go out of her way to help fellow employees. Her motto is 'You're never too old to learn.'"

Urdyne Bryson, 64, director office services, Chicago Board of Trade. "Urdyne can be called upon at all hours of the day or night, weekends included."

Charles Holmer, 74, maintenance department, South Holland Trust & Savings Bank. "Charles' strong work ethic and positive attitude make him an excellent role model for younger employees. We are proud to work with him."

Helen Drozd, 64, press operator, Armstrong Containers Inc. "An employee that every employer dreams of. Helen is quality conscious and industrious and always puts out a 100 percent effort." (Helen's employers value her so much they hired a limousine to take her to the Older Workers Award Luncheon at the Palmer House to accept the award.)

A man can't retire his experience.
He must use it.
Experience achieves more
with less energy and time.

■ ■ ■

—Bernard Baruch
on his eighty-fifth birthday.

Flexible Hours

To take advantage of the new demand for your services, you need to be aware of the great variety of working arrangements currently available. They make it possible for you to construct a work life that meshes with your lifestyle.

Flexitime programs are gaining in popularity, and companies that have such programs say that flexitime improved employee morale. In a flexitime program, an employee chooses, within guidelines, his or her own working schedule for the specified number of hours of work called for. Some flexitime schedules permit workers to work anytime between 7:00 A.M. and 10:00 P.M., so long as they put in the requisite 6 to 8 hours a day and 30 to 40 hours a week.

A few flexitime programs allow workers to carry debit and credit hours into a monthly time bank. Aside from the benefits to the community of reduced rush hours for auto traffic and public transportation, flexitime can increase production as "morning people" and "night people" are able to work when they are most energetic. Older adults favor flexitime work schedules because it allows them to arrange medical appointments, recreation, and shopping at off-peak hours. As they tell it:

> "Being able to drive to and from work in light traffic makes it an easier day."

> "I am personally accountable for my workday—not watched like a kid to make sure I'm at work on time."

> "I'm an early riser so it's no problem getting to work at seven. I'm off at four and my wife and I are there for the 'early bird specials' at the best restaurant in town."

"Temp" jobs. In a single year—1988—the temporary help industry employed 6.5 million workers in more than one million jobs daily. Temp jobs can be obtained by applying directly to an employer or by working through a temporary-help company that places workers on a temporary basis. The temporary-help company is the employer, while the firm hiring the services is the client. The individual actually performing the work is the "employee" or "contractor."

Working for a temporary-help service such as Kelly Services and Manpower Inc. offers the limited involvement and flexible work schedule that many older men and women are seeking. There are short-term assignments, long-term assignments, full-time, part-time, evening, and weekend assignments. Temporary assignments are specific in length, but there is no limit as to how long an assignment can last. While some last only a day or two, others may continue for a year or more. Very often, "temp" work can lead to a permanent position—if that's what you want.

The variety of assignments handled by temporary-help companies means that you won't get stuck in the same old job routine that you tried to escape in your younger days. More than 200 different types of positions are available in office, light industry, data-processing, finance, marketing, manufacturing, health-care, and technical work. *You* decide whether you want to accept or decline a particular assignment.

The diversity of assignments and the variety of job settings can expand your work experience and sharpen your skills. Many temporary-help companies offer training that will allow you to learn entirely new skills, such as word processing, and become eligible for a greater variety of better paying assignments. And remember, you'll also be making new contacts through your different assignments. Meeting new faces can be one of the most rewarding aspects of work.

Younger people use temporary work for immediate income while they are between jobs. For older adults, however, temporary work can be an attractive, permanent way of life.

I asked Jean Martin, for many years my highly skilled secretary at the Chicago Board of Trade, why she now prefers "temping" to taking a permanent position. She summed it up this way: "As a 'temp' I have complete control. I can work when I want. I get to meet new people and learn about different businesses. Best of all, I don't have to make a long-term commitment. If I want to take six months off to travel, I can do just that."

RENT-AN-EXEC

Temp work isn't just for secretaries and bookkeepers anymore. Companies are hiring executive help on a short-term basis. The services of an executive "temp" can be used in a number of situations: when a company reorganizes, when it makes an acquisition or a divestiture, or when it expands internationally. When a key executive suddenly departs a company or is absent from work because of illness, the interim executive can fill in.

Jim Baker, a former vice president of Comsat, completed his temporary assignment at British Aerospace Communications in three weeks. "I've been looking for some short-term opportunities," Mr. Baker explained, "and this has provided me with the best of both worlds."

The existence of many temporary opportunities for high-level people is confirmed by Don Hoffman, vice president of Telesciences CO Systems Inc., which develops systems for phone companies: "We're using interim executives because they bring us the expertise we need to succeed." Telesciences is employing "temp" management for both their Latin American operation and their international activities. Mr. Hoffman is quoted in an article in *The Wall Street Journal* as saying, "We expect to use more interim executives as we expand overseas." According to the *Journal* article, there's a bright outlook in the new world of interim executives, both for the hiring companies and the hired executives.

This optimistic view is echoed by Shelley Votto, manager of the Philadelphia office of Romac and Associates, a national executive-search firm specializing in the placement of full- and part-time accounting, banking, data-processing, and financial-services executives. Romac is now seeking early retirees from executive and management positions to fill temporary positions in the financial and computer fields. Votto reminds corporations seeking experienced, top-level people for unexpected, seasonal, or transitional work that retired managers do not have to be trained. "Senior temporaries already know how to fit smoothly into an existing company structure. The older executive is also more dependable, always arriving at work on time, and willing go the 'extra mile' to get the job done. Whenever we've sent a senior to fill a temporary job, we've received more praise than usual."

Employers seeking help and mature executives looking for work can locate the nearest of the 35 Romac/Temp offices by asking their local telephone operator for the company's toll-free number.

Pros and Cons of Temp Work
for Older Adults

■ ■ ■

Pro

- Provides quick additional income.
- Requires no long-term commitment to employer.
- Work schedule is flexible to match personal lifestyle.
- Work situations are varied.
- Allows for meeting and working with new people.
- Offers an opportunity to learn new skills.
- Provides exposure to many different industries.
- Leads to a permanent position, if wanted.
- Is an income-producing fill-in for people between jobs or planning to move.
- Is a chance for people returning to the job market to orient to new technology and working conditions.

Con

- Hourly rates usually modest.
- Lacks permanent job stability.
- Requires constant adjustment to new people and new situations.
- Transportation to different locations can be a problem.
- Hourly compensation with on-the-job promotion unlikely.
- Benefits below norm and uncertain.

TEMPORARY WORK VS. FREE LANCING AND CONSULTING

Jane Dorkin, a skilled accountant, returned to work after many years as a housewife. She works through a temp employment firm in Denver that specializes in placing accountants. Jane is hired out to the firm's clients on a daily basis.

Linda Vegas, an equally skilled accountant, retired from a 20-year tenure with a large Boston accounting firm and opened her own accounting practice in a suburban mall near her home. She has developed a successful practice providing services for local merchants.

Jane and Linda exemplify the difference between temporary work and free lancing. Jane relies on the temp-help firm to market her services while Linda, a free lancer—or consultant, if you prefer—has to market her own services.

Marketing your services is costly and time consuming. Linda works that way because her earnings potential is greater. Whether you choose temporary employment directly with a company or through a temp agency or as a free lancer and/or consultant depends on the level of your ambition and whether you are willing and able to assume the responsibility for selling your own services.

Seasonal work occurs at certain times of the year when the employer's work load is heaviest. Retail sales positions at the local department store for the Christmas shopping season are typical of the seasonal work available to mature men and women. In addition to department stores and retail establishments, industries with part-time seasonal work opportunities include hotels and resorts, tourism, and transportation.

Seasonal jobs are ideal for seniors who like to spend part of the year up north, near their roots, family, and friends, and spend the winter in the warm and sunny South. Jay Charters, an old friend, has been working in a gift shop in Phoenix every Christmas since he lost his wife ten years ago. He looks forward to working during the holiday season, a season that used to be "the loneliest time of the year," and heads back to Minneapolis in the spring when Phoenix gets too hot to handle.

Home-based work. It is estimated that some 25 million Americans currently work at home. The U.S. Department of Labor predicts that this number will double in the next decade, and some government studies indicate that as much as 75 percent of the work done in this country could eventually be moved to the home.

Home-based work may be just what you're looking for. You can be home based as a salaried employee or as a self-employed individual operating your own business. Your work can be accomplished entirely in the home or can be based from the home but done mostly somewhere else. Sally Elfman, a former neighbor in Ft. Lauderdale, Florida, has chosen the latter course. As a manufacturer's representative, she is on the road three days a week; she spends the rest of the week on the phone at her office in the basement of her home. (The best part, according to Sally, is that she baby-sits her two granddaughters while she's on the phone and working.)

Tele-commuting is a variation of home-based work, made possible by new technology. The new tools available to mature adults who prefer to work at home include personal computers and laptops; modems that transmit documents to anyone, anywhere; versatile telephone setups, voice mail, and telephone conference hookups; copiers and desktop printers.

Jobs for telecommuters range from the highly skilled— editor, researcher, architect—to the more mundane—bookkeeper, customer service representative, reservations agent. J.C. Penney, Blue Cross/Blue Shield and Travelers Insurance are some of the companies that have set up formal telecommuting programs that employ men and women who perform their services at home through the telephone and computer modems.

Can older persons relate to a computer-oriented workplace? According to Dr. Denise Park at the University of Georgia, older adults are very positive about the use of computers and have no phobias or hesitancy about their use. University research showed that mature adults do not lack the ability or desire to conquer computer skills.

Pros and Cons of Working at Home

■ ■ ■

Pro

- Save time and energy by not commuting.
- Living near work is not important—you can live where you wish.
- Spare the time and expense "dressing" for work.
- Solitude.
- Fewer interruptions means increased productivity.
- Home office deduction provides tax advantage.
- Spend more time with children, grandchildren, and family.
- Reduced auto costs.

(continued on next page)

Con

- Workaholics can become more so.
- Border between work and personal life is compromised.
- Evenings and weekends may be interrupted by business.
- Motivation and productivity suffer because of home environment.
- Loneliness.
- Loss of interaction and stimulation from other people.
- Family relationship endangered by "closeness."
- Requires strong self-discipline.

Whether the advantages of working at home outweigh the disadvantages depends for the most part on your personality. The "solitude" listed in the "Pro" column appears as "loneliness" in the "Con" column. And sometimes it's hard to tell which it means to you until you've tried it.

Job sharing. Here's an alternative to the old 9-to-5—a work arrangement with great appeal to older workers. It's called "job sharing," and it means just that. The duties and the income of one full-time job are shared by two persons.

Job sharing is particularly suitable for people with skill and experience in specialized fields. Such individuals can find employers willing to try this arrangement in order to get the job done right. For many years now, teachers, administrators, program developers, secretaries, counselors, re-

searchers, and technicians have been job sharing successfully. Occupations where job sharing has been used include
bank tellers, editors, therapists, ministers, physicians, and
librarians.

In her book *It's Never Too Late to Start*, Dr. Jo Danna
expresses concern that workers in job-sharing arrangements
"can be exploited to handle peak work loads and frequent,
heavy deadlines. They may also be denied access to training
programs, promotions, and other fringe benefits." Despite
the possibility of exploitation, personnel executives believe
that flexible work styles are the wave of the future and, as job
sharing becomes more widespread, such drawbacks will be
minimized.

Phased retirement. For most people, retirement is an either/or
proposition. Either you are employed or you are retired.
Phased retirement programs reduce the work schedules of
older employees during a transition period. Typically, hours
are reduced to 20 to 32 hours per week with wages reduced
accordingly. Full or proportional benefits and a partial pension may be offered. Such programs allow people to retire
little-by-little, with gradual kick-in of their Social Security
benefits.

It makes good sense—for employers *and* employees.
Phased retirement provides employers with the uninter-
rupted services of loyal and experienced workers and, at the
same time, gives workers a chance to make a gradual adjustment to retirement. Everybody gains by adopting more flexible retirement systems that enable older people to continue
working longer, according to their capabilities, financial
needs, and personal desires.

Sociologist R. L. Kahn suggests that modular work
schedules which would enable individuals to define their
own gradual reduction in working time could greatly improve the quality of work life for older employees. The

Swedish Social Security system has incorporated phased retirement, and statistics show an increase in the employment rate among Swedes in their sixties.

How old would you be
if you didn't know
how old you was?

■ ■ ■

—Satchel Paige

Phased retirement programs have been adopted by a wide variety of firms in the United States, from aerospace to high-tech manufacturing, to research and development to financial-services firms. Two programs at the Polaroid Corporation, described in a background paper prepared for The Commonwealth Fund, are excellent examples:

"First, 'rehearsal retirement' at Polaroid allows employees to receive a leave of absence of up to six months without pay and benefits, so that they can experience retirement before making a decision to retire permanently. An employee must be 55 and served with the firm full time for one year to be eligible. The average rehearsal is about three months. About half the participants have returned to full-time work at the end of the period.

"Second, 'tapering off' allows workers approaching retirement age to reduce their work hours per day, work days per week, or work weeks per month for up to three to five years prior to retirement. Arrangements are individually negotiated. Employees are paid according to hours worked and receive full medical benefits and prorated pension credits. They receive other benefits on a prorated basis if they work at least 1,000 hours per year."

Employees can meet the 1,000-hour criteria by working 20 hours a week for 50 weeks during the year.

In addition to Polaroid, the following companies have adopted some variation of a phased retirement program:

Minnesota Title Financial Corporation. The company employs older workers in a job-sharing program that involves working on alternate months.

Corning Glass Works (Research and Development Division). For certain salaried professionals, the "40 percent work option" allows participants to retire, collect their pension, then return to work at 40 percent time, with prorated pay and a combination of full and prorated benefits.

Steelcase, Inc. The company encourages older employees to explore part-time options such as job sharing as an alternative to retirement.

Warren Publishing Corporation. Employees are encouraged to continue working as many hours as they wish. Benefits are prorated.

Aerospace Corporation. Employees nearing retirement may take a leave of absence for up to three months to explore post-retirement options or to elect to work part time prior to retiring.

Pitney-Bowes. After 25 years of service, and for every 5 years thereafter, employees are eligible for a 5-week vacation to pursue other interests.

MONY. Employees 64 years and older with 10 years of service may receive one paid day off each week for the 52 weeks prior to retirement.

Deere & Co. Partial and phased retirement for employees approaching retirement includes leaves of absence for one-year periods.

Teledyne Wisconsin Motor. Employees nearing retirement may take additional vacation time.

Varian Associates. Employees 55 or older are able to work 20 to 32 hours per week. They receive benefits that are proportional to hours at work plus partial insurance, vacation, and sick leave.

Company perks for older workers in the form of special education and sabbatical programs may be seen as a reward for long service or as an incentive to keep them at work and happy. Such programs include awarding the title of senior associate in recognition of superior performance (Corning Glass), facilitating an approaching career change (Control Data), three-month leave of absence for personal growth, (Wells Fargo), counseling to enable employees to make informed decisions about retirement (Travelers), and tuition aid to learn new business skills or a hobby (IBM). Kollmorgen Corporation allows employees who are one year from retirement to volunteer their services to the community while on the company payroll.

YOUR DREAM JOB—IF NOT NOW WHEN?

A large number of older workers simply continue at the work they were doing all along. And that's just fine with them. Most, however, are looking for "something different." A recent study found that fewer than one quarter of the mature people surveyed moved into a job that was in the same broad industry and occupation as their old position. For most people the transition from career jobs to post-career bridge employment involves a change in industry, occupation, or both.

How about you? If you're planning to enter a new field when you leave your career employment and are prepared emotionally and financially to accept the possibility of a different status and a lower wage, the change can be just what you've been looking for at this stage of your life.

Certain conditions that kept you from pursuing your "dream job" earlier in life no longer exist. As a mature adult you may now choose work for reasons different from in the past, when there were fewer choices and your financial obligations were greater.

Dramatic changes in technology and the way that business is conducted has opened doors for mature men and women who want to express their creativity and special talents. Although post-career bridge jobs represent an important transition, they need not be marginal or dull. They range from the off-beat to the downright exotic, and in many situations your age is an advantage, not a barrier.

At the Hilton Riverside Hotel in New Orleans, I met Richard Kelly Baird, a former federal attorney. While I was having my complimentary continental breakfast at the hotel's hospitality suite, Mr. Baird, a gentleman somewhere in his mid-seventies, came over to me in his snappy Hilton uniform and said, "How are you enjoying yourself? Is there anything about the history of New Orleans I could tell you about?" You bet he could. For the next hour and a half, Mr. Baird, who was a member of the hotel's concierge staff, filled me in on the adventures of the Longs—Huey, Russell, and Earl—in Louisiana politics. He also explained how the Cajun and Creole cultures created the New Orleans cuisine.

Mr. Baird told me he's been a history buff all his life. He was lucky, he said, "to find a job that would let me talk politics with people from all over the country. And get paid for it." Once again, I was reminded that your job is what you make it. At another time, Vee Taylor told me about her new profession in a cab we shared from LaGuardia Airport to downtown Manhattan. Vee is a retired teacher living in Sun City, Arizona. At age 62, she studied to be a Parliamentarian.

Now an expert at Robert's Rules of Order and a fully registered professional, she gets paid by corporations to sit at the side of the presiding officer and advise on the rules of order at board of directors' meetings, annual shareholder meetings, and union meetings.

If you never heard of Professional Registered Parliamentarian as an occupation, what other novel ways of making money are out there that you don't know about?

More and more older Americans choose work that captures their interest, without the primary regard for financial considerations. SCORE and the Peace Corps are two examples of the exciting and meaningful work opportunities open to adventure-seeking nonconformists. Here, early retirees, or even older retirees, enjoy doing what they always wanted to do without worrying about how well it pays, or if it pays. That doesn't mean that all purposeful work is in unpaid volunteer jobs. It does mean that if you can afford to forgo the income, there are many situations where the work itself is the best compensation.

Contrary to general belief, many such jobs have few educational or societal barriers. Coming out of the Great Depression, many young people could not afford college and went to work at an early age to support parents and their own new families. For mature adults seeking meaningful work, a college diploma is less important than are specialized skills and experience. In your later years you can enter fields where a lifetime of accumulated know-how is the best credential you can have.

With persistence and resourcefulness you and your dream job will find each other. Like the old song says, "It's nice work if you can get it, and you can get it if you try." Very often it's just a phone call or a letter away.

Here is a sampling of off-beat, nontraditional jobs particularly suited to older men and women. Obviously, these positions are not suited to everyone or available everywhere—there are not many jobs for mature male models in Jackson Hole, Wyoming—but the list will stimulate your thinking about unusual jobs in your area and open up a whole new range of options.

Party Coordinator. Look up party-planning services in the Yellow Pages. Call or write to tell them how good you are at running parties.

Film Extra. Older men and women are needed as extras in movies and TV shows. If you live near New York City or Los Angeles inquire at Screen Actors Guild in that city.

Wine Steward. If you know your wines and want to put your knowledge to work, consider becoming the sommelier in the best restaurant in town. Reach for the phone now.

Gardener. Many people who have been gardening as a hobby for decades are finding out that they can also make money at it. Look up "Landscape Contractors" or "Gardening Services" in the Yellow Pages.

Air Courier. Travel for free and get paid besides. Start by looking up "Air Courier Services" in the Yellow Pages.

Pet Care. Once again, your search starts with the local Yellow Pages. Look up "Pet Care," "Pet Exercising Services," or "Pet Training."

Bridal Consultant. No formal training is needed, but you may want to contact the Association of Bridal Consultants, 200 Chestnutland Road, New Milford, CT 06776 to learn more about the business.

Book Indexer. Enjoy reading? Got an eye for detail? Contact the American Society of Indexers, 1700 18th Street NW, Washington DC 20009, to learn how you can get a job or free-lance assignments as an indexer.

Professional Shopper. If shopping is what you do best, you can make money at it. Your Yellow Pages lists "Shopping Services—Personal." Start there.

Tour Guide. Proud of your city? Want to tell everybody about it? One of the booths recruiting older workers at the Operation ABLE Job Fair was occupied by the Chicago Motor Coach Company. The company was seeking mature men and women who knew the city to work as tour guides.

Cruise Ship Host. More cruise lines are seeking mature men on board to serve as "hosts" by dancing and socializing with unescorted ladies. It's an opportunity for free cruising and many pleasant vacations. Hosts are given a $100 to $200 bar credit to pay for the drinks they buy for ladies. If you're interested, stop in at your local travel agent and get a list of cruise lines to contact. Many men apply for this job—a recommendation from the travel agent will help you beat the competition.

Mature Models. Increased recognition of the spending power of seniors has persuaded advertisers to cast older men and women in their print and TV commercials. Rose Indri (60), John Hoffmeister (60), and Eugenia McLin (56) are among the nation's top mature models. Ford model Carmen (61) says, "Modeling keeps me socialized and in touch with younger people." Interested in modeling? Check with local model agencies, advertising agencies, and companies that produce clothing catalogs for mature people.

WHERE THE JOBS ARE

It's not what you did.
It's what you're doing.

—Allan Fromme

Even during periods of high unemployment businesses face labor shortages in specific areas. Valuable expertise is lost when longtime employees retire early and corporate "downsizing" leaves gaps in staffing.

The result: a "skills drain" that can seriously affect a company's bottom line. To slow the skills drain and fill in the gaps, a number of large companies have installed internal recruitment facilities and implemented flexible work arrangements for retirees and other experienced workers. A relatively new phenomcnon, but one that is growing fast, is the internal labor pool or "job bank" run by large companies with a continuous need for qualified temporary workers.

Since job-bank programs are not always visible or well publicized, it may take some digging to find company-run job banks in your area. But it's worth the search. Finding programs of this kind in your area is a smart first step in the post-retirement job search.

Travelers, Wells Fargo Banks, Cigna Corporation, Digital Equipment, and the Stouffer Corporation are some of the many large corporations that maintain job banks actively recruiting retirees and older workers. A few companies, Aerospace and Grumman, for example, have taken the concept a step further. By referring to their internal temporary pool as a "skills bank," they have widened the scope of the temporary work beyond the traditional "temp" typist and clerk. Their "skills bank" includes high-responsibility positions requiring advanced engineering and technical skills.

THE HONOR ROLL

No single model suits all company-sponsored job banks, but a special report by the Conference Board, a New York-based research organization, provides insight to current job banks and how they operate:

> *Stouffer Foods* maintains two pools of temporary workers. One is for part-time production-line work to augment as required the number of people on the production line of various products. The second pool is for clerical workers and is made up mostly of older workers.
>
> In each of the Stouffer pools, workers are guaranteed employment several days a week throughout the year.
>
> *Aerospace Corporation*, based in Los Angeles and nonprofit, conducts technical studies for the U.S. Air Force. It operates a "skills bank" as an internal temporary pool

that focuses on engineering and technical skills but lists retired secretaries and other administrative-support staff as well.

Wells Fargo Bank's "Retiree Temporary Work Force" is a retiree-only program that draws from a current pool of more than 650 retirees, approximately 110 of whom are actively working at a given time. A Conference Board survey estimates that 80 percent of the pool workers have clerical and teller skills. The number of retirees in the program was greatly enlarged when Wells Fargo merged with Crocker Bank.

Grumman Corporation has a skills bank that draws heavily on its retirees, although it now includes other skilled individuals who have worked for the company. About half of the people in the skills bank are in manufacturing jobs as machinists, inspectors, and other positions requiring similar expertise; the other half are in categories requiring engineering specialties.

Most of the men and women in Grumman's skills bank live near the company's Long Island, New York, facility. They are not hired directly by the company but are employed by outside temporary service agencies and assigned to work at Grumman.

CIGNA Corporation, a Philadelphia-based insurance company with a major presence in Hartford, operates its Encore temporary pool in both cities.

Hewlett-Packard Company operates On Call and On Contract, two forms of internal temporary employment. Both programs include retirees; the separate classifications relate to the nature and length of the work assignments.

Hewlett-Packard has about 3,500 retirees across the nation. A pilot program in Boston was designed to reach out to the company's sizable retiree population in that area.

Combustion Engineering, based in Windsor, Connecticut, operates a Retiree Temporary Employment Program. About a third of the 400 people registered in the program are retirees. When it was started in 1986 the pool emphasized technical skills, but it has since shifted to clerical work. Spouses of retirees have recently been recruited for C-E's job pool.

Western Savings and Loan in Arizona is looking for older men and women for teller positions "because older workers relate better to older customers."

Kentucky Fried Chicken has a program called The Colonel's Tradition that has created 1,500 new jobs for older workers.

Kinder-Care Inc., the nation's largest chain of child-care centers, has a staff of which 10 to 15 percent is over age 55. The chain continues to recruit older workers.

Xerox Corporation has a unique program that allows older workers to switch to a less demanding job within the company if and when the physical demands of their job become too great. Compensation for workers in this program are halfway between the level for their previous position and their new positions.

McDonald's restaurants operate the McMaster Job Training Program designed for workers over 55 who want part-time work. The fast-food chain pays program graduates slightly more than the minimum hourly wage.

Georgia Power Company employs part-time workers over 65 to weatherize the homes of retirees.

Texas Refinery Corporation has a sales force in their sixties and seventies who work as independent contractors.

Sixty-seven-year-old President Wesley D. Sears was quoted in *Modern Maturity* magazine: "Our older sales-people are more disciplined, more self-motivated, and follow instructions better than younger workers. They have enough experience to realize they don't know everything and are more productive as a result."

Corning, Inc., maker of Corning Ware Cookware, Pyrex, and Steuben Glass Products, has been cited by *New Choices* magazine as one of four that deserve "the gold medal for best treatment of older employees." (The others are Johnson & Johnson, IBM, and Aetna Life Insurance Co.) Corning requires all employees to invest 5 percent of their time each year improving their skills. Most of the courses are at the work place, but the company reimburses the cost of outside classes.

Corning has expanded its program for older employees to include job sharing. James Flynn, formerly vice president for finance at the company, is quoted in *New Choices:* "Looking at the heavy commitment, the stress, I decided that life was too short to work my hours." Consequently, 57-year-old Flynn and another recent retiree share the job of director of investor relations. They work out their own schedule and alternate every four to seven weeks. "For me," says Flynn, "it's been a great transition to retirement."

Herman Miller, an office-furniture manufacturer, recruits its retirees for special work assignments and provides a toll-free 800 phone number to assist them with Medicare and other health-insurance claims. Herman Miller and the Metropolitan Life Insurance Company have been honored by The American Society on Aging, the largest association of professionals in its field, for their innovative elder-care and flextime programs.

U.S. West, the global communications giant, has championed "telecommuting" (which allows employees to work at home) and other flexible job arrangements. It also offers older employees opportunities for skills upgrading.

Warner-Lambert, the pharmaceutical company, has alternative work scheduling that includes flexible times and places as well as job sharing.

Walt Disney companies discovered mature adults in the mid-1980s, actively recruiting individuals in their fifties, sixties, and seventies for a variety of positions in the company's recreational parks. You'll find older adults taking your tickets at the front gate, operating rides, serving as salespeople in the shops, and supervising work crews and stage events. (I'm told that the Disney parks will welcome your job application and those of other mature adults.)

Bank of America is known for its flexible time-and-place programs. The banks also offer personal leaves of up to one year, days off for family medical emergencies, and special work place adjustments for employees with life-threatening illnesses for as long as they care to work.

Other companies that have recognized the needs of older Americans and benefited from their experience and skills include American Express, Burpee Seed, Chase Manhattan Bank, Continental Bank, General Electric, Motorola, Levi-Strauss, Combustion Engineering, Standard Oil, Woodward and Lothrop, Dayton-Hudson, General Mills, Northeast Utilities, Digital Equipment Corporation, Harris Trust & Savings Bank, Honeywell, IBM, J.C. Penney, Motorola, Pillsbury, 3M, and Union Carbide.

The preceding is just a partial list of companies across the nation that have been cited for using skills of older workers. Although the formal job-bank programs reside at the larger companies, middle-sized and smaller companies in your area may have similar aims but more modest, informally managed programs. Such programs may be tougher to locate but are worth your effort in searching them out because they are likely to provide more interesting work alternatives. In your search for employment opportunity, middle-sized and smaller companies could be a better fit for you.

The only difference
between a gentleman
and a derelict is a job.

■ ■ ■

William Powell in the 1936
Universal Pictures film *My Man Godfrey*.

Small is beautiful

In the late eighties and the early years of the nineties, hundreds of large corporations were cutting staff and pressuring older workers into early retirement. At the same time, many thousands of smaller firms sprang up creating jobs for the men and women cast off by the big corporate entities. Human resources experts estimate that in the 1990s companies with fewer than 250 employees will account for more than half of the country's manufacturing jobs. And, since companies tend to be even smaller in nonmanufacturing industries, most service-industry positions will also be in small companies.

Although much of the recruitment of older workers— particularly for "temps" and part-timers—exists in large companies, small companies offer some of the more interesting work opportunities. In his book *The Paycheck Disruption*, Dan Lacey extols the small company: "Today's small business entities aren't offering people just jobs; they're offering a new level of occupational excitement and satisfaction."

Because they are less formal in their demands and more flexible in the division of labor, smaller companies are more likely to be receptive to mature workers. Concerned more with the bottom line and getting the job done than with tables of organization and fancy titles, smaller companies appreciate the work ethic, dependability, and the lifetime of experience that older workers bring to their jobs.

GOVERNMENT-SUBSIDIZED JOB PROGRAMS

The U.S. government is an important ally in helping you remain productively employed in your later years. Three important government-subsidized programs provide nationwide employment service and generate job opportunities for older workers:

1. **The Job Training Partnership Act (JTPA).** This act replaced the Comprehensive Employment and Training Act, which promoted public-service employment for individuals 55 and over. JTPA stresses training. And, because the federal government's role is primarily advisory, JTPA gives state government and private industry a much more active role in adjusting the program to meet regional needs.

   Job development, remedial education, work experience, and follow-up services for workers placed in non-subsidized employment are among the many services of JTPA. The program's Employment and Training Assistance for Dislocated Workers helps individuals of all ages who lose or cannot obtain employment due to mass layoffs, natural disasters, high local unemployment, or the closing of federal facilities. Although the program was designed primarily to assist economically disadvantaged workers, it also helps those who have encountered barriers to employment—older workers, handicapped individuals, displaced homemakers, veterans, and so forth.

Before 1986 income eligibility for JTPA was based on the combined income of the applicant's entire household. After 1986 the "Family of One" ruling stated than only the applicant's income was to be considered when determining his eligibility. If you were turned down previously because your income was too high, you may now be eligible. You can reapply at your Area Agency on Aging or your Human Services Information office. They will direct you to the nearest Job Training Partnership Act program office in your state.

2. **The Senior Community Service Employment Program (SCSEP)** under Title V of the Older Americans Act is administered at the Federal level by the U.S. Department of Labor. It is designed to provide part-time jobs in community service for unemployed individuals 55 and older whose incomes do not exceed 125 percent of the federal poverty level. Priority is given to individuals age 60 and over.

SCSEP projects are sponsored by state and territorial governments in all 50 states, the District of Columbia, Puerto Rico, and all U.S. territories. Participants work 20 to 25 hours per week at schools, hospitals, day-care centers, fire-prevention centers, programs for the handicapped, and conservation projects. By law, participants must be paid no less than the federal minimum wage, the state minimum wage, or the local prevailing rate of pay for similar employment—whichever is highest. In addition to wages, participants receive physical examinations and personal job counseling.

3. **The State Employment Security Agencies' Job Service** is funded by the U.S. Department of Labor's Employment and Training Administration and the state and local governments. More than 2,000 Job Service offices serve employable legal residents of the United States. Special assistance available to older persons includes job development, occupational testing, job-market information, employment counseling, referrals to work and training programs, as well as help in finding full- and part-time work. Most Job Service offices maintain up-to-date listings of local job openings.

To contact the nearest Job Service office, find "Employment Service" or "Employment Security Commission" under "State Government Offices" in your telephone directory.

Demand for Older Workers

Unfortunately, many older individuals have bought into the negative myths about older workers. Misconceptions about the value of older men and women and misconceptions about business's attitude toward hiring and retaining older workers has discouraged the older workers from seeking employment.

Age discrimination existed in the past and continues to exist today despite laws that make it illegal, but older Americans should be aware of the great progress that has been made in eliminating age discrimination. Although the law has been a factor, the real reason that so many businesses have done a complete about-face and welcomed the older worker can be summed up in one sentence: It makes good business sense.

9 Myths and 14 Simple Truths About Older People in the Work Place

The myths about older people in the workplace.

1. Less productive than younger workers
2. Cost more to employ
3. Not motivated—just biding their time
4. Preoccupied with the past; little interest in the future
5. Old-fashioned values, traditional thinkers, and overly conservative
6. Mentally and physically impaired
7. Often ill and absent from work
8. Resistant to change
9. Unable to learn new skills and new ways of doing things

The simple truth—older adults make better employees.
Here's why:

1. Dependable—lower absenteeism
2. Able to relate to others
3. High level of productivity
4. Require less supervision
5. Less drug and alcohol use than with younger people
6. Stability that comes with maturity
7. Willing to work part-time and flexible hours

8. Strong work ethic

9. Waste less time on the job

10. High level of writing and math skills

11. Highly motivated

12. Willing and able to learn and acquire new skills

13. Less distracted by outside interests

14. A lifetime of experience dealing with people and changing conditions

The growing demand for older workers has been fueled by the experience of employers in the United States and abroad. The Commonwealth Fund, a private national philanthropy, conducted studies as part of the Fund's Americans Over 55 At Work Program, which prove that older people can be trained in new technologies, do not cost more to employ, and can work as efficiently as younger people.

The studies were conducted in the fall of 1990 and spring of 1991 and included two major American corporations and a large British firm: *Day's Inn of America, Inc.*, the world's third-largest hotel chain with more than 1,100 properties and a nationwide computerized reservations system; *The Travelers Corporation*, based in Hartford, Connecticut, one of the world's largest multiline financial-services companies, focusing on insurance, managed health care, and investments; and *B&Q plc*, Britain's largest chain, with 280 Do-It-Yourself stores—very large hardware, housewares, construction equipment stores—with $1.6 billion in annual revenue and 15,000 employees.

The experience of these three companies supplies hard evidence of the value of older workers. It is the kind of information that should bolster the confidence of older adults searching for work and motivate profit-minded employers building a more effective work force.

Days Inn of America began hiring workers age 50 and over as reservations agents in 1986. The company's reservations system is a sophisticated 24-hour round-the-clock telecommunications operation that handles 23,500 calls a day. Day Inns began hiring mature men and women because it was having difficulty recruiting younger workers in sufficient numbers, and the younger workers' annual turnover rate was nearly 100 percent.

At the Atlanta Center, one of the company's two telecommunications locations, researchers found that

- Older workers can be trained to operate sophisticated computer software in the same time as they can train younger workers—about two weeks.

- Older workers stay on the job much longer than younger workers. They stay an average of 3 years as compared to 1 year for younger workers. The bottom line: $618 in average training and recruiting cost per hire for older workers, compared to $1,742 for younger workers.

- Older workers participate in all three shifts.

John Snodgrass, president and chief operating officer of Days Inn, reports that his company's experience employing mature adults as reservations agents "has been great—they are dedicated and effective salespeople who are certainly just as productive as our younger employees." Because of Days Inn's positive experience at reservations centers many of the company's hotels across the nation have also hired seniors.

The Travelers Corporation, an insurance and financial services giant, operates one of the largest and most active retiree job banks to help fill the company's continuous demand for temporary help. Since its beginning in 1981, the program (TravTemps) has been expanded to include retirees from other companies as well as younger workers. Travelers skilled-retiree labor pool is based in Hartford, Connecticut, where a third of the firm's 34,000 employees work and where nearly half of its 6,500 retirees live.

Currently, about 700 retirees are on call for temporary assignments in positions ranging from unskilled production to data entry and professional duties. Some Travelers' field locations outside Hartford also maintain local job banks.

As can be expected, the demand is greatest for office and word-processing skills. The job bank also places professional retirees, handles all hiring from outside temporary agencies, and monitors the company's use of consultants. (Retired executives now working as consultants will find this a fertile source of leads for consulting assignments—at Travelers and elsewhere.)

In a cost comparison of the TravTemps retiree program versus the cost of hiring temporary employees through an outside temp agency, Commonwealth Fund found that

- Setting up a job bank for retirees has provided Travelers with significant savings in both agency fees and sales tax. Total savings in 1989: $871,000.

- Using job-bank retirees instead of outside temps hired through an agency saved the company $4 to $9 per hour.

- Using retirees as temporary workers gives Travelers maximum flexibility in staffing and expands the available pool for temporary assignments.

The program capitalizes on the retirees' relationship with the company. Retirees are more motivated; they know the company and its work, and the company is aware of each retiree's abilities. The goodwill inherent in this program spreads throughout the company and improves the morale of the entire work force as all employees see firsthand how the company takes care of its own.

In the spring of 1991, when Travelers received a special comprehensive award from the U.S. Administration on Aging for Business and Aging Leadership, Chairman Edward H. Budd said, "At Travelers, we've learned how much we can benefit from the rich pool of talent, experience and productivity that exists among mature Americans."

Elizabeth Burns, an 87-year-old employee of the company, was among those present at the award ceremony in the nation's capital. The oldest employee at Travelers, she works an average of three days a week, putting in a full seven and a half hours each day. Ms. Burns had worked close to 45 years before leaving to care for two sisters. Fifteen years later, at age 82, she rejoined Travelers and has been there for five years since. At the awards ceremony she equated her work situation to a good marriage: "It is definitely a partnership based on mutual respect and commitment."

B&Q plc was having staff problems throughout its vast network of retail stores across Britain. In some locations the entire staff had to be replaced each year. Demographic changes in the U.K. population resulted in expensive and costly recruitment; store employees lacked knowledge of the products they were selling.

Top company management believed that hiring older workers could solve their staffing problems. They responded to the doubts about older men and women by staffing a new store in Macclesfield, south of Manchester, entirely with workers aged 50 and over.

B&Q's all-older-worker store opened in late 1989. A study conducted by the Institute for Employment Research at the University of Warwick and a Washington, D.C., research organization compared the Macclesfield store with five traditionally staffed B&Q stores with similar demographics. The study revealed that

- Macclesfield was 18 percent more profitable than the average of the 5 comparison stores.

- Employee turnover at Macclesfield was nearly 6 times lower than the average of the comparison stores. The older workers at this store were flexible and ready to fill in whenever they were needed. They worked an average of 8 overtime hours per month.

- The older workers were absent 39 percent less than workers in the comparison stores.

- Shoplifting—a serious problem at retail establishments—was less than half the average of the 5 comparison stores. (Management says this is because older employees pay greater attention to customers.)

These findings have significantly affected the store's future recruiting, training, and staffing plans. B&Q chief executive Jim Hodkinson states: "The great results at Macclesfield have led us to open another older worker store at Exmouth. We've also set a corporate goal for older employment at 10 percent by the end of 1991."

The Commonwealth Fund's Americans over 55 at Work program, the sponsors of the study that brought these facts to light, is dedicated to making more opportunities for continued employment for older Americans who want to work and motivating employers to find ways to attract, retrain, motivate, reward, and retain seniors.

According to the Fund's Molly McKaughan, this is an international trend. "We are already in contact with companies in Germany and Japan analyzing their older worker policies."

The many studies confirming the value of older workers furnish the proof you need to convince employers of the value of hiring and retaining you and others your age. The studies reinforce your confidence in your abilities and provide the hard evidence to correct employers' misconceptions.

Over the hill? Hardly. Top of the hill is more like it.

CHAPTER SIX

KNOCKING DOWN BARRIERS

> Discrimination on account of age is
> as bad as discrimination on account
> of sex or race or anything else.
>
> —Claude Pepper

"On or about March, '87, we are going to get rid of all chefs over 40."

That terse memo from an executive of a Black Angus restaurant cost 63-year-old chef Rex Kinney his job. The company, which had discontinued its pension plan some time before, told Mr. Kinney that he was being given early retirement. A charge of age discrimination based on the Federal Age Discrimination in Employment Act (ADEA) was upheld by a California court and the chef was awarded a judgment of $290,932.

In reporting the case, the AARP *Bulletin* quotes Mr. Kinney as saying, "To think the jury vote was 12–0. I was really flying on cloud nine."

Although not all cases of age discrimination end as happily, ADEA, a federal law, has been a major force in preventing employers from denying equal employment opportunity because of age. Joseph Kalet, a Washington attorney, points out, however, that the law has its limitations: "ADEA made it a lot more difficult to discriminate, but it didn't preclude it."

Once practiced openly and without apology in offices and factories, age discrimination is now more subtle and harder to prove. Employers with an age bias usually find a way to terminate older workers or reject older job applicants without being held accountable. It's important that you understand your rights and the ways you can fight back if and when a biased employer tries to circumvent the law and you are denied your rights.

Americans age 40 and over are protected by a federal law, the Age Discrimination in Employment Act (ADEA) and by most state and local laws. The law passed by Congress in 1967 makes it illegal to deny employment because of age and puts an end to mandatory retirement in government and the private sector, except for limited categories of employees. ADEA promotes employment of older persons based on ability rather than on age. The law prohibits arbitrary age discrimination in employment and advises employers and workers in finding ways to solve age-related problems.

At the same time, ADEA allows employers to base a decision on a "reasonable factor other than age" and to "discharge or otherwise discipline an individual for good cause." But when age is the only factor, the law is clear: Age discrimination in hiring, discharge, pay, promotions, fringe benefits, and other aspects of employment is illegal.

Employers are also prohibited from stating an age preference in notices or want ads. Using terms such as "recent college graduate" or "age 25 to 35" in want ads is prohibited. Obviously, such terms are disguised ways of saying, "Older workers need not apply." An employer who retaliates against an employee for complaining about age discrimination or for helping the government investigate such a charge is also violating the law.

Employers have been known to pressure older workers into quitting voluntarily so that they may be replaced by younger workers.

Other employees can be guilty of age harassment as well. An attorney friend of mine was constantly being asked by some of the younger attorneys in the firm why he didn't retire "and give somebody else a chance at senior partnership." It is the employer's responsibility to see that such incidents don't occur, and many older workers are taking action to stop the harassment.

The Age Discrimination in Employment Act applies to private employers of 20 or more workers as well as to government offices, employment agencies, and labor organizations that operate a hiring hall or office that recruits potential employees or obtains job opportunities for its members.

There are exemptions, however, and you should know about them. Some of the exemptions are:

- All elected officials, the elected officials' personal staffs, and all appointees on a policymaking level (and their legal advisers) receive no protection under the age discrimination law.

- Until December 31, 1993, tenured faculty may be retired at age 70.

- Certain high policymaking executives may be retired at age 65.

- The terms of a formal seniority system or employee benefit may be observed.

- An employer may use age as a *bona fide* occupational qualification where it is necessary to the normal operation of a particular business and there are no alternative standards other than age.

In 1986 Congress amended ADEA to permit mandatory retirement of tenured college faculty and public-safety officers. This amendment was made for a seven-year trial period ending December 31, 1993.

In the meantime, the Center for Applied Behavior Sciences at Pennsylvania State University studied the question as it applied to police, firefighters, and corrections officers. Frank Landy, Ph.D., director of the Center said, "We found no basis for the belief that older workers jeopardize public safety. Many of the physical and psychological declines associated with aging are actually the result of illness, injury, and individual lifestyle rather than aging per se."

Charles Meeks, executive director of the 22,000-member National Sheriff's Association, is against mandatory retirement. He says older officers who can perform their duties and want to perform their duties should be allowed to: "When we force them out because of an age rule, we lose a lot of fine people in law enforcement." Meeks, who is 55, says, "Right now I feel I could whip my weight in wildcats. But if I'm not being productive, somebody should tell me, and I'm out of here. Performance evaluations and testing can do that."

A blue-ribbon panel has advised Congress to pass a bill preventing police, firefighters, and corrections officers from being forced off the job at retirement age, but as this is being written, Congress has yet to act.

> To be old in a
> work-oriented industrial society
> such as America is to be relegated
> to being a non-person.
>
> ■ ■ ■
>
> —Richard Mowsesian

THE THIRD MAN IN THE COCKPIT

Age limits on pilots are determined by the Federal Aviation Administration (FAA). For many years, the Airline Pilots Association fought to repeal the agency's mandatory retirement at age 60 for airline pilots. The outstanding achievement of United Airlines senior pilot David Cronin, then a month short of his sixtieth birthday, supports that position. Cronin brought a Boeing 747 to a safe landing in Hawaii with two of its four engines shut down and a gaping hole it its fuselage. Nine passengers were sucked out of the plane when a faulty door exploded an hour out of Hawaii, but 327 passengers were saved. Cronin credits the successful landing to "a huge reserve of that experience."

Despite the life-saving performance of David Cronin and other pilots at or close to mandatory retirement age, the Pilots Association has reversed its position and now accepts retirement at 60 for pilots.

There is a way, however, that pilots can continue to fly after age 60. John Mazor, the Pilots Association's director of communications, told me that pilots can continue to fly past the mandatory retirement age by becoming "the third man in the cockpit." The FAA requires that three qualified people be present in the cockpit during a commercial airline flight—two of whom are pilots and the third, the flight engineer. Since there is no mandatory retirement age requirement for flight engineers, many pilots who want to continue flying after 60 apply for a position as the third man in the cockpit. Even though salaries for flight engineers are lower, many pilots accept the reduced paycheck in order to keep flying.

A recent report, "Alternatives to Chronological Age in Determining Standards of Suitability for Public Safety Jobs," by a team of researchers recommends that police officers and firefighters be judged on a case-by-case basis, rather than relying on an arbitrary cut-off at a specific age. But the long-standing debate about mandatory retirement age for public-safety jobs continues with merit on both sides of the argument.

Perhaps the "third man in the cockpit" approach is the solution where the competence of an older public safety officers is involved. A new level of employment could be created that will allow police officers and firefighters to continue in another less strenuous, less crucial capacity. The "third man in the cockpit" model has implications beyond public-safety jobs. How many other fields are there where a back-up, assistant, or mentor role for older men and women would provide a solution that benefits everyone? Our society loses millions of man-hours of productive work every year—billions of dollars of income—because of age bias. Age bias robs the most respected and cherished members of our nation of their usefulness and self-respect.

7 Ways You Can Fight Age Bias

1. Don't buy into the myths of the age discriminators. Ability is ageless. Your job hunt is a change from one activity to another and has nothing to do with age.

2. Don't refer to age in your job solicitations, resume, or interview. If the employer raises age as an issue, prepare yourself with a response that emphasizes experience and skills.

3. Learn the true facts and be able to correct any misconceptions that an employer may have about the value of older adults in the work place.

4. Never apologize or be defensive because of your age. It's an asset, not a liability.

5. Join organizations and cooperate with others who empathize with your problems and support your work goals: the American Association of Retired Persons (AARP), National Council on Aging, and Gray Panthers, for example.

6. Understand your legal rights to equal employment opportunity and know what action you can take if you come up against age discrimination.

7. Project a youthful image. You do this with your attitude, your dress, your body language, and your young ideas.

OVERQUALIFIED?!?

In spite of laws on the books for over two decades, an insidious and illegal age discrimination keeps energetic older adults warehoused in "leisure villages" and retirement developments. As with many other laws, employers who want to deny jobs to older workers can find ways to get around the law.

By using such slippery charges as "doesn't fit our profile for this position" or "qualifications inconsistent with our requirements," employers who want to deny jobs to older workers find ways to get around the law. The overqualified label is often used as a ruse to turn away an older job candidate. While they know—and you know—that you've been turned down because of your age, a company that doesn't want to hire people past a certain age can find ways of keeping mature people out and the law at bay. (In Chapter Eight, we discuss ways to minimize the perception of over-qualification by a potential employer.)

Similarly, a company that wants to terminate its older workers doesn't have to fire them and risk lawsuits. Pressure on the job and other forms of coercion will usually force resignations and cut higher-priced older workers from the payroll.

Older employees are winning landmark victories in stopping forced "voluntary early retirement." *The Wall Street Journal* reports that a federal jury in Houston awarded $3.2 million to Richard E. Wilson, a 66-year-old former vice president of Monarch Paper Co., who "was demoted to a warehouse maintenance job that included clean-up duty and other menial tasks." Mr. Wilson contended that the demotion was part of a plan to eliminate older managers and replace them with younger hands. Other age-discrimination lawsuits involve early-retirement offers involving workers who contend that they were given little choice in the matter and that the offer was not an option but a requirement. They say that they weren't given enough time to make a decision and that the early retirement plan was not voluntary because it came with the suggestion that their job was scheduled for elimination anyway.

Mandatory retirement
is another form of
compulsory poverty.

■ ■ ■

—Anonymous

Fighting Back

As an older employee or job seeker, you may come up against some form of age bias—sometimes subtle and hard-to-prove, other times bold, blatant, and up-front. Where there is a clear case of age discrimination and you can prove it, the machinery exists to correct the situation. You can file a charge of discrimination with the U.S. Equal Employment Opportunity Commission (EEOC).

The number of claims has grown as older employees and job candidates fight back. University of Houston law professor Mark Rothstein is quoted in *New Choices* magazine as saying that employees are much more aggressive about asserting their rights and adds, " . . . there's the bias against older workers in times of economic hardship. In my view, with the aging of the population, the number of cases is likely to increase from now until as far as one can imagine."

According to the latest EEOC figures, charges of age discrimination nearly doubled during the 1980s and climbed to a record 22,537 new cases in 1990. Since it took over ADEA enforcement from the Labor Department in 1979, the EEOC has filed some 800 lawsuits and collected more than $400 million for victims of age discrimination.

Should you decide to file an age-discrimination claim, you can file in person, by mail, or by telephone at any one of the 50 EEOC field offices. If the commission doesn't have an office in your area, call toll free 800-USA-EEOC to locate the nearest office.

There are strict time frames in which charges of age discrimination must be made. You need to contact the EEOC promptly when you suspect that you've been discriminated against because of your age. They'll advise you on the merits of your claim and give you a specific deadline for any action you wish to take. Here's the kind of information that the EEOC will ask for if you file an age-discrimination claim:

- Your name, address, and telephone number.
- The name, address, and telephone number of the company you are charging with age discrimination.
- The date (or dates) at which discrimination occurred.
- The details of the charge.

Before taking your case to the EEOC, it would be wise to gather additional information, including:

- The names of witnesses who can support your claim.
- Relevant incidents.
- Your job description and your work history with the company, if you are presently employed there.
- The reason the company gave for the action that led you to file a claim.
- How the treatment you received from the company was different from that given to other employees.

When you file a claim of age discrimination an EEOC staffer will interview you to obtain the facts. If your claim meets legal requirements, a formal charge is drafted and the commission notifies the employer of the charge. Information is gathered and witnesses are interviewed. Where age discrimination did occur, the EEOC tries to persuade the employer to eliminate the practice. Remedies may include reinstating you to the job you would have had if the discrimination did not occur, back pay, restoration of lost benefits, and a notice posted by the employer to advise employees that it has corrected the situation.

Where persuasion fails, the commission files a lawsuit in a federal district court on your behalf or you may take private civil action and sue the company yourself. Most charges are conciliated or settled before a court trial begins.

If the EEOC or you personally sue the employer and win the case the court may provide relief for actual damages. It can also get you back pay, front pay, restored benefits, job reinstatement, or job offers.

Even so, you should be aware that age discrimination—in hiring practices or on the job—is difficult and expensive to prove. Balancing a company's right to economize and an older worker's right to be treated the same as a younger employee is a complex legal question, and many lawyers are reluctant to take such cases. Pursuing your claim might temper your outrage but it can be costly and time consuming.

Most important of all, pressing an age-discrimination claim can detract you from your mission: Finding work where you are welcome and appreciated. For every firm that discriminates against older workers, there are ten that welcome the skill, experience, and dedication that older men and women bring to the job. With fewer young people qualifying for jobs that require judgment and experience, employers have begun to appreciate maturity on the job. Throughout this book we cite examples of dynamic and successful companies that actively recruit older men and women.

Many job seekers who didn't get the job because of age bias prefer to look ahead and not look back. They might get it off their chest by writing to the company and telling them about it, but they look elsewhere for opportunity.

Should you decide to pursue the matter through legal measures, two congressional committees monitor the Age Discrimination in Employment Act and should be informed of your experiences.

- U.S. House Select Committee on Aging, House Annex 1, Room 712, Washington, DC 20515

- ▪ Senate Special Committee on Aging, Dirksen Senate Office Building, Room G-31, Washington, DC 20510

For names of attorneys who practice employment law, contact your local bar association or write to the National Employment Lawyers Association, 535 Pacific Avenue, San Francisco, CA 94133.

An Open Letter To Employers

▪ ▪ ▪

Dear Sir or Madam,

Your business has grown, you've expanded your operation, and now you're looking for more good employees to help you achieve your goals.

The people you need are ready and able to go to work for you. They are among the millions of energetic men and women in their fifties, sixties, and even seventies with proven work records and valuable life experience. More and more employers such as yourself have come to recognize these older adults as stable and reliable workers, with high morale and a strong commitment to the company.

James E. Challenger, President of Challenger, Gray & Christmas, one of the nation's leading outplacement consultants says: "The older worker, by virtue of his or her experience, is seen as frequently being able to work 'smarter,' fitting into the workplace rapidly and being able to make an immediate contribution to profitability."

In order to remain lean and efficient in today's market, many companies employ a permanent full-time work force and part-time contingency workers with good skills and flexible wage requirements. Middle-aged workers with families and career commitments have high, fixed salary needs and require full health insurance benefits; older workers with modest needs and income from other sources have more flexible salary requirements and many have their health insurance already covered by private or government benefits (Medicare).

In a study by the Small Business Administration, older workers were rated superior to the average worker, using a number of different measures. More than 65 percent of employers rated workers age 55 and over to be more reliable, punctual, and loyal than the average worker. More than 94 percent of employers said that older workers required the same or less training, were at least as productive, had the same or greater overall skills and the same or greater mental concentration. In general, the employers surveyed were quite pleased with the performance of older workers.

Travelers Insurance, Days Inn Hotels and Motels, Wells Fargo Banks, Cigna Grumman, Hewlett-Packard, and Digital Equipment are just a few of the large and successful organizations that employ older workers in permanent full-time positions and count on them as a contingency work-force resource. Sears actively recruits older workers for certain positions because they are superior workers and because they are willing to work part time. (In fact, most mature adults actually prefer part-time work.)

Today's jobs require sophisticated skills and experience, not muscle power. The Harvard Business Review confirms that older workers outperform younger workers in jobs requiring scholarship and artistic creativity as well as in sales, clerical, and manual work. Many of the jobs you need to fill require math, language, and the basic communications skills that younger work-

ers lack. *Men and women with lifetime experience know how to communicate effectively and get things done.*

You will be interested in a Commonwealth Fund study of the experiences of three firms, two in America and one in Britain. All three companies found that older workers were easy to train, efficient, and productive.

- *Travelers Insurance Co. estimates that using its internal retiree recruitment program saves the company nearly $900,000 in fees and taxes.*

- *Days Inn of America reports that 87 percent of its older workers stay on the job for a year or more, compared with 30 percent of its younger workers. And absenteeism at Days Inn was only 1.4 percent for older workers vs. 3.7 percent for younger people.*

- *When one of the stores of B&Q, a large British hardware chain, was staffed entirely by workers 50 and older, profits went up 18 percent, turnover was nearly 6 times lower, absenteeism dropped 39 percent, and losses to theft and damage less than half than at five comparison stores.*

It is a myth that older workers resist change. In a recent survey, IBM found that employees over age 45 were actually more flexible than younger employees in adapting to job changes. As people age and face new challenges and new experiences, they must learn to change in order to survive. Older workers are ready to learn new tricks and want the opportunity to show off the old ones.

Once recruited and given the opportunity for training, older persons are more likely to complete their training and, once trained, are likely to remain with

*their employers longer than younger trainees are. Work-
ers between the ages of 50 and 60 stay on the job an
average of 15 years, and their attendance rates are equal
to or better than that of most other age groups.*

*Consistency tends to increase with age. According
to the National Association of Manufacturers, older
workers perform better, on the whole, than younger
workers in a wide range of jobs. Older workers have
fewer personal distractions in their private lives and are
therefore better able to focus on the job at hand. They
tend to be more attached to their work and satisfied
with their job because they've established their niche
in life.*

*If your business involves relating to the public and
to customers, you need employees with "people skills."
Courtesy, patience, and helpfulness are not taught in
school. They are the result of lifetime experience.*

*The assumption by some employers that older
workers lack motivation and that they are just biding
their time is simply not so. Motivation or lack of motivation is not a consequence of age, but of personality and
financial need. Thousands of successful companies were
built on the work ethic and drive of older men and
women. Their need and desire to work, their tradition of
a-day's-work-for-a-day's-pay, and their pride in quality
workmanship often serve as a model to younger workers.*

*And, for people on a fixed income squeezed be-
tween inflation and declining return on savings, the
need for additional income spells Motivation with a
capital "M."*

*The very qualities that you want in any employee
are the ones older workers possess. They offer experience,
knowledge, and mature judgment; solid basic literacy
and math skills; commitment to work ethic and interest*

in the job; punctuality, less absenteeism, and lower accident rates.

You should be interested in adding these mature adults to your work force not because age discrimination is illegal but because they are superior workers. Hiring older workers isn't a question of compassion or social justice. It's a matter of dollars and sense.

Yours very truly,

Robert S. Menchin

CHAPTER SEVEN

BEFORE THE HUNT

The man who is too old to learn
was probably always too old to learn.

—Henry S. Haskins

Preparation is the key to finding the right job. In addition to making the search more efficient, preparation and planning will clarify your aims, boost your confidence, and help you overcome any insecurities you may have about looking for work as a mature adult.

Let's review each of the six steps that will prepare you for the job search ahead:

1. IDENTIFYING INTERESTS AND SKILLS

The same techniques that applied to your job hunt at age 40 are valid at age 60—with some crucial differences. You have changed, and the job market has changed. At a recent gathering, Jack Fisher, a former colleague, explained his current motivations: "At 40, I worried about my career and the money I needed to meet the mortgage and pay the orthodontist for my daughter's braces. At 60, I have a completely different set of priorities. I need to keep healthy and remain financially independent. After that, I want to find work that will keep me active and involved."

The job market has certainly changed since Jack was middle-aged and in the prime of his career. Jobs are harder to get now, and the competition is keener. A wave of "rifs" (reduction in force) have created massive unemployment in many areas of the country. In addition, the demands of the job market have shifted from agriculture and heavy industry to service and information processing. Mergers, takeovers, leveraged buyouts, and foreign competition have changed the landscape of industrial America. Electronic equipment and computers are the tools of the modern worker, and the contingency work force employing temporary and part-time workers is gaining popularity.

Where do you stand in this scenario? To determine your current status, check the box or boxes that best describe your situation:

[ ] *Currently employed but contemplating retirement in the future.*

You need to do some serious research and planning. Know your rights as an employee and familiarize yourself with the company's pension plan and health-benefit provisions for retirees—you may have more negotiating power than you realize. If you're contemplating early retirement, you should understand the pros and cons. Talk to retirees about their experiences and learn firsthand what to expect.

[ ] *Currently employed with no intention
of retiring as long as I am physically able
and not forced to retire.*

Good for you. But, just in case your employer has other ideas about your future, you should be aware of the laws prohibiting age discrimination and mandatory retirement at a specific age. If and when you're ready to ease off, you and your employer might consider some kind of phased-retirement arrangement that will satisfy both of you.

[ ] *Unemployed and seeking full-time work.*

Age, as an obstacle to full-time employment, may exist only in your own mind. Even during recessions and periods of high unemployment, there are jobs for older adults with marketable skills, but unless your skills match the demands of the market you must be willing to learn new skills. You may also have to be flexible in your demands.

Consider part-time employment as a morale builder, as a route to full-time work, and as a source of income until you find the job you're really looking for. Contact organizations and support groups that can help you.

[ ] *Unemployed and seeking temporary
or part-time work.*

By supplementing permanent full-time staff with a contingency work force of temps and part-time workers, an employer can operate economically and keep fringe benefits and pension costs down. Consequently, opportunities for temporary and part-time work are plentiful and growing. Temporary or part-time work allows you greater flexibility and more time for leisure. You can construct a work schedule to fit your lifestyle.

Contact the support groups, senior service agencies, the "temp" placement firms, and corporate retiree job banks in your area.

[ ] *Voluntarily retired.*

Like many, you couldn't wait to be free of the old 9-to-5, could you? Enjoy your retirement—keep active, cultivate new friends, and welcome new experiences. But if retirement begins to pall and turns out to be something less than you hoped, there is a way back. Your post-retirement job can be as good—or better—than the one you left.

[ ] *Retired by the company.*

Your company might have acted illegally. There are laws against mandatory retirement and age discrimination. If you wanted to keep working but were forced to retire—and can prove it—see a lawyer and strike a blow for all of us.

On the other hand, it might be best not to look back but to get on with your life. Getting a better job is the best revenge!

[ ] *Enjoying retirement but may be interested*
    in work some time in the future.

Enjoy the freedom and leisure but keep your eyes open for the emerging work opportunities in your area. Do you have the skills you will need if you decide to go back to work? Consider enrolling in classes to learn new occupational skills. In that way you'll be keeping all your options open.

[ ] *Out of the job market for many years*
    and seeking reentry.

Retirees who want to reverse their retirement and men and women out of circulation for years need to update their skills and learn to job hunt effectively. Women who spent most of their lives as homemakers need to reactivate latent interests and match their talent to the job market. Both men and women should seek out support groups to boost their confidence and help them achieve their goals.

Several large companies and government agencies have special programs designed to hire and train older men and women but small, growing companies usually offer more opportunity and greater challenge.

You may have to take a less-than-ideal job while you upgrade your skills and continue your search. If it's practical, consider the possibility of self-employment.

[ ] *Retired, but would want to work if it were the right job.*

OK, be particular. It may take a little longer, but the "dream job" you are looking for is out there. Often the best jobs are unadvertised and filled through personal contact or are created to fill a need.

You should have a firm idea of the "right job" fixed in your mind. The money and the satisfaction that such a job confers is the best motivation for a conscientious job search.

2. SETTING GOALS

One of the advantages of age is that you are now in a better position to live by your own definition of success. You decide which values to maintain and which are no longer important to you. Many older Americans with long and productive careers never before had the luxury of asking, "Will this job give me the satisfaction and fulfillment I am looking for at this stage of my life?" Well, now you can. You can decide when you want to work, in what kind of environment, and with whom you want to work.

Do you want full- or part-time work? Large or small organization? Alone or with others? Under supervision or at your own pace? Salary, commission, or some combination of the two?

Free of the responsibility of supporting a young family, you can set goals that offer ego compensation as well as financial reward. As you look over this list of job related values, try this exercise. Assign a number to each item—10 for the most important, 9 for the next most important, and so on to 1 and 0 for those values that mean little or nothing to you. This is not a test that others will see and judge—it's for your eyes only. If you've been honest with yourself it will give you a pretty good assessment of what really matters to you.

Money

- Making a lot of money
- Making enough money to take care of my needs
- Increasing my income each year
- Accumulating a substantial sum of money

Where

- In a pleasant environment
- Near home
- Working outside
- Working indoors

Relating

- Having a sense of belonging

- Being part of a team
- Working with and for people I like
- Chance to meet new people and make new friends
- Working with people my age
- Working with people of all ages

How

- Being constantly challenged for solutions to problems
- Competing with other companies and fellow employees
- Meeting deadlines
- Being able to make independent decisions on the job
- Chance to exercise leadership
- Working by myself
- Working without the pressure or stress of competition
- Performing similar tasks each day

Time at Work

- Shorter work days
- Regular hours
- Setting my own work schedule
- Working with the least disruption of leisure activities
- Being able to take long vacations
- Work same days each week
- Work different days each week

Kind of Work

- Variety and daily change in work activities
- Chance to learn and grow
- Allows me to perform before an audience
- Work in a field that matches my interests
- Having my work recognized and appreciated
- Being creatively challenged
- Work that involves travel

Job Satisfaction

- Helping other people one on one
- Working with others to help society as a whole
- Working at a job that commands respect
- Relating to many people each day

This is a partial list. Look it over carefully. Have we left out something that's important to you? If we have, it's certain to be an interest high on your list of priorities—an automatic 10!

NOT JUST A JOB—THE RIGHT JOB

When your friends and relatives find out that you're working or looking for work you will, no doubt, hear the usual comments: "Why do you want to work so hard?" or "At this stage of your life you should be taking it easy and having fun."

For those of us who see work as a blessing, not a curse, such comments are hard to understand. What others may see as duty, tedium, stress, and responsibility, we consider one of life's satisfactions. But looking forward to Monday morning will continue only if you like what you're doing. That's why it's so important that you seek not just a job, but the right job.

Of course, the right job means different things to different people. To Peter, the right job means building up a sweat on a farm, while Paul's right job would be a comfortable office with good air conditioning.

The right job is not always the most glamorous or the best paying. Some people prefer repetitious work without responsibilities or stress. No matter how dull or tedious the job may seem to others, it can be a blessing—some might consider it therapy—for the individual who likes work and wants to keep active.

Every day we meet receptionists, telephone operators, waiters and waitresses, librarians, auto mechanics, and salespeople happily at work at jobs that others might sneer at. No matter what the work, there are people with the capacity to elevate and enrich their jobs. They do so through the force of their own personality and respect for the work.

A LOOK IN THE MIRROR

Finding the right job starts with taking personal stock and establishing your goals. What do you enjoy? What have you always wanted to do? What skills do you have and enjoy using most? Explore your interests. A review of your hobbies, sports, and volunteer activities, as well as your cultural and civic interests will steer you in the right direction.

Older Americans with long and versatile careers in several fields make the mistake of trying to be all things to all people. The experts recommend that you decide which skills you want to use in your job and concentrate your marketing efforts only on those skills.

There are practical matters to be considered. You may have health limitations that would eliminate certain jobs. Health problems such as arthritis, high blood pressure, diabetes, back problems, and hearing impairment would keep you from seeking work that requires physical exertion or stress. Jobs that involve more than average amounts of walking, standing, lifting, and sitting would rule out some, but people with limitations are not incapacitated for every type of work activity. It depends on the demands of the job and the severity of the health problem as well as on the individual's ability to cope.

Transportation could be a problem if public transportation is not available and you don't own a car. Family obligations, such as caring for an elderly relative, may limit the number of hours you have available for work.

With pen and paper in hand jot down the answers to some important questions:

What Are My Strong Points?

SKILLS:

APTITUDES:

ACHIEVEMENTS:

EXPERIENCE:

PERSONALITY:

How do they compare with the requirements of the job market? Which occupations are compatible with my interests? Which occupations are compatible with my personality?

Once you've established your strong points and your interests, check off what you need to do to get the work you want. It will provide a calendar of activities for you for the immediate future.

I Need To . . .

[ ] Rethink my priorities.

[ ] Establish goals.

[ ] Review my finances and determine income needs.

[ ] Schedule my job-hunting activities.

[ ] Check my wardrobe for suitable job-hunting attire.

[ ] Get a better understanding of the job market.

[ ] Train to update skills.

[ ] Train to acquire new skills.

[ ] Learn job-search skills.

[ ] Improve my job interview performance.

UNDERSTANDING YOUR NEEDS AND VALUES

When you think about the different job possibilities, you must consider your needs and values as well as your abilities. You must decide many things, including how much salary you want and how the hours and location will affect you and your family. Factors such as an attractive work place and friendly co-workers are elements of any job—how important are they to you?

There are bound to be trade-offs that you have to make in choosing a job. For example, will you take lower pay for higher job satisfaction or will you go for the most money and let job satisfaction come as it may?

The following work sheet will help you organize your thoughts and get a better idea of your priorities. Put an "X" in the box that best describes your needs and values—something you must have in the job, would like to have, don't care about one way or the other, would dislike in a job, or realistically cannot have or do in your job.

Worksheet

■ ■ ■

NEEDS AND VALUES

	Must have	Like	Don't care	Dislike	Can't have
SALARY					
More than $_____					
Based partly on sales or productivity					
Frequent raises					
Linked to cost of living					
Draw against commission					

(continued on next page)

	Must have	Like	Don't care	Dislike	Can't have
BENEFITS					
Vacation weeks per year					
Insurance					
Life					
Health					
Tuition and education					
Child care					
LOCATION					
Reach by public transportation					
30 minutes from home maximum					
Over an hour from home, OK					
Another town/city					
HOURS					
Full time					
Part time					
Flexitime (set own hours)					
Overtime					
Available					
Required					
Shift work					
Weekend work/ Evening work					
Overnight travel					

(continued on next page)

	Must have	Like	Don't care	Dislike	Can't have
EDUCATION/TRAINING					
Additional not required					
Additional required					
Less than 3 months					
3 to 6 months					
6 months to 1 year					
1 to 2 years					
More than 2 years					
Education/training					
Must be full time					
Can be part time					
Available locally					
Cost no more than $_____					
On-the-job training					
Apprenticeship					
OTHER FACTORS					
Competition from other workers					
Job satisfaction					
Same-sex co-workers					
Opposite-sex co-workers					
Help others					
Able to take independent action					
Mental stimulation					
Job security					

(continued on next page)

	Must have	Like	Don't care	Dislike	Can't have
Creative opportunity					
Opportunity to lead					
Pleasant working conditions					
Prestige—status					
Responsibility					
Same-sex supervisor					
Opposite-sex supervisor					
Variety—not routine work					

OTHER NEEDS AND VALUES

Adapted from "Project Have Skills" Handbook, produced under a grant from U.S. Department of Education under the auspices of the Women's Educational Equity Act.

YOU HAVE MORE SKILLS THAN YOU THINK

In analyzing the skills you bring to the job market, you will easily identify those skills based on knowledge and expertise in a specialized subject. The skills of a carpenter, an accountant, a nurse, or an engineer, for example, are easily identified and labeled. There are, however, aptitudes and abilities that are so natural to you and used so frequently and effortlessly that they can be overlooked or taken for granted.

These "hidden skills"—or perhaps "hidden attributes" is a better way to describe them—would include warm personality, leadership qualities, highly creative, good talker, detail-oriented, and good organizer. All these attributes are in demand in today's job market. An individual with a warm personality would be an excellent hotel concierge; someone with leadership qualities would excel at a job that requires supervising others; creative people make good teachers and crafts workers; a good talker can persuade and sell, and a detail-oriented organizer would be a superior office worker.

As you inventory the skills you have and enjoy using, consider those you use for hobbies, sports, and volunteer work, as well as for cultural and civic activities. Which of these statements can you honestly make?

I welcome responsibility and take it seriously.

I'm outgoing, gregarious, and like people.

I'm good with words and an excellent communicator.

I'm good with numbers.

I'm a problem solver.

I can get things done.

I'm fast and efficient in everything I do.

I'm patient.

I'm persistent.

It is important that you identify your hidden attributes as well as your more obvious skills and match them to the jobs, self-employment opportunities, and volunteer-work options available to you as a mature adult.

LITERACY IS AN ADVANTAGE

The increased demand for older adults in the work force is driven to a large degree by the lack of basic skills among younger workers. Today's schools—and yes, even colleges—are releasing into the work force young men and women with poor math skills who can't write a letter or a memo without errors in grammar or spelling. A high-school principal told me that the kind of education we received as high-school graduates back then is equivalent, and in some cases even better, than are college degrees today.

Some workers who are considered literate cannot read or write on an eighth-grade level. Nevertheless, the Bureau of Labor Statistics expects to have the highest growth rate and demand for labor among those occupations that require the most education and training. Your competence in such simple, basic skills as reading, writing, and arithmetic, combined with a lifetime of experience interacting with others, makes you a gray-haired treasure to employers who need to get things done.

How Much Education Is Needed for These Growth Occupations?

Bachelor's degree— or more.

Systems analysts and computer scientists

Physical therapists

Operations research analysts

Psychologists

Computer programmers

Occupational therapists

Management analysts

Marketing, advertising, and PR managers

General managers and top executives

Teachers—elementary and secondary school

Accountants and auditors

Lawyers

Some post-secondary training or extensive
employer training.

Paralegals

Radiologic technologists and technicians

Medical assistants

Physical and corrective therapy assistants and aides

Data-processing equipment repairers

Medical records technicians

Surgical technicians

Cooks—restaurant

Respiratory therapists

Licensed practical nurses

Maintenance repairers—general utility

Teacher aides and educational assistants

Legal secretaries

Medical secretaries

High school or less.

Home-health aides

Human services workers

Personal and home care aides

Corrections officers

Travel agents

Flight attendants

Salespersons—retail

General office clerks

Cashiers

Food counter, fountain, and related workers

Truckdrivers—light and heavy

Nursing aides, orderlies, and attendants

Janitors, maids, and housekeeping cleaners

Waiters and waitresses

Food-preparation workers

Receptionists and information clerks

Gardeners and groundskeepers

Guards

Child-care workers

Secretaries

Cooks—short order and fast food

Clerical supervisors and managers

Stock clerks

—"Outlook: 1990–2005," U.S. Department of Labor Statistics

YOUR SKILLS CAN BE APPLIED
TO OTHER FIELDS

George Wessman's 19 years of service as a foreman in a small appliance factory came to a sudden end in 1989, when the company closed its Providence, Rhode Island, plant and started manufacturing in Taiwan. Out of work at a time when other plants were closing in the area and manufacturing jobs were going overseas, George found himself unemployed, unhappy, and unwanted.

A friend asked him to take a look at a toaster oven she had bought at a neighborhood K-Mart. It was burning the bread instead of toasting it. George was able to make a small adjustment that fixed the problem. The experience gave him an idea. If he knew so much about making appliances why couldn't he use this know-how to sell appliances? After making the rounds, he landed a job as an appliance salesman at a large department store where his knowledge of what goes on inside the appliance won customer confidence and made the cash registers ring. George Wessman is now the manager of the store's extensive appliance department and has added former plant workers to his sales staff.

George went from manufacturing, a depressed, problem area, to retail sales, an active and growing sector of the economy. This is an example of how the skills gained in one setting can be transferred to another. The logic of this transition eludes people with fixed ideas about how and where to apply their skills. If you find yourself in a declining part of the economy, consider the ways that your years of experience can serve you in more robust areas. As in the case of George Wessman, the transition may be easier than you think.

FINANCING THE ADDED YEARS

The good news is that you're probably going to live a lot longer than you think. The bad news is that you'll need substantial income for the additional years of life.

Not very long ago, if you were lucky enough to live past half a century, you would have little time left to worry about money. Today, once past age 55 the odds are that you'll live until you're 77 or more. And, while the life span is increasing, the retirement age is constantly decreasing. Most people now retire at a little over 60, leaving them 17 more years to provide for—and many live a lot longer and need to provide for more years yet.

To get a handle on your income in your later years, list the sources of income and estimate how much they will provide monthly:

Estimated Monthly Income

Social Security   _____

Pensions   _____

IRAs, Keoghs   _____

Sales of assets (business or property)   _____

Income from savings and investments   _____

Home equity   _____

TOTAL: _____

In 1993 the maximum Social Security benefit for a worker retiring at age 65 is $1,128 per month. If you are fortunate enough to have a company pension plan it can brighten the picture, but on average it will account for only another 16 percent of your needs.

There's one more factor to consider—inflation. For the period 1967–1990, the average rate of inflation was 6.3 percent, which reduced the purchasing power of $30,000 to just $7,500.

Income from savings and investments? The risks inherent in stock market fluctuations keep many older persons out of the market and income of bonds and Certificates of Deposit (CDs)—two favored conservative investments of older Americans—have declined sharply with the drop in interest rates.

Estimate your monthly expenses in the list that follows. When you do it's important that you make allowances for unpredictable health-care costs. The cost of serious or long-term illness is a major consideration because Medicare does not cover all health-care costs. You may decide to buy "medigap" insurance to supplement Medicare and long-term health insurance to protect yourself if nursing home or home health care is needed at some time in the future. The premiums for medigap and long-term health insurance are high and rising but it's a cost you will have to accept for the protection it provides.

Recent cutbacks in retirees' medical insurance may add another burden to your budget. As many as 95 percent of employers have either cut back on retirees' health benefits or will do so eventually, according to David M. Walker, a former Assistant Secretary of Labor in the Bush administration. About 13 million retired people over age 55, about a third of Americans of that age, receive health benefits from their former employers. At least 8.5 million have benefits that seem secure, but 4.5 million retirees are at risk. Hit hardest are the tens of thousands of people who retired before age 65 and are too young to be protected by Medicare. If you are in this category be sure that you calculate realistically the cost of medical care in your estimated monthly expenses.

Estimated Monthly Expenses

Rent or mortgage _____

Utilities _____

Food and beverages _____

Clothing _____

Medicines, eyeglasses, dental care _____

Medicare _____

Supplementary health insurance _____

Life insurance _____

Auto and homeowner's insurance _____

Leisure and hobbies _____

Federal taxes _____

State taxes _____

Property taxes _____

Job-related expenses _____

Miscellaneous family obligations _____

Paying off debt _____

Vacation _____

Auto maintenance _____

Gifts _____

Charity _____

Other _____

TOTAL: _____

When you compare potential income with anticipated expenditures and the figures fall short of your needs, the importance of income from work becomes apparent. For more and more older adults all across the country, income from work is a necessary supplement to Social Security, pensions, savings, and investments.

With fixed and inadequate income and rising costs a fact of life, it's worth taking another look at your monthly expenses. How much money do you need? Are there any discretionary expenditures you can cut? Given the range of lifestyles and personal priorities—one man's luxury is another's necessity—you'll have to answer these questions for yourself.

Several mature men and women in my community find it a worthwhile "trade off" to give up cable TV, expensive entertainment, and country-club membership if it allows them to take a job that pays less but satisfies more. They chose to give up lifestyle fun that wasn't important to them in favor of fun on the job.

Then, too, some older Americans are at work today specifically to afford the very luxuries that others don't care about. But it's not an "either-or" situation. Being able to work for less doesn't necessarily insure job satisfaction, and seeking good money doesn't mean you'll have to settle for a dull or unpleasant job. Many have been able to obtain work with a good salary *and* job satisfaction. With adequate preparation, training, and a clear goal in mind, you can create your own perfect mix of money and fun on the job.

The question, "Does it pay to work?" is discussed in full in Chapter Two. Essentially, it is a decision each individual makes based on his or her own financial situation and needs. Obviously, if the need for income is urgent and immediate, you will be obliged to work and take the first job you can get whether you enjoy the work or not. From a job-search point of view, it comes down to this: The less urgency there is for income, the greater the freedom to explore alternative work opportunities and to give greater weight to job satisfaction.

3. A RESUME THAT SHOWCASES YOUR EXPERIENCE

Job seekers who spent the greatest part of their working life with one or two companies rarely have a resume and most lack experience in writing a resume. But no matter how impressive your work record and skills, you need a resume because you have to communicate your qualifications in writing. You need a resume because

1. The resume is your self-inventory on paper. In writing the resume you are forced to recall and organize the facts that document your qualifications.

2. Your resume is a tool for self-evaluation. Thoughtfully prepared, it will help you determine your marketability, suggest new avenues to pursue, and make your job search more productive.

3. Your resume is a basic job-search tool—your calling card, work history, personal advertisement, and sales brochure, all in one. It introduces you to a prospective employer and opens the door to an interview. It presents you in favorable terms and serves as an agenda during the interview. And your resume remains behind to speak for you after you've left the office.

RESUME TIPS

A common mistake of older job seekers, eager to impress, is to include too much. Keep your resume brief and to the point, informative but concise. Your reader is busy and sees many resumes; he or she must be able to cover all the key points within seconds.

Do not include your age, date of birth, or the dates you attended or graduated from high school or college. Resist the temptation to list every job you ever held. Listing jobs held more than 20 years ago makes you seem older than you are. You may eventually have to deal with the age issue at some job interviews, but at least you'll have had a chance to prove yourself in person. Leave out jobs you held early in your career. They usually have little bearing on what you can do today. The fact that you were a camp counselor at a girls' camp in your teens is relevant only if you are applying for work in a similar type of organization.

Here are some additional resume tips specifically for the mature job seeker:

- If you've been out of school for some time leave out detailed educational information. Omit age (it's illegal for the employer to ask), photographs, and irrelevant dates.

- Don't lie about your age, your employment record, or your education. If you don't have the specific educational background the job requires, you're better off explaining why you can perform the job better than any other applicant even though you don't have the formal academic credentials. Lying on your resume—even a white lie—can ruin any chance you had for the job.

- The length and breadth of your experience is an asset, not a liability. Any attempt to apologize, conceal, or lie about your age furnishes ammunition to the age-biased employer and undermines your basic position that it is ability, not age, that counts.

- Use the past to document your qualifications but focus on the future. Your resume should be future-oriented in tone and content. Place emphasis on your immediate goals and objectives. To offset the stereo-type image of older employees, your resume should convey energy and enthusiasm.

- If you've taken courses or training to improve your skills or pick up new skills, include this information in your resume. Aside from the importance of the skill itself, it tells the employer that you are a highly motivated individual who takes the initiative to learn and improve.

- Your resume is you in print. It should be typed or typeset, neat, and clean. Proofread carefully to make sure the spelling and grammar are correct. Management consultant Kevin Murphy advises against colored paper. He points out that colored stationery makes the resume harder to read and more difficult to reproduce if the recipient wants to circulate it. He advises, "Resumes should be printed on good quality white paper and the print should be big enough to read easily."

- Highlight your accomplishments in each of your past jobs and use the strongest verbs you can to describe your experience—words that convey action and power. Refer to this list to find the word or words you're looking for:

Words that emphasize your contribution to profits, productivity, and growth: augmented / broadened / doubled / enlarged / expanded / generated / increased / improved / implemented / generated / launched / marketed / obtained / procured / reduced / saved / sold / streamlined / strengthened / tripled

Words that convey leadership qualities: administered / authorized / communicated / conducted / controlled / directed / delegated / enforced / governed / headed / hired / inspired / led / managed / motivated / organized / pioneered / presided / sparked / stimulated / spearheaded / supervised / vitalized

Words that stress your creative abilities: adapted / analyzed / built / composed / conceived / created / designed / devised / developed / discovered / drafted / innovated / invented / originated / set up / structured

There are literally hundreds of books on writing resumes. If you need help, you might review a few of the many books on the subject at your local library.

SAMPLE RESUMES FOR MATURE JOB SEEKERS

A good resume presents your skills and accomplishments in a way that clearly demonstrates your qualifications. Its purpose is to "sell the interview" by convincing prospective employers that it is in their interest to meet with you personally.

The resumes of fictitious people that follow are examples of three different formats:

1. The functional (or skills) resume
2. The chronological resume
3. A combined resume format

In each case, the format was chosen because it was most suitable for the particular job seeker.

These sample resumes are included as a guide. Resist the temptation to copy the language or borrow words or phrases of job descriptions similar to yours. The more unique and highly personal your resume, the more effective it will be. Utilize the format that works best for you or create your own format and headings. Ideally, the words and the organization of the resume should be your own and tailored specifically to your own qualifications.

Successful resumes are not written, they're rewritten. Your first draft is several drafts away from the finished product. Keep revising and improving, using the comments of knowledgeable friends and prospective employers to make it better. Try writing your resume using the different formats—editing, changing, adjusting, and revising as you go—and pick the one that presents you in the best possible light.

Example I.
Chronological Resume

In a chronological resume the information is organized by employers, starting with the most recent work experience and going backward in time to the earliest. It is easy to follow and the most widely used format. The disadvantages of this format for older job applicants is that when the dates of early employment go too far back it highlights the age of the applicant.

(Alan Wald, a 59-year-old office manager, is the victim of cost-cutting and a massive layoff by an employer he has worked for for the last 11 years. He is seeking a full-time position as a foreman-supervisor in his field.)

Alan Wald
5344 Atlantic Drive
Baltimore, MD 21200
Tel. 410 665 0243

OBJECTIVE:

Carpentry supervisor for construction company, interior remodeling contractors, trade-show exhibit, or theater scenery builders.

EMPLOYMENT:

1981–92	R&K Construction Co., Baltimore, MD
	Supervisor. Actively managed more than 18 major projects per year, on average. Prepared estimates and was responsible for holding down costs, quality control, and timely completion of projects. Devised innovative work methods that increased profitability by 22 percent during a three-year period. Personal hands-on management of staff that ranged seasonally from 18 to 50 carpenters and other construction workers.
1968–81	Exhibit Crafters, Washington, DC
	Assistant Foreman. Supervised staff of exhibit designers and 23 carpenters and plastics craftsmen. Initiated training program that increased profitability and created programs to improve morale and personnel relationships.
1958–67	Delman General Carpenters, Washington, DC
	Hired as carpenter on leaving military service. Promoted to site foreman two years later. Hands-on experience on a range of projects—from architectural woodwork to quality cabinet carpentry.
EDUCATION:	Indianapolis Technical Institute, Indianapolis, IN
	Special advanced courses at Hendricks County Vocational School in blueprint reading, estimating, and drafting.
MILITARY SERVICE:	Sergeant-Major, United States Army, 1956–58

References available on request.

Example II.
Functional (or Skills) Resume

A functional (or skills) resume is organized under functional or topical headings. This allows you to include skills according to your own values and even to include new areas of interest. This format is ideal for older adults and for retirees and homemakers reentering the job market because it does not require dates of employment and other information that may reveal a spotty work record. However, some employers find it confusing and suspect applicants of intentionally leaving out vital information.

(Frances Harris is a 62-year-old homemaker who was recently widowed. A wife, mother, and homemaker, she has been out of the work force for more than 20 years. By using a functional resume format, she is able to emphasize her skills and education. If asked, she can explain the absence of a recent work record during the interview.)

Frances Harris
22 North Clay Avenue
Minneapolis, MN 55445
Tel. 612 883 4201

OBJECTIVE:

LIBRARIAN (part-time or flexible-work schedule) in a specialized business library, school, college, or public library that can utilize my literary knowledge, library-science education, and research training with computerized information retrieval systems.

LITERARY INTERESTS:

Extensive knowledge of books (classics as well as popular fiction and non-fiction), based on a lifetime enthusiasm for literature and reading. Particular interests: history, economics, biography. Led and served as moderator for Community Center Book Club. Served as member and chairperson for Fairfax County Library Board.

LIBRARY AND RESEARCH SKILLS:

Extensive cataloging experience with both Dewey Decimal and Library of Congress Systems. Created program that increased library usage 15 percent each year. As a researcher, assisted author of several American history textbooks in gathering, organizing, and indexing government information. Also assisted in research and on-line searches for doctoral students. Skills include ability with computerized information access services (DIOLOG, NEXIS, AMERICA ON-LINE) and interlibrary loan procedures.

WORK EXPERIENCE:

High school librarian, Baldwin High School, Baldwin, NY

Substitute teacher (English, History) for Kennedy Junior High School, Baldwin, NY

Archive library assistant, Chicago Chamber of Commerce

Volunteer work: Storyteller for children at suburban library, American Literacy Foundation, made recordings of books for American Foundation for the Blind

EDUCATION: Bachelor of Arts, Hunter College, New York City (Dean's List, Creative Writing Award)

Masters Degree, Library Science, C. W. Post College, Brookfield, NY

Supplementary courses in Computerized Library Functions, Information Retrieval, and On-Line Search Functions, Rosary College, River Forest, IL

MEMBERSHIP: Denver Literary Society

Computer Club

References available on request.

THE COMBINED RESUME FORMAT

Operation Able, a Chicago-based organization dedicated to finding jobs for older people suggests that the Combined Resume Format "generally works best for older people." The combined resume format includes the elements of a functional resume (listing skills in order of interest) plus a synopsis chronology of employers and dates.

The elements of Operation Able's Combined Resume Format consist of

1. NAME, ADDRESS, TELEPHONE NUMBER

2. OBJECTIVE OR SUMMARY OF EXPERIENCE. This section tells the employer the kind of job you are looking for. It should stress your immediate objective, not your long-range goal. Sometimes just giving a job title accomplishes your purpose.

3. SKILLS AND/OR EXPERIENCE. According to Operation Able, "For most older workers, this is the strongest selling point. This should be a collective expression of your abilities, rather than each job you have held."

4. EMPLOYMENT. Name of most recent employer, city, state, etc. Job title. Second most recent employer, city, state, etc. Job title. And so on. (List years employed, not months.) Employment history should relate to your objective.

5. EDUCATION. List institution or institutions that would most correspond to objective. (An insurance company would be interested in learning that you attended a business school or college; your studies at music school may be important to you, but are not relevant here.)

6. ACHIEVEMENTS. List any award citations received for outstanding work or community service.

7. PERSONAL INTERESTS. Indicate two or three activities that you engage in during your free time—particularly activity consistent with the image you want to project.

8. REFERENCES. Don't bother listing references. Indicate that references will be furnished on request.

Example III.
Combined Resume Format

(William Simmons, 66, retired for the past three years wants to return to work on a flexible-time schedule. He is seeking work in his own field—financial services sales—but he wants to indicate in his resume that he is versatile and also qualified as a trainer and seminar speaker.)

William R. Simmons
1120 North Avenue
Boulder, CO 80302
Tel. 303 440 4688

OBJECTIVE	SALES REPRESENTATIVE, FINANCIAL SERVICES mutual funds, life and health insurance, annuity plans. TRAINER-INSTRUCTOR of sales representatives and/or SEMINAR SPEAKER at company-sponsored financial-planning seminars to promote sales.
SKILLS	Persuasive salesman responsible for increasing health-insurance sales in territory by 35 percent in one year. Winner of the company's mutual-fund sales contest for three consecutive years.
	Conducted more than 100 presentations and financial-planning seminars at social centers and

condominium-association meetings. This activity produced new business and measurable bottom-line sales results.

Extensive experience training new sales representatives and developing material for company's internal-training program in selling health insurance and annuities. First-year sales of trainees exceeded quota by 18 percent.

EMPLOYMENT

1977–89	Roberts & Bernee, Members of the New York Stock Exchange, New York and Denver offices. Insurance and Mutual Fund Sales—Sales Representative and Trainer
1963–77	Rosedale Financial Services, Denver, CO Insurance sales representative
1963–76	Cleveland High School. Economics and civics teacher. Basketball coach. (Teacher Excellence Award)
EDUCATION	BS (Banking and Finance) Truscon College, Walton, MA Certification: Financial Planners Institute
MEMBERSHIPS	Boulder Toastmasters' Club Association of Financial Planners
LICENSES	Registered Insurance Agent, Colorado Registered Representative, National Association of Securities Dealers (NASD)

References available on request.

4. NETWORK! NETWORK! NETWORK!

Whenever I meet a mature person at work I make it a practice to ask how he or she found the job. Of course, some have been on the job for many years and continue to work at the same place well into their later years. Many, however, are working at new, recently acquired jobs. Almost always they tell me they got their job—or the lead that led to the job—through a recommendation or information about an opening from someone they knew.

My wife's friend Rita got her Saturday-only job as the librarian for the Institute for Social Work in Chicago because another friend Joan Evers worked in the building and heard that they needed someone with a masters degree in library science for a one-day-a-week job. My wife got her job as a marketing representative for Medical Management of America from a lead by Mary Ann Mazur, with whom she worked at a previous job. In both cases, the job was unadvertised and newly created. In both cases, it turned out to be the job that each one was looking for at the time.

That's "networking," a proven and time-honored job-search strategy. Networking provides access to the plum, sought-after jobs that never make it into the want ads. The kind of nontraditional, flexible-hours job you are looking for at this time is more likely to come to you through the grapevine than through the want ads and other regular channels. The best jobs, jobs at higher levels with fatter paychecks, are neither listed nor advertised. They are found through word of mouth.

More jobs are filled because somebody knows somebody who knows somebody than by all the want ads and employment agencies put together. In a survey of members of the Administrative Management Society, 70 percent said that a referral of another employee is the best method for getting a job interview with their firm. Most job openings are filled by word of mouth before want ads are placed or employment agencies get into the picture.

A research team at the University of Southern California found that the more relatives and friends older job seekers had, the more likely they were to find work. Led by Assistant Professor of social work Michal Mor-Barak, the team interviewed Los Angeles-area men and women 55 and over who signed up at public-service agencies for help in finding work. They had retired, lost their jobs, or were trying to reenter the work force for reasons ranging from financial need to escape from boredom. Sixty-four percent found jobs.

The research team found that, in addition to relatives-and-friends-networking, other factors predicting a successful job hunt for older adults included strong motivation and fewer major life changes such as divorce, new marriage, and major illness.

The idea that you need connections with influential people in high places to get the sought-after jobs is not necessarily so. Today, just plain folks are in a position to advise. They have an insider's knowledge of what's going on at different companies, who needs what and when, long before the information is made public.

Because you've lived longer, you have a broad network of people to call upon in your job search. The people you've come in contact with over your lifetime represent a rich source of information about developing situations and unadvertised job opportunities.

It's not enough to tell those on your networking list that you're looking for work. You have to remind them of your skills and give them some idea of the kind of work and schedule that you're looking for. Encourage others to help you be creative on your behalf—your future job may not have a name or a job description. It may be something that you and your employer design to satisfy mutual needs.

WHO DO YOU KNOW?

Before you start your job hunt, make a list of people who will become your personal job-hunting network. Pick up a package of 3" × 5" index cards and jot down some names in each of the categories in your network.

Men and women you know from previous jobs—those you've worked with and those you've worked for, as well as suppliers, customers, clients, and competitors

Relatives, friends, and social contacts, current and past

Members of your church, synagogue, social and athletic groups, charitable or public-service organizations

Influentials and professionals—bankers, lawyers, accountants, doctors, dentists, and so forth

Others

Get in touch and stay in touch with the people on your personal network. Expand your network by asking the people on your list to suggest others who are as knowledgeable as they are. Leads for jobs can come from the most unlikely sources.

Once the people on your list know that you are looking for work, and know the kind of work you want, they become your eyes and ears. An active grapevine is the best job hunting tool.

ORGANIZATIONS, SUPPORT GROUPS, AND JOB CLUBS

Job hunting can be lonely and frustrating. It's easier if you have the help of your personal network of friends, family, and former co-workers. The cooperation and emotional support of age peers who understand the special problems of finding work as a mature adult is particularly important. Without that support, many individuals give up before the pay-off. The largest number of "discouraged workers" are older men and women who stopped their search because they thought they would not be able to find suitable work.

Enter the job club. A job club is a peer group of job seekers who meet regularly in a friendly place to discuss and apply their job-search skills and exchange job leads. Members review one another's resumes, hold job interview practice sessions, and exchange information.

Jack Esterlan, who obtained his job as program director for a community center in Toledo, Ohio, with the guidance of a local club, told me that the tips he received from other members of the club were invaluable during his job search. In addition, "Regular contact with others my age who monitored my search efforts gave me the discipline I needed to keep to my game plan. I would get discouraged and throw up my hands. They provided the moral support when I needed it most." One of the tips he received at the club led him to a great job, and even though he is now happily employed Jack shows up at a job-club meeting from time to time to see if he can help new club members.

Chapter Twelve includes a resource list of private and government organizations ready and willing to help older Americans in their search for work.

5. KNOW THE CURRENT JOB MARKET

After looking inward and identifying your ambitions and the skills you have mastered, look outward and identify organizations and businesses that can employ your skills. Choose from a variety of possibilities:

Business and industry

Government—Local, state, federal, military

Education—Schools, colleges, universities, libraries

Nonprofit organizations—hospitals and clinics, social agencies, trade associations, member organizations

Percent of 55+ Employed by Occupational Group
1991 Annual Average (Current Population Survey)

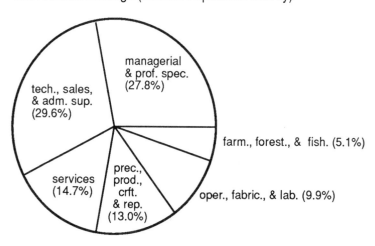

Percent of 65+ Employed by Occupational Group
1991 Annual Average (Current Population Survey)

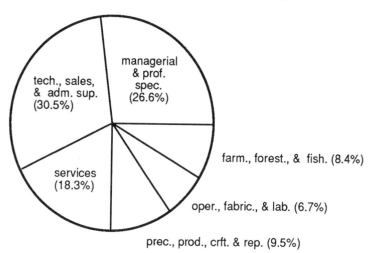

The greatest demand for help is in the service field, but "service" is a big field. Job salaries vary and require different levels of education. There are modestly paying salesclerk positions, moderate-paying jobs as aircraft technicians, and high-paying jobs such as investment bankers and financial advisers, which require advanced degrees.

In her "Jobs" column in the Sunday Chicago *Tribune,* Carol Kleiman reports that the sector presents real employment opportunities, "not only in percentage of increase but in real numbers. Among them are registered nurses, retail salespeople, cooks and chefs, accountants, computer specialists, and health-care workers."

The job market is constantly moving and changing with the times. For the rest of this century and well into the next, the hottest jobs will require vocational or undergraduate-level training, common sense, and a human touch. Prestigious law firms, economizing and downsizing in order to compete, are hiring fewer lawyers and taking on paralegals to handle the routine legal paperwork for a lot less money. Tremendous growth in health care has created a shortage of nurses, and hospitals are paying bonuses to get qualified nurses. Other areas where the Labor Department expects greater-than-average growth include computer specialists, managers, security guards, and truckers.

The answers to these questions will help you research the job market and zero in on the companies you would like to work for.

- What changes have occurred in my industry? How does it affect my job chances?

- Which companies and industries offer the best job opportunities?

- Is the job I want available in my area? Do other parts of the country offer a better chance to land the right job?

- Which companies have a good record of hiring and maintaining older workers?

- How many employees does the company have over age 55?

- Has the company redesigned jobs or changed the work environment to accommodate older workers?

- Is this the opportunity I've been looking for to go into a different field?

Target the job you want. Sometimes this means starting out with a foot-in-the-door job to get the training, experience, and contacts to be ready for the job you're aiming at.

Number and Percent of 65+ Employed—by Industry
1991 Annual Average

	Total Employed	Percent of That Industry
All industries	3,384,000	
Mining	12,000	4.0%
Construction	123,000	3.6%
Manufacturing	309,000	9.1%
Transportation and public utilities	124,000	3.7%
Trade (wholesale & retail)	733,000	21.7%
Finance, insurance, and real estate	247,000	7.3%
Services	1,440,000	42.6%
Agriculture	268,000	7.9%
Public administration	129,000	3.8%

Figures do not total 100% due to rounding.
Source: U.S. Department of Labor, Bureau of Labor Statistics.

Career Information Sources

Most local libraries contain extensive collections of materials for job seekers and individuals seeking work opportunities. While most of the material is directed at young adults or middle-aged career changers, it is just as useful for older adults.

Library resources can be used to find information on specific companies or information about developments, trends, compensation, and other matters relating to specific occupations and industries. Most libraries contain directories that are useful in compiling lists of companies by geographic location or by industry. Other books are devoted to job-hunting skills and strategies such as resume preparation and interviewing.

Some of the larger libraries have study guides for many civil service entrance and licensing examinations. These guides are arranged in occupation groupings:

> *Agriculture / Agribusiness and Natural Resources / Business and Office Occupations / Communication and Media / Computer Occupations / Construction / Consumer and Homemaking Related Occupations / Environment / Health Occupations / Manufacturing / Marine Science / Marketing and Distribution / Military Careers / Personal Services / Public Services / Recreation and Hospitality / Transportation*

Directories are a valuable resource for job seekers. Many libraries contain U.S. and foreign industrial directories. You can find specialized companies in specific geographic locations by using the Standard Industrial Classification Code (SIC). Some typical directory titles are:

> *Directory of Corporate Affiliations*
>
> *Dun & Bradstreet Million Dollar Directory*

Dun's Employment Opportunities Directory

Standard & Poor's Register of Corporations

Thomas Register of American Manufacturers

Directory of American Firms Operating in Foreign Countries

Dun & Bradstreet Principal International Businesses

National Trade & Professional Associations of the United States and Canada

Specialized directories in your library include directories of accounting firms, consultants, executive-search firms, advertising agencies, import-export firms, insurance companies, research libraries, and securities dealers.

Sources of want ads can be found in several publications. National Ad Search compiles executive, technical, and management ads from 68 Sunday newspapers. Other job-finding sources include *National Business Employment Weekly, Federal Career Opportunities,* and *Community Jobs.*

NEW JOB, NEW PLACE

Trading in the old snow plow for a new set of golf clubs is an idea whose time has come. This may be the change you've been looking for to move to a warmer climate *and* find the job you want.

When the last child leaves home, family responsibilities lighten and priorities change. Relocation to another part of the country is no longer just a dream. With your newfound freedom, you can choose what you want to work at and where you want to do it.

Older adults pick up stakes and move because they want a change of scene, because the weather is better, and because many of their friends have already resettled in the

Sunbelt. To these we add one more reason that will appeal to the older adults who want a second chance at work—many places in the Sunbelt are enjoying an economic boom. In fact, the Sunbelt is defined in Webster's Dictionary as "that part of the United States comprising most of the states of the South and Southwest, characterized by a warm, sunny climate and regarded as an area of rapid population and economic growth."

The development of aerospace and electronics industries in the Southwest has been a stimulus to economic growth. Thriving tourism and retirement living has generated business activity and jobs in places such as Florida and Arizona. A recent report by the Small Business Administration indicates that new hiring of older workers by small business is greatest in the South (39 percent), followed by the West (33 percent), the Midwest (16 percent), and the Northeast (11 percent). Forty-two percent of the newly hired persons age 65 and over were within metropolitan areas. Woods & Poole Economics, Inc., forecasts that the Phoenix-Tempe-Scottsdale, Arizona, area will produce the greatest number of new white-collar jobs between 1990 and 1995.

For several decades, seven states—Arizona, California, Florida, New Mexico, North Carolina, South Carolina, and Texas—have attracted half of all the older adults who pulled up their stakes and moved to another state. Nevertheless, fewer older adults move to another state than you would guess. David Savageau, author of *Retirement Places Rated*, reports, "Each year fewer than half a million people 60-and-over pack up and relocate to another state." Even when they move, most older adults prefer to move close to home: "For every 94 older adults, only one moves to another state."

Retirement Places Rated is a valuable source of information for those who want to relocate. The book profiles 117 places and rates them by seven factors—financial considerations such as taxes and the cost of living, housing, climate, personal safety, services (including health care), recreational and cultural facilities—and work opportunities.

When I met David Savageau at a conference in Montgomery, Alabama, he told me that ratings on work opportunities were added to his book *Retirement Places Rated* in response to readers' demands. In the preface he gives three reasons for adding ratings on work opportunities:

1. Nearly one in four people continue to work part-time for a few years immediately after they start receiving Social Security benefits

2. An additional quarter of their contemporaries indicate they, too, would work part-time if they found a good opportunity

3. A successful strategy for weathering future inflation is to build wealth in the early retirement years by working part-time.

Your consideration of a particular place to relocate may have been prompted by past visits or by the urging of a friend or relative who lives there. Even so, you'll want to visit it again—and possibly many times—before you make the big move. To make a sound relocation decision and conduct a long-distance job search you'll have to do some careful research.

Mature job seekers who live in an area heavily populated with work-deprived seniors may face tough competition for suitable jobs. There is greater competition for such jobs and fewer job opportunities for mature adults in St. Petersburg, Florida, or in Sun City, Arizona, than there is in Seattle or Minneapolis, where seniors make up a lower percentage of the population. It's not impossible to find work in areas heavily populated with seniors. It may just take a little longer.

You can learn a great deal about a location before you get there. Contact the Chamber of Commerce as well as appropriate state, county, and local government agencies. Develop personal contacts in the area—friends or friends of friends, people in your line of work, church or synagogue members, and others who can give you an insider's perspective on the place.

It's nice to be wanted. States and cities throughout the country offer all sorts of tax breaks in order to attract mature people to their area and keep their current seniors in the area. Property-tax deferral, sales-tax givebacks, state-tax-free, municipal-tax income, and exemption from state taxes on pension income are their way of welcoming you to the area. If any or all of these advantages are important to you, check it out with the state's tax agency before you move.

Subscribing to the local newspaper is another good way to find out about a new place. The classified want ads contain important clues to the job opportunities in the area.

Mature adults seeking new work adventure in an idyllic Caribbean setting will be interested in an announcement by the new El Conquistador Resort and Country Club in Puerto Rico. The 926-room luxury resort built on 500 acres on the top of a cliff overlooking the Atlantic Ocean and Caribbean Sea is seeking 500 or more mature adults for positions as managers and staff in more than 100 occupational specialties to be filled before the opening in September 1993. I stayed at the El Conquistador in the late Sixties and if there is a more magnificent setting for a resort anywhere in the world I have yet to see it.

In an interview, Lawrence Stalcup, director of employee recruitment for the resort, said "I have seen the benefit of mature managers and workers in our other hotels, and age will be no barrier when we're selecting the best person for any job."

Stalcup believes that mature managers and staff can contribute to the resort's success, "Mature adults have faced challenges before, and we'll be looking to them to provide leadership and maturity and to be positive role models for the other staff."

Asked about the cost of living in the region, Stalcup said that food, clothing, and many other items are less costly than they are in the states. He assures applicants that "You won't be alone in a strange land. There are Wal-Mart and KMart stores in town, and you can rent your videos at Blockbuster."

9 "Hot Areas" for Older Adult Employment in the Nineties

1. Information technology—computer sciences
2. Travel
3. Food services
4. Hospitality industry
5. Health care
6. Biotechnology
7. Sales and marketing
8. Loan services
9. Pharmaceuticals

6. CONSIDER TRAINING

Older Americans are frequently offered low-paying jobs that require little or no skills and provide little in the way of job satisfaction. They are disadvantaged not because they are old but because they lack the up-to-date skills that employers require. Older men and women who haven't kept up with changes in technology will find a job; they will have a hard time finding a good job. Even highly educated seniors may find themselves unemployed or underemployed because their education is irrelevant to current needs.

That being the case, you have two choices. You can accept a low-paying, low-satisfaction job or you can acquire the skills that qualify you for a better paying, more interesting job.

For most unsuccessful job seekers, age is not the problem. Experts agree that the only way to remain marketable in today's environment is to embrace change and be willing to learn. Your capacity to learn is as great as it ever was, and the training is accessible. If, for example, you're an office worker, learn to use the latest word-processing equipment. If you're an accountant, brush up on recent changes in the tax law. Free or inexpensive training specifically designed for older workers is available through employers, trade associations, unions, local educational institutions, and government programs. Many companies subsidize occupational courses and on-the-job training.

In addition to the newly acquired skill and knowledge, training gives you fresh achievements to list in your resume and talk about in your job interview.

There are more than 160 adult-education and training centers serving thousands of mature people at colleges and universities. Classes in computers and business management are among the most popular programs.

A number of states have tuition-waiver programs for older adults. Currently, 29 states have statutes that allow older people to take courses tuition free at state higher-education institutions on a space-available basis.

Resources For Education and Training for Mature Adults

Colleges and universities
  for professional and business training and academic degrees.

Public vocational schools and trade schools
for training in office and computer skills, nursing, culinary arts. Some courses offering hands-on experience are sponsored cooperatively with employers under government programs.

Private business schools
for secretarial training, accounting, data processing, paralegal, fashion, travel-agent skills, drafting, electronics, etc.

Private trade and technical schools
usually specialize in a specific trade: secretaries and office workers, hairdressers, commercial art, air-conditioning mechanics, modeling, etc. Some of these schools promise to place the student when he or she finishes the course.

Home study programs
correspondence courses available for a great variety of occupations—travel agent, TV repair, commercial artist, and just about any other field you can name. Manuals, video tapes, audio cassettes, and computer-network support make it easier to train without leaving home.

ON-THE-JOB TRAINING

Companies with successful training programs for older workers build on the individual's experience, allowing self-direction and self-pacing, and providing feedback along the way. When these factors are included in the design of the training program, mature adults can learn new skills as readily as younger people can. As new skills are added to their previously acquired experience, seasoned judgment, and reliability, retrained older workers become a valuable asset to the firm.

The companies that provide training programs to upgrade the skills of older workers are among the most successful in the nation.

> *Control Data Corporation* has developed an internal, expanded life-planning and education system for employees 55 and older.

> *Grumman Corporation* retrains older employees through midcareer training programs.

> *General Electric* offers after-hours courses to upgrade the skills of engineers.

> *AT&T Bell Laboratories* provides older workers with training opportunities, from graduate study to business-skill development. The company offers 500 courses of study, including highly specialized courses not typically available in the general academic community. Bell Lab employees teach 35 percent of the courses.

> *Crouse-Hinds ECM* has several training programs for older workers. College tuition is reimbursed for general-subject courses and second-career preparation as well as for training for changing technologies.

> *Pitney-Bowes* contributes up to $300 annually and a total of $3,000 for books and tuition for employees aged 50 and over. No required length of service and few restrictions on subject studied.

JOB GROWTH

If you are training to better your employment opportunities make sure that your training is relevant to the needs of current employers and in an area of job growth. Here is the U.S. Bureau of Labor Statistics' list of 30 occupations with the greatest projected job growth between the years 1990 and 2005. (The figure in parentheses is the number of new jobs projected by the Bureau during that period.)

Salespersons, retail (887,000)

Registered nurses (767,000)

Cashiers (685,000)

General office clerks (670,000)

Truckdrivers, light and heavy (617,000)

General managers and top executives (598,000)

Janitors, maids, housekeeping cleaners (555,000)

Nursing aides, orderlies, and attendants (552,000)

Food-counter, fountain, and related workers (550,000)

Waiters and waitresses (449,000)

Teachers, secondary school (437,000)

Receptionists and information clerks (422,000)

Systems analysts and computer scientists (366,000)

Food preparation workers (365,000)

Child-care workers (353,000)

Gardeners and groundskeepers (348,000)

Accountants and auditors (340,000)

Computer programmers (317,000)

Teachers, elementary (313,000)

Guards (298,000)

Teacher aides and educational assistants (278,000)

Licensed practical nurses (269,000)

Clerical supervisors and managers (263,000)

Home-health aides (263,000)

Cooks, restaurant (257,000)

Maintenance repairers, general utility (251,000)

Secretaries, except legal and medical (248,000)

Cooks, short-order and fast-food (246,000)

Stock clerks, sales floor (209,000)

Lawyers (206,000)

THE SENIOR-FRIENDLY COMPUTER

In a column in his organization's monthly publication, Horace B. Deets, executive director of the AARP, tells of a recent ad for a large company showing a young woman sitting at a computer keyboard. "The difference between my mother and me?" she is saying. "My mother thinks software is a nightgown."

It's a joke based on myth. These days mother is likely to know as much or more about computers as is daughter. Nearly 60 percent of all women aged 45 to 64 are in the work force, with a clear majority of them in managerial, professional, and administrative positions. Surely, the word "software" is not foreign to them.

If it is foreign to you, it's important that you learn the language. When you started your career, computers didn't exist. Today, as if you hadn't noticed, they are everywhere. It is not possible to overstate the extent to which the computer's widespread use is changing the nature of work, the location of the work place, and the qualifications of workers. One in eight workers uses computers in one form or another.

Lots of older adults are intimidated by the computer. They watch in awe as their children churn out financial spreadsheets and their grandchildren do their homework on computers but, as one retired gentleman told me, "it's too late to learn this new-fangled computer stuff."

There is no basis for this attitude. Mary Furlong, a professor at the University of San Francisco and executive director of SeniorNet, an "international community of computer-using seniors," believes that older adults are ideal candidates for operating computers and that seniors empowered with computer skills "will contribute their knowledge and wisdom to the Information Age."

Many people, including the seniors themselves, think that older adults are not interested in learning about computers. In her book *Computers for Kids Over Sixty*, co-authored with Greg Kearsley, professor Furlong challenges a widely held belief that older adults are not interested in learning about computers. "From our experience teaching thousands of seniors to use computers, we have found that they want to know what all the fuss is about!"

Does it take older people longer to learn to use computers? Professor Furlong and her colleagues have reached the conclusion that "most older adults can learn to use a personal computer in about the same time and with as much ease as anyone else. In fact, we have found that seniors possess two important learning qualities that many younger people lack: *patience and persistence*. In addition, older adults have much knowledge to share using their new technological tools."

Life is something like this trumpet.
If you don't put anything in it,
you don't get anything out.
And that's the truth.

■ ■ ■

—W. C. Handy,
Father of the Blues, at age 85.

More than 15,000 people have joined SeniorNet, a six-year-old San Francisco-based organization. Members are part of a network of men and women 55 and over who are learning to use computers "to write or publish everything from a newsletter to an autobiography; manage personal or business records and communicate with other members across the country." SeniorNet members communicate from their own computers in their homes or from computer-equipped SeniorNet centers in more than 40 cities, from New York to California and Hawaii, and from Florida to Washington State and Alberta, Canada.

The simple fact is computer competence is fast becoming a basic requirement for most jobs. It is the one skill that cuts across all fields of endeavor. Yes, of course there are jobs that don't involve computers, but your job hunt will be easier and your pay higher if you have the required computer skills. Princeton economist Alan Krueger calculates that anybody who uses a computer earns 15 percent more than an equally skilled co-worker who does not. Even Americans with a lifetime of experience in a particular occupation will find that they need computer competence to find work in their field, even though the computer is only a small part of the job.

To prepare yourself for work in this computer age, you should know exactly what computer skills—if any— might improve your chance for employment. Then decide whether you'll need computer training in advance of getting work or if you can get the training after you're hired.

It is easier to become computer competent than you may think, and the extent of the training needed depends on the way the computer is used on the job. Technical computer applications and programming take a high degree of skill but most computer use on the job is quite basic. Less than 1 percent of all present jobs call for extensive computer training. Most computer-related skills require only a few hours' to a few weeks' training, followed by a period of learning on the job. You can get your introduction to operating a computer in a classroom but your computer skills are perfected on the job.

Seventy-two-year-old E. B. Clark, a semiretired investment adviser living in Seattle, received a computer from SeniorNet—part of an experiment sponsored by Apple Computer. With the organization's help and his own self-tutoring, Mr. Clark became proficient on the computer. "Now," he says, "I'm even teaching computering!" Any advice for his age peers? "Jump in the water and just start to swim," is his reply. Another SeniorNet member, 69-year-old Gerry Ohrt, is confined to a wheelchair. He still practices his former profession, designing industrial tools—on a Tandy Computer at the Park Hill Medical Center in Chillicothe, Illinois. "This makes life tolerable for me," says Mr. Ohrt.

Some employers assume that you and other older men and women are computer illiterates and that you are not capable of learning computer skills. You can disprove this assumption by taking the time and making the effort to relate to the new world of computers. It's the first logical step toward making yourself competitive in today's job market.

Computer training is available at local schools—particularly vocational schools—and by computer-equipment manufacturers. Computer courses are available at adult-education centers free of cost or at a modest tuition fee. Federally funded computer-training courses may be available to you in your community under the Job Training Partnership Act.

SeniorNet, the organization mentioned earlier, is designed to train older adults in computer skills. The objective of SeniorNet is to allow seniors to communicate with one another, but the skills acquired through SeniorNet are applicable to the job market.

Skills taught at SeniorNet Learning Centers and applicable to the job market include:

Word Processing. The computer keyboard is almost the same as the typewriter keyboard and you see what you are writing on the computer screen. The advantage that the computer has over the typewriter is the ease with which you can correct, change copy, move copy around, and store text. You can change, correct, and rearrange your text before and after you print it out.

Telecommunications. With a computer and a modem (a modem is a "telephone for the computer") you can send and receive messages and information over networks of computers that are linked with telephone lines. With a modem you can communicate with an employer in a different location and with customers and sources of information. It's a kind of instantaneous electronic mail.

Spreadsheets. Computer spreadsheets are a valuable tool for managing business or personal finances and organizing other kinds of numerical data. With a spreadsheet you can track investments, prepare cost estimates for jobs or repairs, balance a checkbook, prepare tax information, and handle any number of fact sheets based on numbers.

Databases. Computer databases enable you to store information so that it can be retrieved quickly and in any format. You can print out address labels or lists of customers, print out a list of people in your database of a certain age who live in a particular zip-code area, and store inventory and any other information in an organized and easily retrievable format.

When you become proficient on the computer, besides acquiring a valuable skill in itself you can use a computer and modem in your job search or to start your own home-based business. For example: You can use it to circulate your resume. Tap into bulletin boards that list job openings. Maintain a database of prospective employers. Work at home, telecommute, and send work to your employer through the modem hookup. With your own personal computer you can start your own business doing word processing, mailing-list management, desktop publishing, billing services for doctors and dentists, and tax-return preparation for individuals and small companies.

Although computer competence is just one kind of skill, it is a skill that has application in many fields. Here are examples of other skills that do not require extensive training, jobs that older adults can ease into with training from one week to a few months depending on the individual's aptitude and the degree of expertise required. The following jobs require licenses or certificates, but there are other equally rewarding occupations that do not.

Cosmetologist, Beautician, Hairstylist. Small beauty salons will continue to have employment opportunities for men and women who can help people look good. National hairstyling franchises is one way to go into your own business. All states require licensing to shampoo, cut, and style hair but one to two years' apprenticeship training is available so you can work while you train. This field of personal services is particularly appropriate for mature women with a flair for hairstyling and makeup.

Real Estate. Through good times and bad there will always be a call for real-estate agents and brokers. Mature adults with a "feel for real estate" and a talent for sales will find this a rewarding occupation. You get to meet a lot of people and you can make very good money. Agents who sell real estate owned by others must have 30 hours of classroom training. Brokers who manage and develop new properties must have 90 hours of classroom training. Agents must pass a written exam to obtain a state license.

Insurance. Mature adults with previous business experience in finance, mathematics, and accounting have a head start toward a lucrative job in insurance sales. They have a decided advantage in selling supplemental-health and long-term care insurance to other mature adults. Some classroom training is necessary to pass the written exam and continuing education is mandatory. Intensive on-the-job training sponsored by large insurance companies is available at local agencies.

Although none of the occupations listed here is directly related to computer technology, computer competence is an adjunct to the daily activity of each. Beauty-salon operators use computers to keep track of appointments, maintain a database of customers, and keep business records; real estate agents use computers to list properties, match buyers and sellers, and work up financial worksheets and mortgage information for buyers; insurance agents provide computer-generated premium quotes and calculate estate-planning alternatives and benefits comparisons.

THE JOB HUNT

*Men don't stop climbing mountains
because they get old;
they get old because they stop
climbing mountains.*

—Finis Mitchell,
naturalist and author

Until you get the job you're looking for, your occupation is job hunting. Target the position you want and go for it. Job hunting is a skill in itself. Get good at it. Learn the strategies and techniques that have proved successful for others and adapt them to your situation. Approach job hunting with the same single-mindedness that you would employ on the job.

The search for meaningful work at this stage of your life is a challenge to be met and conquered. Be adventurous. Take up the challenge.

To start, you must commit to a realistic schedule for accomplishing specific tasks. Decide on the hours you will spend each day on your job hunt. An overly ambitious schedule of more hours than you can handle will leave you worn out and frustrated. Devoting too few hours to job hunting is equally self-defeating and likely to drag on and possibly end in failure. A full schedule for job hunting will improve your chances.

Information about emerging job opportunities for older adults surfaces, regularly, and special programs and recruitment campaigns are reported in your local newspaper, senior publications and magazines (*Modern Maturity, New Choices*), and the bulletin boards in senior centers and social agencies. Keep informed and follow up on the information you read about. While you're at it, look for job opportunities that include training and allows you to upgrade your job skills on the job.

ACCENTUATE THE POSITIVE

Lawrence Kamisher, a New York-based executive recruiter, told me about an applicant who opened up the discussion with "I know that you're probably looking for someone younger, but ... " Very often in an interview, a self-conscious older person unwittingly raises the matter of age. Mr. Kamisher says, "Don't—you may be raising an issue that wasn't there to begin with. Don't apologize for your age and don't use it to win sympathy. It's demeaning, counterproductive, and won't get you the job."

Laid-off older workers and retirees often suffer from a diminished sense of self-worth. They blame themselves. Convinced that they are "over the hill" and no longer wanted, their unemployment is a self-fulfilling prophesy.

The greatest barrier that job seekers in their fifties and sixties face are their own insecurities. In the popular comic strip, Pogo sums up their situation: "We have met the enemy and it is us."

Insecurity and low self-esteem can be overcome by analyzing your work record and discovering how valuable your lifetime of experience can be to the right employer. Your age and your years of work make you the kind of employee that successful companies depend on to get the job done. Years of experience learning "people skills" make it easier for you and your age peers to get along with other workers and satisfy customers. You know when to cooperate, when to negotiate, when to be part of the team, and when to use your own initiative.

Although the main thrust of this book is to promote the value of work for older Americans, it would be unrealistic to present all work as a glorious experience. There are jobs that are unpleasant and tedious, where people are overworked and underpaid. Some older Americans need the income and are forced to accept any kind of work they can get. Sometimes job satisfaction is a luxury that only the well-to-do can afford. If you need immediate income, you will probably go for the best offer you receive, whether it offers job satisfaction or not.

That is understandable and is part of the behavior pattern that makes you a survivor. But too many older adults are insecure about their chances competing in the job market and are unacquainted with the new and emerging positions constantly opening up for seasoned, experienced workers. Because they are unaware, they settle for low-paying jobs that offer little in the way of job satisfaction.

Your alternatives at this stage of your life are clear. You can work for modest compensation at a less-than-satisfactory position or you can acquire the skills that enable you to get the job you want. If you need training to get the kind of work you want, go get it. Training programs for older Americans are usually free. If not free, they are inexpensive.

Millions of men and women enter maturity with enough savings and investments to free them from money pressures. If you are among this fortunate group of financially secure older Americans, you can put salary lower down on your list of priorities. People who spent most of their lives as breadwinners trying to make ends meet have a hard time adjusting to new priorities. They continue to seek work that pays the most money, whether they need the income or not.

This is a question worth thinking about: Isn't this the time in your life when job satisfaction should get a higher priority?

JOB-SEARCH METHODS THAT WORK

Over the years job-search strategies have evolved to help conduct the search as efficiently and quickly as possible. Since it is not possible to determine which strategy will produce results for you, it makes sense to use as many of them as practical and all at once: answer ads, send letters, increase your contacts and network, make telephone calls. Any one of these activities can pay off for you.

Successful Job-Search Methods

Applied directly to employer

Asked friends about jobs where they work

Asked friends about jobs elsewhere

Asked relatives about jobs where they work

Asked relatives about jobs elsewhere

Answered local newspaper ads

Private employment agency

School placement office

Civil service test

Asked teacher or instructor

Placed ad in local newspaper

Union hiring hall

The top three methods, in order of effectiveness, are (1) Applied directly to employer, (2) Private employment agency, and (3) Answered local newspaper ads.

YOUR MAIL CAMPAIGN

The mail carrier is your ally. Use the mail to spread your net wide and reach hundreds of potential employers—or you can communicate with a selected few at specific companies. Let's look at the techniques for using letters in your job search.

1. BROADCAST LETTER TO A LARGE MAILING LIST

Although there is an advantage to "mass marketing" yourself to a large number of employers and having the percentages work for you, this is an expensive, time-consuming way to go. If you use the shotgun approach, scattering your mailing to a large number of companies, your letter will be just one more in an avalanche of job-seeking letters. The results of such a mailing are seldom fruitful considering the time spent in producing such a mailing and the cost of postage. The response could be disappointing. Even if you have something very special to offer and have a very effective letter, you'll be doing well if you get two responses for every hundred letters you mail.

Careful selection of your prospect list reduces the cost of mailing and improves the response. You can also increase the effectiveness of your mass mail campaign by following up on the phone to as many companies on your list as you can handle. Your follow-up call should be made within a week to ten days.

The most difficult—and at the same time, most important—aspect of a mail campaign is addressing your communication to the right person. Most job applicants make the mistake of addressing their application to the head of the organization. Top executives seldom participate in employment decisions except at the highest levels and then only after all the necessary screening has been completed by others.

Where a corporation lists an assistant to a president or top executive, it may be best to address your letter to that individual. Screening employment applications is often part of his or her job.

Unless you have a unique approach and a powerhouse of a letter, you would probably be more successful with a rifle approach, targeting your letter to a particular individual at a specific company.

2. TARGET A SPECIFIC INDIVIDUAL IN A SPECIFIC COMPANY

If you've researched the company, have the name of the individual doing the hiring, and can match your skills to the company's needs, this is by far the most effective way to use the mail in your job quest. Researching the company and writing a letter tailored to the specific interest of the employer may be more time consuming, but the response to this focused approach is bound to be greater than from the shotgun mailing.

3. NETWORKING LETTER

Just as you network in person and on the telephone to let people know that you're looking for work and asking for help, you can use the mail to put additional steam in your networking. Your networking letter, accompanied by a copy of your resume, should

- Remind the individual who you are and describe briefly your background, skills, and employment goals.

- Ask specifically for information about job opportunities he or she may know about, ask for ideas about whom else to contact, and ask for referrals to individuals who can help.

- Acknowledge that he or she may not know of immediate openings but ask the person to keep you in mind for future openings.

- Tell the individual when you will call to discuss the matter further.

4. RECOMMENDATION REQUEST LETTER

You'll find that most people are flattered by your request for a recommendation and are happy to comply. Tell them about the kind of work you're seeking so that they can stress applicable skills and attributes in their recommendation. Your main purpose here is to get a letter of recommendation, but your request notifies them of your job search and becomes part of your overall networking activities.

5. LETTER TO ACCOMPANY RESUME

You've called a prospective employer. He expresses interest and asks you to send a resume. When you do, it should be accompanied by a short, attention-getting cover letter. The purpose of the cover letter is to encourage the employer to read your resume and grant you an interview. You may send your standard letter to many employers, but when there is an expression of interest, the cover letter should be a personalized message to the employer. Remember to send an original letter, never a photocopy.

Address your cover letter to the person (by name and title) who can make the hiring decision. Use the language of the field to which you are applying. The cover letter should reflect your familiarity with the organization and call the reader's attention to qualifications that match the employer's requirements.

> Aspects of my background are particularly relevant to your needs at this time. You will note in the third paragraph of my resume the sales campaign I conducted for the Excell Corporation and the results I was able to achieve for them in a short six-month period.

> The computer courses I refer to in my resume relate to the type of problems we discussed on the phone. My successful completion of the computer courses gives me the know-how to improve your current computer system.

> I am particularly interested in working for ConTrac because my familiarity with the area you are opening enables me to identify the areas of greatest potential for your new facilities.

If throughout your life you've been told that it's inappropriate to boast about yourself, that's one bit of advice that's best forgotten. Modesty is a virtue, but not here. Your cover letter is essentially a sales letter and the product is you—and your ability. You have to sell yourself. Employers receive thousands of resumes in the mail. To stand out above the competition, you need a well-written, compelling cover letter.

**6. LETTER ANSWERING A CLASSIFIED
WANT AD.**

Many mature job applicants have had success responding to
a classified want ad with what can best be described as a
"letter resume," which combines aspects of a job response
letter with the essential facts of the resume. This hypothetical
ad is answered in the letter that follows:

> Seeking experienced individual for one-person personnel depart-
> ment for small, growing health-care company. Full-time, part-time,
> or flexible hours arrangement. Knowledge of labor department
> report forms and word processing skills required. Must have "peo-
> ple skills" and be dependable. Respond to P.O. Box 4866, M22,
> Chicago, IL 60611.

Here's an example of a "letter resume" responding to
the ad:

Sir or Madam:

> *This letter is in response to your classified want ad
> in the October 10 issue of the Chicago Tribune.*
>
> *My background, skills, and experience are
> uniquely matched to the position described in your
> advertisement.*
>
> *For the past eleven years, I have served as assistant
> personnel manager of National Office Services in Ev-
> anston. My duties there included interaction with em-
> ployees on diverse matters, from health benefits to
> vacation schedules. I was also responsible for completing
> and sending out labor department reports on time. My
> ability in word processing (WordPerfect 5.1) enabled me
> to fill in and assist the secretarial staff, which I was often
> called upon to do.*
>
> *Prior to my employment at National Office Ser-
> vices, I worked at the human resources section of a large*

Chicago bank. I started in a clerical capacity processing employee health claims and was promoted to group manager where I was responsible for grading employee performance reviews and other tasks requiring experience and judgment.

The ability to get along with people and to communicate with fellow employees and customers is a matter of personal pride. I am a self-starter and able to work independently or as part of a group.

Because of my experience in personnel and my ability to handle a large volume of work quickly and efficiently, I can deliver full-time results on a part-time or flexible hours arrangement. In any case, I am open to any arrangement that meets your needs.

Please call so that we can discuss further how I might be of service to you and your company. I look forward to meeting with you at your convenience.

Your very truly,

Rosalyn Edwards

Note that all the qualifications called for in the ad are covered in the response letter. The ad calls for experience; the applicant demonstrates experience. Knowledge of labor department reports and word-processing skills are mentioned in the ad; the response letter covers both points. The ad asks for "people" skills; the applicant writes about her interaction with employees and her ability to get along with others. And, finally and most important, the applicant implies that she can get the job done on a part-time basis, thus saving the employer a full-timer's salary.

The preceding is just one format for a "letter resume" responding to a want ad, but there are other equally effective ways of accomplishing the same purpose. Whether the information is organized in columns, numbered paragraphs, or graphic tables, its purpose is the same: to reduce your communication to the essentials, giving employers the facts they need to determine your qualifications. Remember, the purpose of your letter is to "sell" the interview.

USE THE TELEPHONE

By itself, or in combination with the mail, the telephone can produce quick success for individuals seeking part-time work or flexible-hours work. Job hunting by telephone lets you cover a lot of territory in very little time, and a cold call to a company that is growing and changing can reveal openings before they are generally known.

Five Tips for Using the Telephone Effectively

1. Write out a script. Even if you're glib and articulate, a written script you can refer to during the conversation will make sure that all points are covered.

2. Don't lead off with your age or volunteer information that will date you. Bob Tell, a highly successful Detroit recruiter specializing in the health-care industry, told me: "I get many telephone calls from doctors who start right off by telling me, 'I'm not a kid, you know. I've got some age on me.'" Tell's reaction: "First of all, it's against the law for me even to be talking about that. Second of all, I don't care. My clients are looking for competent doctors, no matter what age."

3. Don't be vague about the purpose of your call. Ask for the interview. And give the individual a choice of

"when," not "yes or no." ("Would the morning or the afternoon be more convenient for you?")

4. Give enough information to win you the interview but try to avoid conducting the initial interview over the phone. You want an eye-to-eye meeting with the person doing the hiring.

5. Call early in the day when the man or woman you're trying to see is fresh and when there is less likely to be a secretary guarding the gate. Even when calls are screened, you're more likely to get through if your voice reflects confidence and authority.

Life is like riding a bicycle.
You don't fall off
until you stop pedalling.

■ ■ ■

—Claude Pepper

CONSIDER TEMPORARY WORK AS A STARTER

"Temp" work is usually available through temporary employment agencies or directly from the company itself. Besides being the quickest and easiest way to overcome the psychological hurdle from retiree to worker, temporary work allows you to test your skills, determine whether you need further training, and if so, what kind. Temporary work lets you become familiar with the work environment without making a long-term commitment.

LOOK FOR OPPORTUNITIES
AMONG SMALL BUSINESSES

Even if your background is with large companies, you will find that the best new jobs are with small businesses. The change will be good for you—and that's where the jobs are. A Small Business Survey conducted by the accounting firm of Arthur Andersen & Co. reports that "the role of small business is becoming increasingly important in the U.S. economy. There are over 17 million small businesses today, accounting for 55 percent of all existing jobs and the creation of almost all new jobs since 1980."

According to James C. Challenger, president of the Chicago outplacement firm of Challenger, Gray & Christmas, "As large employers downsized, many thousands of the managers they discharged found new work at small- to medium-sized firms." Small, rapidly growing companies and new businesses employ a significant share of workers aged 65 and over and are primary targets for older men and women seeking part-time work. Part-time employment opportunities for older workers are more plentiful in small firms. The Small Business Administration reports that more than half of workers 55 and over employed by firms with fewer than 100 employees were working part time.

JOB SATISFACTION IN NONPROFITS

The world of nonprofits—the 1.3 million charities, church groups, foundations, think tanks, agricultural co-ops, and quasi-governmental agencies, plus arts, health, social service, educational, and membership organizations—represent a wealth of work opportunity for older Americans who "want to make a difference."

Many people mistakenly believe that nonprofits are staffed only by unpaid volunteers. Fact is, this segment of the population employs more than 20 million people and generates $750 billion a year in revenues. If you're seeking a salaried position in a nonprofit organization, you should be familiar with the staff structure of the prospective employer—how many paid, how many volunteers, and who does what.

Full-time and part-time office jobs such as receptionist and mailroom worker at these organizations are usually advertised in the "want ads" or placed through employment agencies. These and other jobs at nonprofits usually pay minimum wage or a little better. Even high-level executive positions at these organizations demand more and pay less than comparable positions in the commercial world. But for many people the satisfaction of identifying with the goals of the organization makes up for the difference in compensation. Among the larger, more prosperous nonprofits, the paid staffs enjoy a stimulating and pleasant work environment without the stress that goes with highly competitive sales jobs. When she turned 58, Helen Bradley left a high-paying position as a sales representative for a handbag manufacturer and went to work as an administrative assistant at the county Center for Performing Arts. She told me, "I don't take the job home with me every night the way I used to."

THE GOVERNMENT IS AN EQUAL OPPORTUNITY EMPLOYER

As a longtime taxpayer you are painfully aware that the government employs many people. You've been helping to pay their salaries for years. This is a good time to be on the receiving end. The federal government employs more than

3 million people, many of them 55 and older. When you create your list of potential employers, you might consider including Uncle Sam and the state and local governments. Although some government jobs are civil service and obtained only through competitive examinations, many older persons obtain jobs through special government programs or are appointed to jobs by office holders. Part-time opportunities, in particular, are expanding on all levels of government. To learn more about government jobs, contact your local legislator's office or the agency or government department that interests you.

SEEK OUT THE COMPANIES THAT SERVE SENIORS

The 62 million—one of every four people in the United States—aged 50 and over have a combined annual income of more than $900 billion. That in a nutshell explains businesses' renewed interest in "the mature market." New divisions and new products and services are being introduced to cater to this huge and profitable "mature market." Since a mature individual is better at relating to older customers, the companies are actively recruiting people with some gray showing to help them lock on to this lucrative market segment.

Travelers Insurance Company, American Express, and the Marriott Corporation are among the leading companies actively recruiting older men and women to help them win the patronage of mature customers.

With so many companies aggressively searching for mature staff to relate to older customers, doesn't it make sense to apply for work where your age is an asset? In behalf of its members, The American Hotel & Motel Association has launched a campaign to recruit older people for hotel staff jobs. Industries actively courting the patronage of older adults include banking, tourism, health care, and retirement housing.

GIVE LUCK A CHANCE

We all know somebody who was lucky to be in the right place at the right time. You can improve your chances of getting lucky by doing your homework and increasing your job-search activity. Read business publications, attend trade exhibitions, and keep your eyes open for job leads in your field. Seek out companies with expanding sales and new product lines. Do something every day and devote enough time to job hunting. Make telephone calls, make contacts, spread the word, write letters, and schedule appointments. The harder you look, the luckier you'll get.

Even an interview for a job you're not sure you want serves a purpose—it gives you a chance to practice and improve your performance. After a while you'll develop intuitive feelings about job openings in activities you observe in your neighborhood or in a newspaper item. Act on your intuition—you would be surprised at how many situations are discovered that way. Don't allow yourself to get discouraged. Many seniors faced with a few rejections just give up and rationalize, "Who wants to work anyway?" Men skip the shave; women don't bother washing their hair. Pretty soon, rejection and unemployment is a self-fulfilling prophecy ("Nobody hires people my age.").

My unemployed neighbor Chris would stop for a pick-me-up after an unsuccessful interview or whenever he was feeling down. After a while, Chris, who was a social drinker all his life, became a heavy drinker. Job hunting can be traumatic so you'll need to avoid some of the obvious but dangerous ways of escape. A similar warning applies to drugs. It can start with a few tranquilizers, then uppers and mood-elevating pills, then stronger stuff, and eventually a serious drug dependency. For some it's alcohol, for others, drugs; instead of solving problems, they just add to their problems. With adequate planning and a clear target in sight you can avoid the pitfalls; persistence and patience will pay off.

Watch for Employment Scams

Dishonest operators are always out there ready to take advantage of the desperate and the gullible. Many seniors are so eager to get work that they fall for these scams.

Mail-order business. There are legitimate ways to enter the mail-order business in special niche markets, but most of the ads promising instant profits in mail order are making money for themselves, not for you. Some mail-order scams involve selling you catalogs that you mail at your own cost. They are using you to pay for the postage and the labor of mailing.

Earn big money stuffing envelopes. Unscrupulous operators charge you to get into their business—selling instructions on how to place ads to attract other suckers who want to make money stuffing envelopes. Automated mailing facilities make such work obsolete. The post office puts thousands of these con artists out of business every year, but the scam goes on.

Arts and crafts. Make good money selling your arts and crafts. The company will buy it from you. But first, you'll have to buy their equipment, which ranges from sewing machines to sign printers. Naturally, your work fails to meet the standards of the company so the company is not obligated to buy your work as they said they would.

Work at home. Con artists take advantage of disabled or elderly people with newspaper ads promising huge profits for clipping news items, raising rabbits or chinchillas, doing home sewing, and other seemingly honest activities. All these companies want to do is sell you advice and equipment. In most cases you must buy something from them before you can start to work.

FLEXIBILITY IS AN ADVANTAGE

In targeting prospective employers, your job goals need to be well defined but broad enough to allow flexibility within that goal. For example, a lower-level job at a company you want to work for could put you in a position for advancement to the job you really want. And don't rule out other fields. Your job search will be more productive if you are willing and able to move or change industries. Employers are now more open to "outsiders"—people from other industries who can apply their skills to solving the company's problems.

TAX BREAKS

Unless you are seeking work for the first time or have been out of the labor force for a long time or are changing fields, most of your job-hunting expenses are tax-deductible. Travel, printing stationery and resumes, and employment-counseling expenses are tax deductible.

In addition, if you meet IRS requirements, you can deduct reasonable costs of house-hunting trips before moving, temporary lodging, moving expenses, and selling and buying a place to live. Be sure to keep receipts and keep careful records of all your job-search expenses.

THE INFORMATIONAL INTERVIEW

Informational interviews have become an integral part of modern job-hunt strategies. The purpose of the informational interview is to ask for information, advice, and referrals, not to ask for a job. Here, you are the one asking the questions. If approached diplomatically, most people will be happy to cooperate and will be flattered that you asked them.

In addition to discovering useful information and gaining the benefit of a knowledgeable individual's advice, he or she may refer you to others, offer suggestions on how to improve your resume, and remember you for future reference. While it is not the purpose of the informational interview to solicit a job offer, many such interviews have ended with a genuine job offer.

THE APPLICATION FORM

It looks pretty harmless but the application form tells the employer more about you than you think. Aside from the information itself, the application form tells the employer whether or not you can follow directions, if you're sloppy or neat, whether you can spell simple words, if you're well organized, and whether you pay attention to details.

Filling out application forms will be easier and take less time if you jot down relevant information on an index card and carry it with you in a pocket or handbag. The data that should be on the index card for quick reference includes:

- Social Security number
- Driver's license number
- Educational institutions attended/address/dates
- Names and addresses of former employers/dates
- Military service (if applicable)/dates
- Volunteer Service
- Membership in professional, civic, and social organizations
- Name, address, and telephone numbers of references

Be prepared with carefully thought-out replies to questions that may appear on the application form: "Why did you leave your last position?" "Have you ever been dismissed from any position? If yes, please explain." "May we contact your present or former employer?"

Additional tips on applications:

- Mature job seekers should be especially careful that their handwriting is clear, legible, and firm. You may prefer to take the application with you to complete at home and mail in. Many companies allow you to do so.
- You are expected to answer every question. On questions that are not appropriate to your application, write in "Not Applicable" rather than leave a blank space.
- If you're asked for references, three should be sufficient. It helps if one or more of the references are well

known and respected in the industry or community. Call the person you're giving as a reference, so the inquiry about you doesn't come as a surprise. You need to check with your references to make sure that their comments are positive and convincing.

- The application is a legal document. Make sure the information you provide is accurate and avoid any temptation to stretch the truth. Any lies or misinformation you give on your application is just cause for dismissal.

THE JOB INTERVIEW

Feeling a little insecure about going out on interviews? You are not alone. Most job applicants have qualms about facing an inquisitor; mature adults are particularly insecure. "I resent having to prove myself all over again" was the way a retired bank manager expressed it at a job-club meeting. He and many others like him bring negative attitudes with them to the interview. And it shows.

That's why adequate preparation *before* the job hunt is so important. If you're prepared, you should be able to walk into the interview with confidence, knowing the job you want and ready to prove your claim to it. The story of the employer looking for someone 30 years old with 40 years of experience is not just a joke. Many employers are ambivalent about age when hiring—they value experience and mature judgment but cling to the outdated myths about older workers. Whether it is openly expressed or not, you must correct any misconceptions they may have about age and about your ability to do the job.

> **W**hatever a man's age,
> he can reduce it by several years
> by putting a bright colored flower
> in his buttonhole.
>
> ■ ■ ■
>
> —Mark Twain

First impressions are important, and here things count that you may not have been aware of. Your appearance. Your posture. Your body language. How you shake hands. These are a part of your image. Because many employers have a stereotyped image of older job seekers, you have to take special care to project good health and a high level of energy.

Relating to Younger and Lower-Level Interviewers

It is possible that your job interview will be conducted by someone younger than yourself. Don't let this throw you. If you're over 55 most working people are younger than you. Just as you don't want to be judged on the basis of your age, don't underestimate the ability of younger people simply because they're younger. (Have you noticed the age of your doctor?)

Similarly, don't be upset if the person interviewing you is at a lower rank than the position you're applying for. It is common practice at many companies for lower-level personnel-department people to guard the gates and screen potential employees for positions at all levels.

You can go a long way toward overcoming any prejudices that a young interviewer might have about age differences by appearing comfortable and amiable during the conversation.

When you start to work you will probably be working with many men and women younger than you. The chance to work with people of all ages is one of the benefits of work, and the ability to relate to younger people—or to work under the supervision of people younger than yourself—is a reality of working later in life.

INTERVIEW TIPS

- Be prompt—allow yourself plenty of time to get to the interview. Plunging in breathlessly is not the way to make a good first impression.

- Greet the interviewer with a firm handshake. The impression you create with your posture, body language, and energy level can be crucial to the success of the interview. Make eye contact and speak with confidence and enthusiasm.

- Be sure your answers to the interviewer's questions are clear and concise. Whenever possible indicate the positive aspects of your claim to the job—seasoned judgment, good work ethic, good health and high energy, flexibility, and lifetime experience working with people.

- Older job seekers have to take particular care in dress and grooming. A wrinkled sports coat and worn-out heels can undo you before the interview starts. Note what others are wearing in the company and dress appropriately for the job you are seeking. You need

to look smart, stylish, and up to date—for men, a
dark suit, a light-colored shirt, and a conservative tie;
for women, a tailored dress with a jacket is best. Keep
the jewelry simple.

■ Avoid like the plague the self-deprecating phrases
that focus on age: "Back then we did things much
different . . . "; "When you get to be my age you'll
understand how I feel"; "I remember when we used
to . . . "; "When I was younger I was able to . . . "

You may have used similar phrases in conversation
with friends without realizing the implications. They
are a dead giveaway; they tell your interviewer you
are living in the past.

When you say things such as, "At my age . . . " "When
I was younger . . . " "Way back when . . . " you're
sending the wrong signals. Nostalgia is fine in a
social setting, and there's nothing wrong with being
a proud grandparent, but talk of grandchildren
doesn't belong in a job interview. You may be justi-
fiably proud of your World War II military service
but reference to it doesn't belong in your resume or
in the interview. Keep the conversation focused and
relevant and, if possible, avoid talking about personal matters. Even if the interviewer gets nostalgic,
try to shift the conversation from the past and talk
about the future. The immediate future.

■ Let the interviewer lead the discussion. You have to
listen carefully so that anything you say will be
responsive to the interviewer. In his book *On Hiring*,
Robert Half, president of Robert Half International,
one of the largest placement firms in the country,
lists "poor listener" on the top of his list of most
disturbing applicant behavior during an interview.

- Don't set limits on how long you plan to work. A frequent criticism of older workers is that they are disinterested in the work and just biding their time. Statements such as, "I plan to work only another two years," feed the charge that older workers don't want to make a commitment and are just holding on until they can stop working.

- Even employers who value older workers want to hire healthy, reliable people. They want people who are going to be on the job at scheduled hours and who are physically able to get the job done. Chronic complainers and people who are often out sick need not apply. That's why in all your contacts with a prospective employer, you accentuate the positive and present the image of an energetic and vigorous individual.

- If you've had a long, varied career, you'll be tempted to tell the interviewer about all of it. Don't. During the interview highlight the experience and skills that relate to that job.

- Be prepared to answer some of the most frequently asked questions: Why did you choose this organization? Have you done this kind of work before? Tell me about your strengths and weaknesses. Tell me something about yourself. That last one is tricky. It could lead you into saying things about yourself that perhaps should not be said. To avoid the trap, *think in terms of what the interviewer wants to hear*. Keep that in mind and you'll do just fine.

- Don't just answer the interviewer's questions; ask questions of your own. Speak up and make eye contact. Your questions will raise some issues that could help you and might not have been raised otherwise. Also, the interviewer's answer to your questions make it easier for you to decide whether you want the job or not.

- Try to anticipate questions in possible problem areas. A question about your age, the state of your health, gaps in work history, and related matters can be dispatched easily if you've thought about it and prepared an answer.

- You should have a firm idea of your salary parameters before going out on an interview. Hourly wages for lower-level positions are often advertised with the job descriptions. Salaries for mid- and upper-level positions are usually discussed at a second or third interview but be prepared to discuss salary if the interviewer brings it up.

- Rehearse the interview with a friend or a job counselor, particularly if you are nervous or uncomfortable interviewing. Interviewing skills improve with practice. The more you rehearse and prepare your answers to the hard questions, the better your chance for success.

- If there are no jobs currently available, call back periodically. Employers are favorably impressed by friendly perseverance and eagerness to work.

WHAT EMPLOYERS WANT

You and your contemporaries can help solve the employers' most troublesome staffing problems. Companies are afflicted with high turnover and the cost of training new employees; they want employees who will stay with them for a reasonable amount of time. On average, older workers stay at the job three times longer than younger workers do.

The high rate of absenteeism hurts production and affects profitability. Studies show that older workers are reliable, miss fewer days at work, and are punctual.

Employers are appalled at the inability of many young job applicants to handle simple arithmetic and communicate effectively on paper. You and your contemporaries have good basic math and writing skills and are better educated and more highly trained and skilled than any generation before you.

Employers appreciate conscientious employees. Your generation takes pride in the quality of its work. Its work ethic is based on a full day's work for a full day's pay.

Sticky issues—responding to the age barrier

Although an employer is not allowed by law to ask an applicant's age, the interviewer may look for clues that reveal your age. (When did you get your degree? What did you do at your first job—and when was that? Will you fit in here?)

Other questions (How do you feel about working with others who are a lot younger than you? We don't have many employees your age. Would that bother you?) usually imply that you are too old for the job. Sometimes an interviewer not familiar with the laws against age discrimination will be more blunt and tell you outright, "We were thinking in terms of a younger person for this job." These are among the best answers I've heard to sticky age questions:

> I am a better worker now because of my experience over the years working with many men and women of all ages—some younger and

some older than myself. I respect the supervisor's role in making things work smoothly, and the supervisor's age is irrelevant to me.

I have no problem working under a supervisor younger than myself because I don't believe that leadership has anything to do with age. I can learn from and follow someone who is younger or older than myself, and I respect the abilities of other workers, including my boss.

I'm applying for work at this company because people tell me that it's competence and ability that count here, not age. Is there any question of my competence or ability to do the job?

If you're looking for someone who can be productive right from the start, you need someone with experience. My track record working with people of all ages and my zest for work outweigh any reservations you may have based on age.

My maturity can be a great advantage to your company. Many of your best customers are seniors. I can relate to them and win their confidence better than a young person could.

If I understand correctly you're looking for someone who can apply seasoned judgment and stay cool under pressure. Those are the very qualities that come with life experience.

If my background and experience are important, are they less important than my age?

You can stick to your legal rights and refuse to answer questions relating to age or you can decide that it's best to be forthright about it and address the issue right up front:

I know that legally we're not allowed to talk about age. But since it's come up, I don't mind talking about it. My health is excellent, and I have many good years to give to your company. Frankly, my services would be a bargain to your company since my experience and knowledge has already been paid for by many years on the job.

If you're applying for a job after being retired for a period of time, be prepared to respond to a direct question—"Why do you want to go back to work after being retired for two years?"—with a direct answer:

> I took some time off to travel and do some free-lance work but I never thought of myself as being retired. I like work and I like to interact with people. My background and experience are a perfect match for this job and if I get the chance I would expect to spend many years making a real contribution to the company.

Retirement is a state of mind, and if you were actively involved in work as a volunteer or working on a meaningful, self-directed project, then you weren't retired.

MOTIVATION AND STAYING POWER

Some age discrimination is based on the misconceptions of otherwise well-meaning employers. Among other things they assume that you don't need the income and therefore have less incentive to work. Or that you will want more money because you have more experience. (If the income is important to you, say so. It tells the employer you're motivated. If you're willing to work at the going rate, say so and put that objection to rest.)

Employers may assume you lack the stamina to do the job. And most will assume that fringe coverage—life insurance, health insurance, and pension benefits—will cost them more than fringes for younger applicants. (If you're covered by Social Security and Medicare and already have a pension plan, this is a tremendous advantage to your employer. If you have such coverage, make it known.) Employment specialist Dan Lacey told me that health-insurance costs have become such a burden to employers that if he were an older person seeking employment he would purchase his own health-care insurance: "If you can tell a prospective employer that he doesn't have to cover you for health care, that you've already taken care of it personally, that could be the most important thing you could say to clinch the job for yourself."

Whether they come right out and say so or not many interviewers, when faced with a mature adult applying for a job, think to themselves, How long will this person stay on the job? They worry that you will not remain on the job long enough to justify the investment in orientation and training. And yet, study after study confirms the fact that older workers stay on the job longer than many younger people. If you sense that this is a concern, don't fail to set the record straight:

> I think it's important that you know that I am in excellent health and expect to continue working for many years.

RESPONDING
TO THE "OVERQUALIFIED" CHARGE

Employers will use the "overqualified" ploy to let you down easy when they really mean that you're too old for the job.

Also, employers worry about hiring highly experienced applicants who feel superior to other workers or will grow bored and above it all.

> If, when you say I'm "overqualified" you mean that I have a lot of experience, perhaps you are right. But I am willing to work at the going rate and I bring experience and skill to the job. That means I will be more productive and cost you less.

Once an employer understands that your career interests are different from what they were at an earlier age and that you are now seeking a job that is suitable to your current status, your superior qualifications become an asset, not a liability. Another appropriate answer to a charge of overqualification could be:

> In a business such as this I'm not sure you can be overqualified— there is so much to know, and things are always changing. If you

are concerned that I will be bored or restless working at this level, I can assure you that this is not the case. I like the work and there are challenges on every level to keep me on my toes.

THE HEALTH QUESTION

As an older job applicant, your health is a matter of greater than usual concern. For your own sake, do not apply for any job that will endanger or risk your health, but if the issue is raised unfairly don't hesitate to correct the matter.

> As for my health, I am very fortunate. I am in excellent health and can cope with a hectic pace. I welcome the challenge that this job represents.

> I am healthy and have a lot of energy. If there's anything old about me it's my old-fashioned work ethic. I like work and I look forward to a long and productive future here. The work of this company fits nicely with my own goals.

You need to reassure the employer that your health will not affect your performance. If you have physical limitations, explain how you manage them and why they will not prevent you from doing the job.

> I have some obvious physical limitations. Let me describe how I plan to handle them on this job . . .

Employers set against hiring someone past a certain age will find other reasons for turning you down. And then it's time for you to ask yourself: Do I really want to work for a company that will turn down a qualified person because of age?

CHAPTER NINE

WORK AND THE OLDER WOMAN

IMMEDIATE OPENINGS for mature,
responsible homemakers interested
in careers leading to economic
independence. Program needs displaced
homemakers who seek paying
jobs because of divorce, separation,
the death or disability of a spouse,
or loss of public assistance. Career
guidance, support groups, and job
counseling offered to women
willing to transfer household skills
to the work place. No Age Limitation
Equal Opportunity Program

The hypothetical ad above was conceived by the National Displaced Homemakers Network, a Washington-based organization that disseminates information, provides technical assistance, and acts as a link to the more than one thousand agencies that provide job training and other vital services to 15 million displaced homemakers.

The term "displaced homemaker" describes a woman who fits one or all of the following:

- She has lost her spouse through divorce or death.

- She needs to supplement family income.

- She considers employment when children leave home and her obligations as a full-time homemaker end.

The term "displaced homemaker" applies to any woman who decides for any reason to give up full-time housework and take outside employment—or, as I've heard one woman describe it, "get into the real world."

As a mature woman looking for work for the first time or returning to paid work after spending many years as a homemaker and volunteer, the odds may seem overwhelming. Age bias, sex discrimination, and the absence of a work record makes the job search more difficult, but the highly visible and growing number of mature women at work today—many of whom entered or reentered the work force in their later years—tells you that it can be done. You have learned a great deal from unpaid work in the home and the community. Government and private organizations such as the National Displaced Homemakers Association stand ready to assist you.

Truckin' on Down

"I didn't pick the work, it picked me," says Esther A. Williams in a recent letter to the editor of *Modern Maturity* magazine. Her family refers to it as "Grandma's strange occupation" but she doesn't think so. Mrs. Williams is a truckdriver.

"Oh I knit, crochet, play a violin, and bake," says Mrs. Williams, who contends she does all the "normal" grandmother things but is just as content perched high in the cab of her huge 18-wheeler.

Esther and her husband Bob own a commercial trout hatchery in Utah and Bob spent a great deal of time delivering live trout to destinations all over the country. When the last of the four children left home she started riding along with him. As the company grew, another driver was needed and Esther figured she could just as well be that other driver. She hasn't regretted a single minute since:

"I never get tired of my view from the cab: deserts, mountains, prairies, wildlife, city lights—all part of the endless pattern of life we see on our trips. And we're together. You couldn't ask for a better life."

Whether they were motivated by the need to make money, by career ambitions, mental stimulation, or some combination of these reasons, the extent of women's participation in the work place is unprecedented, a post-World War II phenomenon that is considered the most spectacular change in the work place in decades. Thirty-nine million women, more than half of all American women, now hold some form of employment outside the home. Their participation will grow to over 60 percent during the 1990s. Economists predict women will account for two thirds of the growth in all occupations. The Women's Bureau of the U.S. Department of Labor expects that almost all the new jobs women will hold will be in the service sector—in career fields such as finance, transportation, telecommunications, real estate, and other work offering good salaries and a bright outlook for the future. Women will also make inroads in the nontraditional job sectors, especially in production and management, and they will join the growing army of small business owners.

In her book *The 100 Best Jobs For the 1990s and Beyond*, Chicago *Tribune* "Jobs" columnist Carol Kleiman says that "the 'old boy' network in which white males share inside information and power only with other white males" will be challenged by the influx into the work place of women and other minorities. "The result," she writes, "will be more parity in hiring, wages, training, and advancement for all qualified employees."

The Mature Woman

A skyrocketing divorce rate, greater educational attainment, and the women's movement are among the forces that have encouraged mature women to return to the work place. Women in their fifties and sixties are returning to work after many years as wife and mother at home; some are joining the work force for the first time in their lives. In the past women were content to live their later years on the wealth accumulated by their husbands. Today's woman, with her greater life expectancy and her enlightened sense of independence, wants to be self-sufficient throughout her life.

The entry of older women into the labor market will be driven by the need for more income in order to cope with inflation and to maintain a reasonable standard of living. Economic need as the prime motivation for older women at work is supported by the facts.

- More than 70 percent of the nearly 4 million persons over 65 in the United States living in poverty are women.

- Social Security income, with average benefits of less than $5,000 annually, are the only source of income for 60 percent of older women.

- Only 20 percent of mature women receive pension benefits from former employers. And those who do usually receive smaller benefits than men since most pension benefits are based on earnings, and women typically earn less than men do.

- Some older women never expected that they would have to work again but divorce or the death of a spouse have made it a financial necessity. Aside from their own needs, many older working women are also responsible for the care of one or more elderly parents.

According to the U.S. Department of Labor Bureau of Labor Statistics, the median annual earnings of full-time female wage and salary workers (based on first quarter 1992 averages) was . . .

55 and over	$19,344
55 to 64	$19,552
65 years and over	$17,888

Median annual *part-time* wage and salary of female workers 25 years of age and over was $6,916. (The Bureau does not publish equivalent data on women 55 and over.)

In addition to their need for income, women share the same psychological and social needs as older men. They too seek mental stimulation, social interaction, and the self-esteem and dignity that come with work. According to *The 100 Best Companies to Work for in America*—a Signet book—Control Data, Federal Express, Hallmark Cards, IBM, Levi Strauss, Mary Kay Cosmetics, Nordstrom, J. C. Penney, and Time, Inc. are among the best places for women to work.

Although women seeking work face the double hurdle of sex discrimination and age bias, the real problem—the major barrier to finding work—is the lack of marketable skills.

Recognition of this fact is a vital first step in your job search. Your solution to this problem is close at hand. It includes awakening your latent abilities and acquiring the skills to keep pace with the changing needs of the job market. That done, you'll have to learn to sell yourself in a competitive job market.

Obviously, if you have spent many years as wife and mother at home and are entering the job market after a hiatus of many years, you are in a different position from the retired woman with recent experience and an impressive work record. To start, you need to analyze your reasons for seeking work and need to establish your own goals. Your reasons for going to work at this time, although shared by others, are personal and unique to your situation. Are you seeking the highest income, work at a convenient location, interesting work, or a chance to meet and work with interesting people? "Yes" to all of the above? Women are asking themselves if they "can have it all"—career and family. As a mature woman having it all may have another meaning, but the answer is the same: You can have it all. You can have the added income *and* the job satisfaction.

Personnel managers and job-placement professionals offer these tips to "displaced homemakers" and all older women looking for ways to get a foot in the company door.

1. KNOW WHAT YOU WANT

Early in this century Sigmund Freud asked, "What does a woman want?" Today employers are echoing Freud's question. Their major complaint about mature women job-seekers is that they "don't really know what they want." Sounds simple enough, doesn't it, knowing what you want? Yet many women walk into an interview with only the vaguest idea of what they want. Mature women who spent most of their lives caring for others are inclined to neglect their own ambitions. But this is the time to identify who you are and go for what you want.

Even if your search takes you in new directions as your job hunt progresses, you should start out with the answers to some fundamental questions fixed in your mind:

What kind of job do I want?

What kind of people do I want to work with?

What are my salary parameters?

Can I afford to work for less in order to break into a field I prefer?

Am I setting my sights on the next year or two, or am I looking five to ten years down the road?

Think it through *before* you get to the interview, not during the interview.

2. HOME, INC.

Many women feel that because they have been homemakers, at-home mothers, and volunteers, they do not have the skills that are useful in paid jobs. It is typical of women who have been out of the job market for an extended period of time to underrate their skills and abilities. The connection between the activities of a homemaker and community volunteer and the needs of the job market elude them.

If, as a homemaker, you handled the family's finances, comparison shopped for the things your family needed, and tutored your children and your neighbor's children, you were engaged in activities that the working world calls "bookkeeper," "buyer," and "teacher." If, as a volunteer, you helped with the fund raising, wheeled the bookmobile in a hospital, or drove a van providing transportation for the elderly, you were engaged in activities that the working world calls "salesperson," "librarian," and "driver."

Don't sell yourself short. Running a household is like running a small business. Much of your past experience in the home or at voluntary community work can be translated into marketable skills with a specific job title. You may have held an elected or appointed position in your community, such as serving on a school or library board or a condominium association. You may have been an unpaid officer in a religious, fraternal, or community organization. You may have worked in a civil-rights campaign, a consumer-advocacy movement, or you may have lobbied for new or changed laws.

You may have taught Sunday School in your church or synagogue or supervised quantity cooking for a bake sale or supper. One of the skills you acquired during years of unpaid work could be the very skill that your new employer is seeking—but you can't depend on the employer to make the connection. You have to identify your talents, aptitudes, and interests and show prospective employers how they correspond to the job.

Here, for example, are the typical homemaker activities matched to job titles used in the workplace:

- Maintaining an adequate supply of home necessities (inventory control)
- Managing family activities (scheduling and coordinating)
- Overseeing family members (supervision)
- Making family plans (setting production goals and corporate planning)
- Settling family disputes (conflict management)

- Getting members of the family to handle tasks (assignment delegation)

- Keeping track of family income and spending, preparing tax returns, paying bills, managing family's savings and investments (controller, accountant, bookkeeper)

- Maintaining home files and family records, handling correspondence, helping with schoolwork (clerk, secretary, administrative assistant)

- Organizing parties, setting up car pool (project manager, schedule planner, conference coordinator)

- Shopping for family needs—groceries, clothing, furniture, home appliances (purchasing agent)

- Sewing, decorating, arts-and-crafts projects (jobs calling for eye-brain-hand coordination)

- Fixing up home, repairing toys, changing electrical switches, installing new fuses. (custodian, building maintenance)

- Volunteering as driver, tutor, team coach, caregiver, fund raiser, clerical worker (comparable jobs in the work place)

Employers are increasingly using volunteer work and other unpaid work experience as a way of "screening in" rather than "screening out" employees. An article in *BusinessWeek* describes how several women used volunteer work experience to become paid employees:

- B.S. drew on the administrative experience she gained from homemaking and volunteer work to become the director of Historic Denver, Inc.

- E.R. used her 16 years of volunteer experience, including four years volunteering with the Atlanta

Public Library, to get a job at the library as a public information officer.

■ P.B. combined her paid work experience as a teacher and her volunteer work skills to become an industrial relations representative for Memorex in California, where she runs training and management-development programs.

In testimony before the U.S. House of Representatives, Judy Hybels, an expert on women's issues, described her research on adult women currently holding paid jobs. She reported that 44 percent of the women in jobs involving public relations said that they developed their job skills partly or totally through volunteer work experience, as did 39 percent of women in management jobs, 28 percent in counseling, 25 percent in teaching, 23 percent in bookkeeping, 22 percent in clerical work, and 20 percent in research and writing.

There are numerous opportunities for older women interested in part-time work. The percentage of women working part-time is greater than that of men, and this holds true for older women as well. Homemakers returning to paid work after many years shouldn't overlook the educational background and work experience acquired before marriage and children. Many have advanced academic degrees and impressive work records that can be the foundation for a new career.

3. OLD SKILLS, NEW SKILLS

It is to your advantage as a mature woman that the work of today calls for more brain power and less brawn. But the changes in the work place and technological advances make training more important than ever. Even though many basic homemaking skills can be applied to today's work place, you will probably need job-related education and training to get the job you want. Continuing-education programs and community-sponsored job-related training programs are either free, subsidized, or available for modest tuition costs.

When your choice is between working for less or earning more because of new and improved skills, doesn't it make sense to take action to acquire the skills?

For women entering the work place for the first time the need to acquire marketable skills is obvious. The need for training may not be as evident to those who worked when they were younger and are now reentering. Women returning to the work force after many years should not expect to return at the same level as when they left if their skills are obsolete. Resourceful mature women who take the initiative to get training can reenter the work force and rise to higher levels as they become more proficient.

I really hate it
when people say to me
"Are you still working?"
Am I still *walking*? *Breathing*?
Who decided you're supposed to stop
at a certain point?
I've worked all my life.
Why should I stop now?
What else would I do?

■ ■ ■

—Lauren Bacall

---

4. DON'T BE INTIMIDATED BY AGE BIAS

The world of work is, after all, a male-dominated world, and there is just cause for complaint by women being forced to retire before they want to or being turned down for a job because of age. But just as the proportion of women in the work place has changed dramatically in the last few decades, so too has the attitude of employers toward older women in the work place.

Billie Higgins Preston writes to me from Waco, Texas: "I have given up arguing with one lady who tells me she is discriminated against in our city. No one will hire her. Every company wants 21-year-old blondes. Funny, I am not a 21-year-old blonde, not by a long shot. She insists no one hires older women. They don't? We just hired a 72-year-old lady to work in the university bookstore who is working out wonderfully."

As employers gain experience with older workers, their appreciation of the qualities that mature people bring to the job spreads among other employers. Older women are generally out of touch with this new reality and are uninformed about new openings for women in a great variety of fields.

Here are sample resumes for two hypothetical job seekers:

Mary Service, a homemaker active in volunteer work entering the job market for the first time in her mid-fifties. She is seeking part-time work and prefers working at a nonprofit organization.

Alice Comeback, returning to paid work as a mature woman after many years as a homemaker, wife, mother, and caretaker. She worked for doctors and at a hospital before marriage and wants to return to the medical/health-care field.

Mary Service
8622 Riverside Court
LaGrange Park, IL 60525

Tel. (708) 555-2084

Objective: A part-time or flexible-hours position as clerk or assistant
bookkeeper at nonprofit organization or company serving the community.

EDUCATION

B.A., De Paul University, Chicago, IL
Certificate of Achievement, Bookkeeping and Accounting
Marshall Business School, Indianapolis, Indiana

SKILLS

Financial	Prepared budget and administered income and disbursements for crafts fair.
	Complete responsibility for budget and management of annual budget of $875,000.
	Developed plans and supervised financial accounts for 275-delegate national conference.
Administrative	Interviewed, hired, and organized staff assignments for semiannual crafts exhibitions.
	Assisted in formulating policy and agenda for Concerned Parents Action Coalition.
Supervisory	Supervised annual fund-raising drive for Cultural Center, each time going above stated goals.
	Served as chairperson at Condominium Association. Supervised the implementation of major renovation of building.
	Supervised paid staff and coordinated the activities of 28 volunteers at crafts exhibitions.
	Recruited and supervised the work of volunteer staff at local Cultural Center.

EXPERIENCE

Assistant to the director
Crafts Exhibition Enterprises
Park Forest, IL 60611

Chairperson,
Great Oak Condominium Association
LaGrange Park, IL 60625

Staff supervisor,
Illinois Cultural Center
Chicago, IL 60610

References available on request.

Alice Comeback
3301 North Avenue
Merriville, IN 46410

Tel. (317) 555-2612

Objective

Family head with a teen-aged child still at home, in excellent health, seeking a full-time position as a receptionist and aid to a physician, professional health-care association, or at a clinic or hospital.

Skills Summary

Experienced receptionist. Friendly personality with excellent "people skills." Knowledge of medical billing procedures and insurance claim forms. Word Processor (IBM or compatibles). Knowledge of medical procedures and terms.

Work Experience

Receptionist and aid to Dr. Arnold Bry and Dr. Jane Sweetser. Billing clerk at Parish Hospital (outpatient surgery). Senior billing clerk at 475-bed hospital.

Volunteer Work and Community Service

Volunteer sales clerk Masonic Hospital Gift Shop
  (voted outstanding "Volunteer of the Year" three years in a row because of
  sales record.)

Secretary of county Little League and chairperson of Parent-Teachers
Association.

Homemaker Skills

Responsible for maintaining household, handled all family finances and tax
returns, tutoring children. In addition, I served as caretaker and administered
injections to elderly parents. Supervised major renovation and rehab of vintage
farmhouse over a seven-year period.

Education

BA degree, Loyola University, Chicago, IL

Continuing education courses in professional medical office administration,
health-care insurance, and Medicare procedures, Columbia College,
Chicago, IL

References available upon request.

---

5. DON'T GRAB AT THE FIRST OFFER

Mature women with urgent and immediate needs, desperate
to get to work—any work—jump at the first offer. If it later
turns out to be a miserable job for which they are totally
unsuited, they use the experience to confirm their worst fears
about work in the later years.

There is, of course, no foolproof way to avoid getting
stuck in a bad job but there are ways to lessen the possibility:
Ask questions before accepting a job. Remember, just as they
are interviewing you, you are interviewing them. Take reasonable time to think it over before accepting and resist

pressure for an immediate answer. If you've been conscientious in your job hunt, you should have several offers and should be able to choose the best of several instead of accepting the one and only offer you've received.

6. CONSIDER SELF-EMPLOYMENT

That pet idea you've had for starting your own business? This may be the ideal time. Your own business will allow you to put your experience and mature judgment to work for you—and you don't have to cajole a personnel manager to give you a chance.

The federal government reports 3.5 million women-owned U.S. businesses. The National Association of Women Business Owners challenges that figure and says that if counted properly it would be closer to 5.4 million women-owned businesses in the United States. Rieva Lesonsky, editor of *Entrepreneur* magazine, estimates that 7 million women now own their own businesses. In any case, it is a formidable number and growing at an unprecedented rate. In 1991 women started businesses one and a half times more frequently than men did, and some experts predict that in the next decade women will own half of all the country's businesses.

Women who spent many years with a company only to come up against the "glass ceiling" that blocks them from the upper floors of the corporate tower look for a new start in a business they can call their own. Felice Schwarz, president of Catalyst, a women's advocacy group, says that many women are "going off on their own where they can control their own hours and chart their own courses." For whatever reason they were started, women-owned businesses make up an increasingly important segment of the economy, generating as much as $500 billion in annual revenues. Women are starting businesses in a wide variety of industries, from agriculture and manufacturing to professional services and retail. According to the National Association of Women Business Owners, by the end of 1993 women-owned firms will employ more workers than all the Fortune 500 companies combined. Legendary female entrepreneurs such as Debbie Fields (Mrs. Field's Cookies), Mary Kay Ash (Mary Kay Cosmetics), Frances Lear (*Lear's* magazine), and Jennie Craig (Jennie Craig Diet Centers) provide the inspiration, but your business will stand or fall on your own abilities.

The disadvantages: long hours; blood, sweat, and tears; risk of failure. The advantages: self-determination and the potential for earning more money. Above all, it's a chance to make that dream a reality. You'll never know until you try.

Resources for Women Only

The Displaced Homemakers Network (DHN) is the only advocacy organization on a national level that addresses the specific concerns of displaced homemakers. (According to Executive Director Jill Miller, a "displaced homemaker" is "an individual who has lost her source of income because of divorce, separation, death, or disability of a spouse or the loss of public assistance."

Employment, older women, age discrimination, and adult dependent care as an employment issue are among DHN's major concerns. The organization works to increase displaced homemakers' options for financial self-sufficiency.

Currently, there are more than one thousand programs in the nation providing counseling, workshops, skills training, and job-placement assistance to displaced homemakers. Located in womens' centers, YWCAs, vocational education institutions, community colleges, and universities, these programs are funded through state revenues, federal programs, community resources, and private contributors.

DHN offers nationwide referral services to displaced homemakers and older women seeking training and employment. Contact the Washington headquarters for information on local programs.

Displaced Homemakers Network
1411 K Street NW, Suite 930
Washington, DC 20005
(205) 628-6767

The Older Women's League (OWL), with a national membership of more than 20,000 midlife and older women. Its programs are designed to improve the image and status of the older woman. OWL is active in disseminating information, training, and mutual support. It seeks the equitable division of Social Security benefits so that women working in the home can accrue benefits.

Among OWL publications: "Older Women and Job Discrimination," "Employment Discrimination Against Older Women: A Handbook on Litigating Age and Sex Discrimination Cases," "Making Ends Meet: Midlife and Older Women's Search for Economic Self-Sufficiency through Job Training and Employment."

Older Women's League
730 Eleventh Street NW, Suite 300
Washington, DC 20001
(202) 783-6686

Women's Research and Education Institute, founded to conduct research and policy analysis on issues of concern to women, holds conferences and briefings and issues an annual report on the status of women.

Older women and employment is a primary concern. The organization publishes "Older Women: The Economics of Aging" and "Older Women at Work."

Women's Research and Education Institute
1700 18th Street NW
Washington, DC 20009
(202) 328-7070

Zonta International is a private, nonprofit, international service organization with 35,000 members—executive women in business and female professionals in 48 countries. It is divided into 21 Districts, each of which is subdivided into Areas.

From its inception in 1919, Zonta has grappled with the problems of women and aging. The organization has developed several programs with UN agencies, and numerous projects to benefit aging women have been initiated by local clubs worldwide.

> Zonta International
> 557 West Randolph Street
> Chicago, IL 60606-2284
> (312) 930-5848

Catalyst works directly with corporate policymakers in behalf of women's leadership development. A career publication brochure is available by writing to the organization.

> Catalyst
> 250 Park Avenue South
> New York, NY 10003

The National Association for Professional Saleswomen, 5520 Cherokee Avenue, Alexandria, VA 22312, (703) 256-9226 publishes a newsletter called, "Successful Saleswomen." The association has chapters across the country. If you're interested write for information about a chapter near you.

Job-search advice and information for women is available in the literature and programs of the following organizations and government agencies:

> Women's Bureau of the U.S. Department of Labor, 200 Constitution Avenue, Washington, DC 20210

> Wider Opportunities for Women, 1325 G Street NW, Washington, DC 20005

Your Own Business- At Last

You're never too old to make a million.

—Nora Wolfson, 83-year-old creator
of the Maison de Nora fudge sauce

For the past seven years now John Nickolson, the 75-year-old owner of New York's popular neighborhood restaurant, Cafe Nickolson, has closed his 10-table restaurant whenever the climate isn't to his liking. He also closes on Thanksgiving and many other days when other restaurants do a brisk business. He doesn't give patrons notice of his future closings because they just don't expect him to be there all the time. Despite the erratic schedule, the business is profitable. Mr. Nickolson says, "There's no waste. I watch everything."

John Nickolson's story illustrates the benefit of owning your own business: You make your own rules. While few businesses carry the privilege that far, the freedom to make your own rules—not just in work schedule, but in everything else connected with the business—is attractive to mature persons starting or buying a small business.

No boss looking over your shoulder. No employee manual. No board of directors. No outside shareholders. To anyone who has labored in the corporate vineyards—at whatever level—this much freedom must seem like paradise. But freedom is a double-edged sword. You have the freedom to fail. Failure in business can empty your bank account and play havoc with your ego.

Despite the Risks

Entrepreneurship is in. And it is catching on with older Americans who are trying to decide what to do with the rest of their lives. Studies confirm the trend toward consulting and self-employment—as opposed to salaried employment—as the preferred post-retirement work experience. In 1988, while 10 percent of all workers were self-employed, *over 25 percent of workers aged 65 and over were self-employed.*

Men and women who "have had it" working for others decide that what they really wanted all along was to own their own business. Even with a less-than-vigorous economy and the high failure rate for start-ups (nearly two out of every three new businesses fail within five years), more and more Americans are becoming entrepreneurs in their later years and finding that it suits them just fine. They want to put something together that they can call their own, something that meshes with their personal goals at this stage of life.

More than half of the estimated 1.3 million new businesses that opened in 1991 were sole proprietorships with no more than two employees, typically operating out of the garage, basement, or spare room. The same recession that put big-company people out of work and forced early retirements opened up new windows of opportunity for many small-business ventures. Cost-conscious companies often replace full-time employees with free lancers, consultants, and outside contractors. Markets abandoned by large companies because they are too small and unprofitable can be a feast for small firms.

Self-employment is not a realistic option for all mature adults. It takes a special temperament to run your own show, and some individuals weren't cut out for it. They are not comfortable in the role of small business proprietor and miss the prestige and perks of working at a large organization. A former colleague of mine retired from the Chicago Board of Trade, the largest futures exchange in the world, and opened his one-man executive-search firm. Before his first year in business was over he realized how unhappy he was and just what it was that he missed: "I miss the meetings where important decisions that affect the world economy are made. I miss the lunches with important VIPs visiting from all over the world. I guess being a one-man band is not for me. There's nobody here to bounce ideas around with and, to be honest, it gets pretty lonely. I had to try it. I did. Now, I'm giving it up to look for the kind of work I prefer at a good-sized company."

There's more to succeeding in your own business than just printing business cards with the word "President" after your name. It takes money, savvy, hard work, and a little bit of luck along the way. Even with a thorough understanding of the negatives, if you believe that you have what it takes and your health and financial status permit, it's a route to consider. In maturity you can bring to your business experience, seasoned judgment, dedication, and other special attributes that it takes to win. It's revealing that some of the most successful entrepreneurs (Ralph Lauren, Elizabeth Arden, Mary Kay, for example) do not have the college degree required for a job with a large company.

As an older adult you have—or should have—a good grip on reality. You know yourself and your capabilities. Not only are you in a better position to understand the risks involved, but if you were conscientious about building your savings, you are now in a better position to contribute all or a good part of the capital needed to start or buy a business.

Bill Farley is a typical example and an interesting contrast to the disenchanted entrepreneur discussed earlier. When Bill's dream of reaching the top corporate ranks were dashed because his branch of a major New York bank was closed, the chairman "suggested"(!) that Bill take early retirement. After 25 years of faithful service, Bill was understandably disenchanted with salaried employment, and as he puts it, "I wasn't ready to retire."

Like so many others before him, Bill left the corporate world and joined the large and growing army of the self-employed. He used part of his $54,000 severance to start his own business—a computer school for children, which he runs with his wife Denise. At first he was afraid of failure, "Now I wonder why I didn't try this sooner. It's a new life."

James E. Challenger, president of Challenger, Gray & Christmas, a Chicago-based outplacement service, reports that a large and growing number of recently discharged managers have become entrepreneurs rather than risk going back on another payroll. Challenger says, "About one out of six discharged managers are currently starting their own business."

7 Reasons Older Adults Give for Self-Employment

1. Being my own boss
2. Liberation from a rigid schedule and ability to set my own hours

3. A chance to earn more money.
4. Realizing a lifelong dream
5. Building a business that has a value and is saleable
6. Dislike of company politics
7. Don't have to persuade a prospective employer to give me a chance

First, Ask Yourself . . .

The decision to join the ranks of the self-employed should not be made lightly. SCORE, the Service Corps of Retired Executives Association, an organization that counsels retired and working executives on small-business opportunities, provides the following ten questions to ask yourself before going into business:

1. Is my product or service different from others already in my market area?
2. Do I have the right kind of business experience?
3. Can I prepare a detailed, credible business plan for the first three years?
4. Am I able to take responsibility?
5. Am I a good organizer?
6. Am I ready to put in the long hours that might be necessary?
7. Am I ready to stick to it even during rough times?
8. Do I have the support of my immediate family?
9. Do I have adequate resources and credit—and maybe a little bit more?
10. Is my health up to the tasks ahead?

Of these questions, those with the greatest relevance to you as a mature person concern the possibility of long hours, the importance of family support, and the state of your health.

If you're trying to balance work with leisure, you must weigh the certainty of long work days. It's worth remembering, however, that when you enjoy what you're doing, long hours may be one of the benefits. Christopher Ruks, a retired insurance executive in Columbus, Ohio, tells me that he doesn't mind the long hours he has to put in at his recently acquired bookstore. To Chris, who has had a lifelong love affair with books, the long hours just mean more time surrounded by his mistresses.

The support of immediate family is vital for older men and women planning to start or purchase a business. Unless your spouse and others in the family understand your need to work and are willing to cooperate, business ownership can cause stress in your family life.

Finally, you should realistically gauge your ability to handle the hard work and commitment that business ownership imposes. John Nickolson, the restaurateur with the erratic schedule cited in the opening of this chapter, is the exception. Small-business owners usually work long and regular hours. Older persons with an old-fashioned work ethic may push themselves further than their stamina allows. In your later years, good health is the one asset you don't want to risk.

Then, there are situations where work and the responsibility of business ownership actually promote good health. After his retirement, Jim Slodner became a "fixture" at his doctor's office, constantly complaining about aches and pains and vague illnesses that had no name. When his brother-in-law moved to the Sunbelt, Jim was forced to take over the family's farm-equipment business; there was no one else to do it. Jim hasn't been to the doctor for almost a year now. He's too involved in making the family business work. Are the aches and pains gone? Hard to tell. As any doctor will tell you, psychosomatic symptoms can be very real, but they can disappear as quickly as they came if the patient hasn't got the time to worry about them. Work as therapy—not a new idea, just a good one. Many older men and women who thought they were "giving out" made remarkable recoveries when they found their way back into the economy again.

Is THIS THE RIGHT TIME?

These are uncertain times. Yet as I write this sentence I am struck by the fact that I could have written the same sentence at any time of my four-decade career and it would have been just as valid. I am also aware that anyone in the future can be just as comfortable writing that sentence. The times are always uncertain. As mature adults we know from life experience that change is the one constant of which we can be sure. If you are reading this during a period of economic hardship, things will change and get better. If you are reading this during an economic boom, you can be just as sure that it will not stay that way.

So, if you're putting off owning your own business because this isn't the right time, it will never be the right time. Even during the worst of times, there is a place for small businesses that can solve problems. Small businesses can move fast and penetrate niche markets for products and services.

Risk is real for anyone who starts or buys a business, but there is much to be said for the idea that the later years can actually be a time for greater risk taking. Former President Jimmy Carter and his wife, Rosalynn, address this in their book *Everything to Gain: Making the Most of the Rest of Your Life.* They favor taking chances in the second half of our lives: "Not foolish or pointless risks, but risks that offer the hope of both real adventure and real reward, for ourselves and others. While some of our physical powers may be diminished, we have survival skills younger people may not have learned, a different kind of endurance that comes with the passage of time."

Brave words, but your decision on whether to start or buy a business depends on your own attitude toward risk. Are you a risk-averse individual who prefers to play it safe, especially at this stage of your life? Those who are not emotionally or financially able to handle risk would be better suited to salaried employment or volunteer work. Those who like being their own boss but want to minimize the risk should consider a sideline or franchise business.

If you take all the experience
of men over fifty out of the world,
there wouldn't be enough left
to run it.

■ ■ ■

—Henry Ford

Pursuing Personal Passions

There are both advantages and disadvantages for the older individual who is trying to turn a hobby or a personal passion into a post-retirement business.

On the plus side: Running a business that reflects your interests is deeply satisfying. Furthermore, your business stands a better-than-average chance of success if you are already attuned to the market and are knowledgeable in the field. When Leo Altman, who had been an amateur yachtsman for 40 years, talks to prospective sailboat buyers at his newly acquired Fort Lauderdale charter business, he speaks with enthusiasm and a genuine understanding of the features that generate sales. His natural tendency to think like his customers keeps him abreast of the market and by any measure—personal satisfaction, working conditions, and profitability—the business is a success.

But mixing business with pleasure can have its drawbacks. The hobby gardener may underestimate the difficulty of operating a gardening firm for profit and overestimate the demand for his products and services. An antique collector doesn't necessarily make the best antique dealer. A similar statement could be made about anyone who wants to turn an avocation into a vocation. It's easy to be swept away by your passion for a particular product or service, but just because you love your product doesn't mean that the world shares your infatuation. Analyze your product objectively and avoid being blinded by personal interests.

Success in business is not always determined solely by the intelligence or competence of the owner. Circumstances beyond anyone's control can make or break a business. A case in point: After 24 years in high public office Senator George McGovern, the 1972 Democratic presidential candidate, invested most of his earnings to acquire the Stratford Inn in Connecticut. The year was 1988 and the Senator was 66 at the time. He said, "Hotels, inns, and restaurants have always held a special fascination for me. The Stratford Inn promised the realization of a longtime dream to own a combination hotel, restaurant, and public conference facility—complete with an experienced manager and staff."

Within a few years The Stratford Inn went bankrupt. According to Senator McGovern, it was the victim of a generally bad economy, regulatory guidelines set too high, and his own naiveté. "In retrospect," he says, "I wish I had known more about the hazards and difficulties of such a business . . ."

SIDELINES

A conversation overheard from the next table during lunch at a restaurant gave me a new perspective on the kind of businesses older adults want: "My whole life, while I was working full-time jobs, I always made extra money moonlighting in my spare time. I always had a sideline. I liked the money but most of all I liked the variety of being in different businesses as well. Well, now, my occupation is retirement. And now I am moonlighting from retirement. I still have a sideline . . ."

You're retired and you like it. Great. But think about it: Why not a sideline? Many sidelines are ideally suited to retirees. Such ventures can fit your lifestyle and give you additional income. These are ventures that are accomplished in your spare hours and make few demands on your retirement lifestyle.

Sidelines don't require set hours and days. You work when convenient. The income, too, is flexible, limited only by the time and effort you choose to expend. A sideline venture is different than starting a business or buying a business or franchise; this type of business is usually more modest. Such businesses as mail-order sales, tax preparation, vending-machine servicing, tutoring, packaging and mailing services, and home preparation of food specialties and catering allow older adults to have something going for them on the side without a major investment of time and money. There are numerous cases of sideline ventures expanding into large nationwide enterprises but most remain small businesses that give their owners spare-time income and work satisfaction.

"Don't quit your day job," is a common expression directed at actors, artists, and writers with uncertain chances for success. As a retiree, your "day job" is recreation, leisure, and rest. A sideline allows you to try something without quitting your day job. So to speak.

Freelance and Consulting

At age 61, Barry Sullivan took early retirement from his $770,000-a-year position as chairman of First Chicago, the tenth largest bank in the United States, in order to devote more time to community service and his family. After retirement he was hired by the bank as a consultant at an annual retainer of $780,000 plus "incidental benefits, such as the use of a car, office space, and secretarial support." He is paid more in annual consulting fees than he earned as head of the bank.

Mr. Sullivan could swing this deal without help from this or any other book. Few—very few!—older men and women are in a similar position. But every year, retired individuals become self-employed, free lancing or contracting their services as a consultant to the firm they retired from or to any other firms that want their services. Their compensation is considerably more modest than Mr. Sullivan's but they have succeeded in making their life better. They have found a way to deliver their expertise without compromising their retirement lifestyle.

Because so many former managers and executives have decided to become consultants, in some circles the word "consultant" has come to be a euphemism for "unemployed." Despite the cynics, the call for such services does exist, and many mature men and women take the risk and hang out their shingle as consultants. According to the 40+ Club, it is "only for those older executives who are truly skilled and have specialties for companies which would not hire full-time, in-house specialists." In the club's official handbook, members are warned that consultancy can be a feast-or-famine proposition and that even established consultants have difficulty selling their services in hard times. Accordingly, the handbook advises that to make consultancy work, you must:

1. Have marketable skills.
2. Know how and be able to sell yourself and your services.
3. Have enough financial reserves to get through the tough beginning stage.
4. Produce the results your client desires when you do sell your services.

Years ago free-lancing was limited to writers, artists, and other creative types. Today more and more people in a variety of fields are free-lancing and consulting. Engineers, financial advisers, bookkeepers, editors and other professionals not ordinarily associated with free-lance pursuits work on a contract basis.

My neighbor Glenn Oster retired at age 63 and subsequently built a successful consulting practice as a retail sales trainer. When I asked him how he went about soliciting clients and building his business, Glenn told me that he was able to sign up his former employer, a large Chicago department store. "That was the base I needed. I went on from there and approached several department stores in other cities. But I really needed that base. After that everything else was relatively easy." Although signing your former employer as a client is a good way to make the transition, it is not the only way. Lots of retirees who go into consulting do so in fields entirely different from their former careers.

A friend who did not succeed in free lancing talked to me about his experience. "Maybe it didn't work because I went into it because I was tired of looking for a job. What I didn't realize was that being a free lancer means that you're always looking for a job." In his classic book *What Color is Your Parachute?* Richard Bolles calls free lancers and consultants, "perpetual job hunters" who must constantly seek employment.

If you're ready to be a perpetual job hunter always pursuing new clients for your services, free lancing and consulting can be a perfect fit. Men and women who have succeeded in consulting practices in their later years say that it can be challenging, exciting, and rewarding work, "if you are emotionally constituted for the financial ups and downs." If not, there are other means of self-employment better suited to your temperament.

Buying a Franchise

As an entrepreneur, you can start a business, buy a business, or as more than 28,000 people did last year—you can buy a franchise. Franchising is the great American success story. More than 540,000 franchises operate in the United States, with a new one emerging every 16 minutes. Franchises brought in about $760 billion in 1991, about 6 percent more than the previous year.

Most people think about franchises in terms of hamburgers and fried chicken. (Both of which, by the way, can be pretty good franchises; they have made a lot of people very rich.) In reality, franchises sell a large variety of products and services, from hamburgers to computers, from income-tax preparation to carpet cleaning. McDonald's, Pizza Hut, Computerland, 7-Eleven, Pier One Imports, Budget Rent-A-Car, and Aamco Transmission are among the highly recognized franchise businesses.

What does a franchiser do for you that you cannot do for yourself? A modern franchise has three main ingredients—an identity, based on a trade name; an operating system or business format; and a continuous financial relationship between franchiser and franchisee. When you buy a franchise you are buying a prepackaged business with a proven well-known product to sell, training, guidance, and access to low-cost supplies and equipment. For these and other support services, the franchisers charge substantial fees.

The equity capital needed to open a franchise business ranges from a thousand dollars to over a million dollars and more depending on the type of business and location. Some typical equity requirements: H.R. Block, $5,000 to $8,000; Aamco Transmissions, $48,000; Dunkin Donuts, $27,000 to $40,000; Supercuts Hair Care, $54,000 to $133,000; Baskin Robbins, $50,000; Radio Shack, $40,000 to $62,000; Benihana of Tokyo Restaurant, $550,000; Wendy's, $600,000 to $1.3 million.

Once you have decided that you can handle the investment and that the initial fee fairly reflects the franchiser's costs of putting you in business, you still have to consider the franchise royalty you have to pay every month from your gross revenues. After deducting your royalty payments, will you still be able to make a decent profit?

Operating a franchise business is particularly suitable for people in their mid-fifties and beyond. Even though franchising, like every other business, is loaded with treacherous twists and turns, John P. Hayes, the president of the Hays Group Inc., a Pennsylvania-based franchising consultancy, believes that "franchising is the safest way to go into business." He points out that franchise owners buy a proven format and that the franchiser's help in avoiding mistakes "such as choosing the wrong retail location or mispricing products—that commonly put new entrepreneurs out of business."

Since most older persons cannot afford the risk associated with new ventures, the fact that franchises offer opportunity at reduced risk explains why so many of the owners of the nation's franchise outlets are bought by mature individuals.

With many businesses deep into recession, franchising looks like a pretty good deal. While the nation's GNP increased by a limp 0.9 percent from 1989 to 1990, the sales in franchise businesses grew over 10 percent. Of the thousands of franchises that open each year, according to the U.S. Department of Commerce, 95 percent stay in business, while small businesses usually fold in the first five years.

Still, there are plenty of "horror stories" about franchises to remind us that the risk is still there. Helen Darkin, a Los Angeles housewife, put most of her savings and her husband's pension—into a fast-food franchise and lost it all. She blames the franchiser for failing to provide the promised advertising and promotional support. Mrs. Darkin's enterprise was one of the 70 percent of the chain's franchisees that went belly-up after sales fell drastically. "I thought that if all else failed, we'd sell the franchise," she said. "I didn't imagine that the whole thing would be worth nothing."

At the same time, *Working Woman* magazine reports that Peggy Klonowski of Appleton, Wisconsin, invested less than $50,000 in a personnel-services franchise. In the first two years of business Peggy was in the profit column with $1.5 million in sales. She is now expanding into two more locations.

Franchise executives agree that in order to make it in a franchised business you have to be eager to learn, willing to work long hours, and able to handle stress. They believe that men and women with sales ability and "people skills" have the best chance at success.

Obviously, buying into a franchise does not automatically ensure success, and success or failure is not necessarily related to the amount invested. Business professionals who have seen it all—the good, the bad, and the scam—advise the franchise buyer to proceed with caution. They suggest that before purchasing a franchise you talk to those in the best position to know and provide unbiased advice: the people currently operating the franchise you're looking at. Companies are required by law to give you a list of current franchisers.

Ask the franchiser how long it took to break even and how profitable the business is currently. Find out whether the company charges franchise owners an advertising fee and whether the advertising is carried in local markets or just for national image building. You're going to need all the local support you can get.

The caution flag should go up immediately if the failure rate for franchises is greater than 5 percent. And don't accept the franchiser's figures on the failure rate without confirming the figures independently. One way to do this is by comparing the current list of franchises with a list several years old. What about those no longer operating? What happened?

A friend who owns an answering-service franchise in Sarasota, Florida, tells me that when he was shopping for a franchise the most important question he could ask a current franchise owner was, "Would you buy the franchise again?" The answer to that question told him all he needed to know.

Dos and Don'ts in Considering a Franchise

■ ■ ■

Do

Give serious thought to self-evaluation. What interests you about owning a business? And what type of business should it be?

Attend franchising expos, answer franchise ads and request information, check franchise directories in the library. Become thoroughly familiar with the full range of franchise opportunities before you choose your spot.

Be realistic about how much money you have and how much you can afford to invest in a franchise.

Examine the track record of the franchiser—look behind the fancy brochure.

Get a copy of the disclosure statement of companies and go over the ones that interest you with your accountant and/or lawyer.

Contact International Franchise Information Services, Washington, D.C., and other data sources about any franchise you are interested in.

Don't

Buy into a business without understanding its nature and its demands.

Sign documents or commit funds without meeting the firm's top executives.

Be afraid to ask questions—a lot of questions. Ask the franchiser and ask other franchise owners.

Get involved with a franchiser that fails to investigate your background, including credit, references, former employers, and so forth.

Get involved with a franchiser that is not registered in your state.

If you want to know more about the franchises available in a business that interests you, you can start by pouring through:

Franchise Opportunities Handbook, U.S. Government Printing Office, Washington, DC 20402.

The Franchise Annual, Info Press, 736 Center Street, Lewiston, NY 14092.

Franchise Yearbook, 2311 Pontius Ave., Los Angeles, CA 90064

Franchise opportunities are advertised in the business section of your local newspaper and in national publications, including *The Wall Street Journal, Forbes Magazine, Barron's,* and many others.

STARTING YOUR OWN HOME-BASED BUSINESS

According to Link Resources Corporation, a research consulting firm studying the role of technology on home and work, 11.8 million self-employed people work at home.

Many of the pros and cons discussed in Chapter Four on jobs that permit you to work at home apply equally to home-based businesses. Working at home as the employee of someone else's company suits many older men and women just fine, but individuals with entrepreneurial ambitions have something more in mind. This hardy breed of self-starters figure that they've "paid their dues" as employees and have now arrived at that stage of life when they can be their own boss.

Starting your business at home is an economical way to test your ideas and operate your business without assuming expensive overhead costs. Thousands of home-based businesses can be started for as little as a few thousand dollars. Whether it involves selling or specialty manufacturing, you can start your new business quickly and easily, enjoying the comfort and privacy of your home and verifying the profitability of your venture as you go.

This is a good time to start your own home-based business. Modern technology makes it easier to communicate with customers, clients, and suppliers. More business is initiated and completed by telephone, computer modems, FAX, and overnight delivery services than ever before. With these tools the whole world is your territory. You can run an international business from your home. While the beginnings may be modest there is no limit to the potential.

WORKING LATE AT HOME

Your new home-based business enjoys many advantages. Personal efficiency is increased. You work at your own speed rather than at the pace set by others. You have freedom and flexibility in hiring, when and if you need help. You set your own hours and your work schedule. You can work at your home-based business full time, part time, or as a "sideline" to your official occupation as a fun-loving retiree. "Morning people" can start work after breakfast, and "night owls" can work while the rest of the world sleeps. The energy otherwise spent commuting and traveling to work can be used to make your business a success.

Older men and women have the profile for success in an at-home business: self-discipline, life experience, and patience.

Thinking practically, many older persons are already paying for the space a business would occupy. Many own homes larger than their current needs, and the space for a home-based office already exists.

Depending on your plans and resources, your business can occupy a space as modest as a desk and telephone partitioned off by a screen from an existing room or a facility as grand as a fully equipped state-of-the-art office or studio in a wing of your home. Or anything in between. Don't go overboard—an expensive set-up does not guarantee success. Lots of prosperous at-home businesses are modestly furnished. A home-based business does unfortunately add to the feeling of isolation that troubles many older men and women. You can alleviate the solitude of a home-based business by attending conferences and social events where you can mix with young and old, male and female, people in your field and in other fields.

Residential areas have zoning laws that restrict the kind of activities you can have at your home. Local authorities are generally tolerant, however, of home-based businesses that don't disrupt the neighborhood. Gil Gordan, a telecommuting consultant in Monmouth Junction, New Jersey, says he has tracked "a fairly steady trend" of local authorities revising their zoning ordinances. Communities have always been more tolerant of certain professionals, notably doctors and dentists, than of noisier or more visible businesses. But now communities are taking an even more accommodating approach. Home-based business owners can do virtually anything in a residential area as long as it doesn't create a hazard or upset the neighbors over parking, noise, or commercial signage.

Some places give home businesses favored treatment. Davis, California, afraid of losing its "budding geniuses" to Sacramento, 17 miles away, exempted a home-based software programmer from paying local business fees for the upkeep of a shared parking lot. "She had no parking associated with her business," says associate town planner Lisa Pysel. "It was just her whipping out software programs."

Why Businesses Fail

■ ■ ■

Ken Edwards of Your Own Business Inc., a company that counsels individuals interested in self-employment, lists the reasons why many new independent start-ups fail:

1. The principal (or principals) didn't know enough about the business.
2. The principal lacked self-knowledge.
3. The principal made incorrect assumptions about the demand for the product or service.
4. Management was poor and bad decisions were made on marketing, site, or controls.
5. The venture was undercapitalized.

TAX ADVANTAGES FOR HOME-BASED BUSINESS OWNERS

Home-based business owners enjoy several tax advantages. To qualify as a tax deduction your home office must be used for work exclusively and on a regular basis and you must either run your business out of it or see clients or patients there. Then you can deduct a percentage of your home mortgage interest, house insurance, and utilities; all office and business costs; and depreciation of the office equipment and the office itself.

As an employee working at home for someone else, you must be able to verify that you are working at home for the convenience of your employer, because of inadequate work space at the primary place of business, or for some other compelling reason. For tax purposes, your work space—large or small—must be clearly delineated from the residence. As the owner of a home-based business there is no such requirement, since there is no employer-provided work space.

These tax advantages apply to renters as well as to home owners. The renter is allowed to deduct a pro-rata share of the rent based on the percentage of the total space that is occupied by the business. The home owner can deduct a pro-rata share of expenses associated with the home, including such things as mortgage interest, maintenance, and repairs.

HOME-BASED ENTERPRISES

The range of work-at-home possibilities for self-employed older individuals is limited only by the imagination: consulting services on everything from wedding planning to investment management; food services, from baking cookies to catering gourmet dinners; lodging services and bed-and-breakfast operations; travel agencies and shopping services.

Here are home-based businesses in several fields that you may find attractive.

Sales-related: brokers; syndicators; manufacturers representatives

Professional services: therapists; tutors; counselors; engineers; accountants; consultants.

Production and specialty manufacturing: precision tooling; catering; desktop publishing; gifts and crafts.

In the past, businesses in the home were the domain of traditional services and "cottage industry" production. Doctors, dentists, insurance agents, accountants, and tax preparers commonly practice their profession in the home. Now, people who make things in their workshop, in the garage, and on the kitchen table are among the estimated 30,000 self-employed "manufacturers" who make clothing, gift items, and crafts that they sell at fairs, flea markets, and shopping malls.

Included in the listing of resources on pages 297–326 is a description of Elder Craftsmen Inc., an organization with consignment shops across the country selling handicrafts made at home by people 60 and over. There's a steady demand for their best-selling items.

When I asked a mature gift-shop owner in Door County, Wisconsin, how her new business was working out, she summed it up for me: "It was a little tougher getting started than I thought it was going to be, but if I had to make that choice again, I'd go right ahead and do it."

Buying a Business

In some respects buying an existing business is like buying a franchise. You don't have to start from square one without a road map. Ken Edwards, an attorney and a consultant with Your Own Business, Inc., a Chicago firm that helps people locate and purchase businesses, says that "buying an existing business is a viable alternative for older individuals." A large percentage of his clients looking for businesses are 55 and over.

Ken Edwards believes that buying an existing business (franchise or independent) at the right time and price and with room for sales growth and greater profit potential is a safer bet than starting a new business: "The business's known track record reduces a lot of unknown factors—the appeal of the business, the income stream, the value of location and the marketing needs." An existing business has an ongoing relationship with customers, and Edwards believes it is easier to expand and improve an existing business than it is to create one.

You might want to talk to a business broker to explore the possibility of buying a business. A business broker can give you an overview of the businesses for sale and help with the numerous transactions including searches, valuation, negotiation, financing, and legal matters. If you don't know a business broker, there are many listed in your local Yellow Pages.

Although it makes obvious good sense to buy a successful existing business, many successful business buyers have looked for a business that had not realized its potential. Such a business can be purchased for less money, and if the new owner can bring enthusiasm and energy to the operation and is able to supply the ingredient that kept the business from succeeding, the chances are good for turning the business around.

When my friends Harold and Betty Shulman moved to Florida, they were both in their late fifties. Tired of Philadelphia winters and optimistic about the Florida economy, they relocated for the express purpose of buying a business. The Shulmans purchased a small floundering telephone-answering service at a sacrifice price. Business was bad, and the owner wanted out.

Harold and Betty are warm, friendly people uniquely equipped with the marketing skills and the capital for promotion that the business needed to make it profitable. In my last visit to Florida I was pleased to see that the business had grown beyond anyone's expectation. There were now several branches serving thousands of subscribers. The business operates 800 and 900 numbers for corporate clients, sells beepers, portable phones, and other allied products to its large and growing client base. At this point Harold and Betty are phasing themselves out of the business as their sons and daughter take over, but neither can see a time when they will be out of the business entirely. They genuinely love the business. If I were asked why the Shulmans succeeded as mature adults purchasing a business later in life, I would have to reply that they and the business they bought were perfectly matched.

Whether you are considering the purchase of a floundering business that you hope to make profitable or an already successful business, matching interests, background, education, location, investment required, and income needed is key to the future success of the business.

Men and women interested in starting their own business will find a rich treasury of books on the subject at the local library. There are books on such subjects as small-business management, venture capital, marketing, franchising, finance, accounting, personnel, and taxation. To complement these information sources, there are directories, bibliographies, pamphlets, and periodicals with information and advice on starting a business.

FOR THE PUBLIC GOOD

The older the fiddle,
the sweeter the tune.

—Australian folk saying

In a scene in sharp contrast to the splendor of the White House, the former President of the United States and his wife, Rosalynn, donned hard hats and went to work as carpenters renovating city tenements. The Carters are active volunteers in several nonprofit endeavors, particularly Habitat for Humanity, a program that renovates old, dilapidated buildings in order to create clean, livable apartments for poor families.

Their work for this project in New York City was not the usual presidential "photo opportunity" staged for publicity. It was dirty, dusty, gritty, and dangerous work rebuilding roofs and replacing structural timbers. And yet, Mr. Carter says, "Of all the activities we have undertaken since leaving the White House, it is certainly one of the most inspiring."

President Carter exemplifies the retired individual (involuntary retirement, in this case) who finds new purpose in volunteer work. Jimmy Carter's post-presidency activities, his hands-on labor at Habitat for Humanity and other worthwhile programs, have earned him greater respect and admiration throughout the world than any of the high offices he held before.

The former President and his First Lady are not alone in their dedication to volunteer work. A survey by the Commonwealth Fund reports that of the 52.4 million Americans aged 55 and older, 13.7 million (26 percent) provide direct one-on-one care and volunteer their services through various organizations. About four in ten volunteers serve more than one organization. Although the typical mature volunteer serves four hours a week, one million volunteers in this age group contribute 18 or more hours per week, and 243,000 serve 35 or more hours. Some 4.7 million mature volunteers also do paid work. (Employers who question the energy level of older adults, please note.)

Volunteer work can be an important part of your later years. A commitment of significant time on a regular basis makes your work more important to the organization and more meaningful to you. One sprightly gray-haired lady who supervises the game room in a South Chicago children's hospital four days a week and six hours each day told me that she likes having a "regular" volunteer job where they depend on her and she has to show up at a specific hour. It gives her "a place to go and to dress for . . . and makes me hustle to get there on time."

Wʜᴏ BENEFITS FROM VOLUNTEER WORK?

A speaker at a national conference for retirees said it best: "Everyone benefits. The talents, wisdom, and energy of our retirees are badly needed by our communities. Retirees who are active and involved have a new sense of self-worth and a source of daily enrichment. The aging process is slowed."

American men and women are living longer and healthier lives, and many maintain their full vitality into their seventies and eighties. For many, voluntary service provides a great deal of what they're missing after retirement—involvement and interaction with others, plus a sense of personal worth. Volunteering is a way to put a lifetime of experience, knowledge, and wisdom to good use.

Your age peers do a lot of volunteer work—and would like to do a lot more. Better than two out of five men and women aged 60 or older perform some volunteer activity, according to polling by ICR Research Group. ICR estimates that about 15.5 million people in that age group are volunteers, providing 3.6 billion hours a year of service.

Almost one fourth of those not serving as volunteers say they would donate time and effort if asked; two out of five say they might. One fourth of those already engaged in volunteer work say they would prefer to give even more time than they do. Of those who volunteer

- On average, 60-and-over volunteers work one day a week.

- Three out of five give time to church or religious organizations, while one third work with social-services agencies. Civic and cultural organizations and schools and other educational groups are also favorites.

- Fewer than 10 percent give time to political parties or campaigns.

If you are among the potential volunteers, what are you waiting for? They need your services and you need the satisfaction that comes with useful work. Volunteers provide companionship, through visits or phone calls, help to raise funds and tutor or give other aid in the educational field. Most cite "helping others" as the reason for volunteering, and more than half say they also want to be useful and productive. Women volunteers outnumber men but the proportion of men over 60 who volunteer is higher.

Many older adults start volunteering because of a genuine desire to do good for others; they continue because they enjoy their volunteer job—the activity itself and the people they meet. Al Bolatti, a retired accountant who relocated to Arizona and provides free tax services to seniors explains, "I have a lot of new friends that I met through my volunteer work. It's really made the transition to a new place easier."

Most charities and nonprofit organizations view mature people as a valuable resource. The efforts of older people is coveted by nonprofit organizations because they are available during the daytime. They fill a gap left by homemakers who went to work at a salaried position.

Older volunteers are usually actively involved in a number of different activities: socializing, organized exercise, travel, reading, and so forth. They also have strong family ties and go to church or to synagogue regularly. Many mature volunteers are wealthy and well educated; their prestige and tangible skills make them attractive to all kinds of organizations. But affluence and educational background are not a prerequisite for voluntary service. In fact, some of the most meaningful volunteer work is being done by seniors who are not wealthy or highly educated. All kinds of people at all stages of maturity are needed and appreciated, especially in church-sponsored activities. More than half of all volunteers 55 and older are active in religious activities.

If you find yourself spending too much time in solitary activities—watching television, listening to the radio, reading newspapers and magazines—and if you have become more sedentary and less social, you owe it to yourself to explore volunteer work. Voluntary work allows you to continue to be productive and do work that you like to do. It is only when volunteer work has served *your* purpose that it is most effective in helping others.

To be seventy years young
is sometimes far more
cheerful and hopeful
than to be forty years old.

■ ■ ■

—Oliver Wendell Holmes

YOUR CHOICE OF VOLUNTEER WORK

Voluntary work can include anything from helping to care for one sick child to running the local charity's flea market to several years in West Africa teaching the natives how to improve their agricultural output. The right kind of volunteer work can add years to your life and meaning to your years.

You'll note that we stress "the right kind." Since your work is entirely voluntary and there is no financial incentive to stay the course, you can walk away from it at any time. Consequently, you have to like what you're doing and enjoy the people you're working with. That should not be a problem. One of the best things about volunteer work is that *you* are the one who decides whom you will work with, how you will participate, and what skills and talents you will contribute.

More than 15 million Americans 55 and older provide direct volunteer care to sick or disabled family members, friends, or neighbors. The typical caregiver spends 5 hours per week—2.4 million caregivers spend 18 or more hours per week. The Commonwealth Fund estimates that the total amount of direct volunteer care to the sick or disabled is equivalent to the hours of 2.7 million full-time workers.

Other volunteers contribute their services through organizations. Their roles include staff support or clerical assistance to implement direct service; advocacy and political volunteering; administrative volunteering, which includes work on committees; and managing, planning, and policy-making.

When you decide to give your time and energy, you can choose from a large number of worthy organizations.

- Group cooperatives (United Way, The National Center, American Council for Voluntary International Action)

- Social services (Covenant House, Red Cross, Family Service America, Volunteers in Service to America, Goodwill Industries)

- Organizations serving older Americans (Senior Citizens Centers, National Council on the Aging, American Association of Retired Persons, Gray Panthers, etc.)

- Education-oriented organizations (Great Books Foundation, Literacy Volunteers of America, Parent-Teachers Association)

- Cultural Groups (Public Television, National Public Radio, local library, museum, performing arts center)

- Health-care organizations (American Cancer Society, Alzheimer's Disease and Related Disorders Association; Arthritis Foundation; local hospitals, clinics, nursing homes, and hospice facilities)

- Churches, synagogues, and religious affiliations (Catholic Charities, B'nai Brith, Salvation Army)

- Environmental groups (Sierra Club; Keep America Beautiful; National Audubon Society; local parks, zoos, and gardens)

- International organizations (Peace Corps, Amnesty International, Freedom from Hunger Foundation)

Opportunities for international volunteer work offer travel and adventure in far-off places. Virtually all provide board and lodging, and some grant modest remuneration. The trade-off is hard work and often difficult living conditions, especially in Third World locations. These volunteers are required to live and work away from home and make a full-time commitment ranging from several months to several years.

FINDING VOLUNTEER OPPORTUNITIES

In *Everything to Gain: How to Make the Most of the Rest of Your Life*, by Jimmy and Rosalynn Carter, the former first couple describe how they went about finding volunteer work: "We decided it would be a good idea to look around one afternoon to see what is available in our immediate area for anyone who is interested in getting involved in community affairs or working as a volunteer, or just doing something different for enjoyment. Rosalynn volunteered to make a tour of our local college, library, hospital, and mental health center and we were surprised at the opportunities right here in our own backyard."

When you come upon an activity or learn of an organization "in your own backyard" whose work you admire, pick up your phone and tell them: "Your work interests me. Can I help?" Many fruitful days and much good starts with just such a call.

Under "Social Services" in your local Yellow Pages you'll find a listing for Voluntary Action Center, a community service whose purpose is to match you and other volunteers with the needs of worthy organizations. If there is no such Center in your community, there are other organizations that provide a similar service. Contact the mayor's office, the Chamber of Commerce, or your local United Way office.

A national hotline on volunteer opportunities—(toll-free 800-424-8867—is waiting at the other end to help you and other potential volunteers connect with a volunteer job to match your interests. The hotline is run by ACTION, the Federal Volunteer Agency in Washington, D.C.

MATCHING INTERESTS

To find the right kind of volunteer work you have to analyze your interests and match them with the appropriate organization. In the following examples, the left column lists typical reasons why older Americans volunteer; on the right, an appropriate match:

Why Older Americans Participate in Volunteer Work

Motivation	Matched volunteer activity
Compensate for loss of work role and/or family responsibilities	Athletic coach at youth center
A way to meet new people	Usher at fundraising events, receptionist at a community facility or clinic
Opportunity for socializing	Volunteer worker at senior center
The desire to help others	Helper in hospital or clinic, answer hotline calls from people in trouble
Opportunity to do worthwhile and interesting things	Recording books on tape for the blind
A chance to learn	Docent at a museum, zoo attendant, library assistant
Strong interest in the goals of the organization	Fundraiser for cancer research, Alzheimer's, etc.
Religious interests	Volunteer at church or synagogue
Prestige and recognition	Sightseeing guide, fundraiser for cultural organization, museum docent, sports coach at youth center, crossing guard

Travel opportunity	Peace Corps, National Park Service
To once again practice career skills or profession without concern for compensation	Conduct musical programs for the elderly, provide *pro-bono* legal services, give language courses for immigrants
To stay active	Staff the phones during a telethon, bus driver for nonprofit organization
Emotional rewards	Foster Grandparents, Meals on Wheels
A chance to effect change	Work at political-party headquarters, election campaigner, volunteer lobbyist
Gain experience in a particular field	Travel coordinator for senior group, cook/nutritionist at home for children

There is one more practical reason for volunteering. If you are a retiree who wants to ease back into a field you left years ago, or a homemaker returning to work after many years, you can work as a volunteer in just about any field you wish. Working as a volunteer allows you to polish your job skills, develop contacts, and gain on-the-job experience to add to your resume. Employers appreciate the value of volunteer work. Although it isn't something you can count on, volunteer workers often end up in salaried positions at the same organization.

Rights . . .

As a volunteer you have certain rights and obligations. You have a right to know the kind of work you will be doing, the hours you are expected to contribute, and whom you will be working with. The job you are assigned as a volunteer should be worthwhile and productive. You should expect that your time will not wasted because of poor coordination within the organization.

You have the right to get answers to these and other important questions:

What is my job? Is it worthwhile and challenging with an opportunity to use my skills? Will I have a chance to develop new skills?

Will I be able to decline work not acceptable to me?

Will I receive training and supervision and told why I am doing a particular job?

Will I be reimbursed for out-of-pocket costs? If not, will I be able to declare allowable nonreimbursed out-of-pocket costs for federal (and some state and local) income tax purposes?

. . . And Obligations

You get the most out of your volunteer work when you are serious about your responsibilities and honor your commitment to the organization. Your obligation is to:

Accept only as much responsibility as I can handle.

Use my time wisely and don't interfere with the work of others.

Follow the guidelines of the organization as it applies to dress code, decorum, attendance, etc.

Notify my supervisor early enough if I cannot fulfill my commitment so that it can be assigned to someone else.

Be considerate, respect the work of others, and work as a team with the staff and other volunteers.

Volunteer Opportunities—A to Z

Adult Literacy Project
2020 Main Street
Aliquippa, PA 15001

Big Brother/Big Sister
470 Mamaroneck Avenue
White Plains, NY 10605

Child Abuse Hotline
80007 Discovery Drive
Richmond, VA 23229-8689

Dogs for the Deaf
13260 Highway 238
Jacksonville, OR 97530

Environmental Action Foundation
1525 New Hampshire Avenue NW
Washington, DC 20036

Forest Service Volunteer Program
1375 K Street NW
Washington, DC 20013-5090

Give Them a Hand Not a Handout
P.O. Box 15486
Washington, DC 20003

HOST (Hands of Share Time)
3438 Olney
Laytonsville Road
Olney, MD 20832

Intergenerational Project for
   Service Learning
600 Maryland Ave. SW
Washington, DC 20024

Joint Educational Project
801 West 34th Street
Los Angeles, CA 90089-0471

Keep America Beautiful
9 West Broad Street
Stamford, CT 06902

League of Women Voters
   of the U.S.
1730 M Street NW
Washington, DC 20036

Martial Arts for Seniors
1400 Fenwick Lane
Silver Springs, MD 20910

National Alliance of Senior
  Citizens
1700 18th Street NW
Washington, DC 20009

Older Americans as a Growing
  National Resource
1017 North Third St., Suite 20
Phoenix, AZ 85004

Parkinson's Institute for
  Caregivers
5121 East Broadway
Mesa, AZ 85206

Quality Education Program
UAW-GM Human Resource
  Center, Region 1C
Flint, MI 48501

Retired Senior Volunteers
5165 Merriam Drive
Merriam, KS 66302

Sierra Club
1730 M Street NW
Washington, DC 20036

Toll Free Hotline Information
  (a Ralph Nader program)
P.O. Box 19404
Washington, DC 20036

United Way/Crusade of Mercy
701 North Fairfax Street
Alexandria, VA 22314

VISTA (Volunteers in Service
  to America)
1100 Vermont Avenue NW
Washington, DC 20525

Wellness Center
4320 Seminary Road
Alexandria, VA 22304

Xerox Corporation Community
  Affairs Office
Stamford, CT 06904

Yes Program (Youth-Elderly
  Services)
101 Rock Street
Fall River, MA 02720

Zero Population Growth
1601 Connecticut Avenue NW
Washington, DC 20009

This **A** to **Z** listing will give you some idea of the length and breadth of the volunteer opportunities open to older Americans. The organizations listed here are culled from some 2,000 listings in *Volunteerism: The Directory of Organizations, Training Programs and Publications*, Harriet Clyde Kipps, editor, published by R. R. Bowker. Your local library has this directory—it's a great place to explore the many interesting and challenging volunteer opportunities open to you.

POWERFUL ALLIES

A society that gives to one class
all the opportunities for leisure, and
to another all the burdens of work,
dooms both classes to spiritual sterility.

—Lewis Mumford

A large number of organizations and support groups across the nation stand ready to help you in your search for work. The employment network for older Americans includes state, county, and local agencies, as well as the area agencies managing private-employment services and federal-government-employment programs.

These agencies offer a variety of services to job-seeking older Americans and employers looking for mature people to fill open positions. The services include:

- A central job clearinghouse
- Screening job applicants

- Job-search training for applicants
- Referrals to other appropriate facilities

Most are nonprofit, offering their services at no cost; a few have modest fees.

I resisted the suggestion to separate resources for compensated employment from those for voluntary work. I did not want in any way to suggest that one is more important than the other. Some of the most important and meaningful work being done today is being done by skilled and conscientious volunteers. What President Bush referred to as "a thousand points of light" is more accurately millions of points of light—one for each of the dedicated men and women working as caretakers, drivers delivering meals to the indigent elderly, and people serving as museum docents, teaching the handicapped and the underprivileged, raising funds for charity, and providing any one of the hundreds of community activities where the psychic and emotional rewards are greater than money.

Many of the headquarters of the resources listed are located in the nation's capital. That doesn't mean that their help is beyond your reach. Most also maintain field offices across the country. By writing or calling the Washington, D.C., base, you can obtain information about branches or local offices close to you. These organizations can be powerful allies in your search for suitable work. They make an excellent starting point as you explore all the options open to you.

The interaction between the following organizations is nothing short of amazing. As a result, if the people you contact can't help with a specific problem, they can probably refer you to the right person or organization. Whether you are looking for work or need information about a particular work-related problem, if the organization you call or write can't help, press for a referral to the appropriate resource.

Some of the resources listed here disseminate information to help in understanding and overcoming barriers to the employment of older workers and in research or lobbying for older-worker issues. Here again, if they can't help you directly, they will know someone in the "aging" network who can.

It isn't possible to list all the local organizations and support groups across the country that can help. There are too many, and new ones surface regularly. Use this list as a guide to the kind of support that's available in your area—resources that you didn't know were there. Once you start looking around, you'll be surprised at how many people are out there ready and able to help.

Resource Roster

Operation ABLE (*A*bility *B*ased on *L*ong *E*xperience) provides the support, training, and job-search assistance to help older job-seekers find work. ABLE is a not-for-profit Chicago-based agency affiliated with more than 40 community-based city and suburban older-worker employment centers. Together, they place more than 5,000 older workers annually.

Among ABLE's specific services are:

A very active telephone hotline for applicants looking for work and employers who want to hire older workers. There is no cost to employers or job seekers.

ABLE's Pool of Temporaries (APT) places experienced office workers in temporary assignments.

ABLE Institute is a job-search assistance program that specializes in assisting professional, managerial, technical, and skilled clerical job seekers. The Institute offers group training, individual career assessment, testing, and guidance, and maintains a library of business- and career-resource information. Frequent workshops are conducted on job search and career change, and individual counseling and assistance in preparing resumes is available. (There is a modest fee for group training and individual counseling.)

Job Club is an ABLE-sponsored support-group job-search program for men and women seeking full- and part-time employment.

Operation Able sponsors an annual Job Fair in Chicago and a number of Chicago suburbs that brings together older job seekers and employers. The organization also offers subsidized training and tuition assistance that enables qualified individuals to upgrade their skills and develop new qualifications. ABLE's Subsidized Employment Program provides subsidized employment to economically disadvantaged individuals 55 and over.

Since it was established in 1977, Operation ABLE has served more than 60,000 older workers and more than 5,000 employers.

Call or write for information on this organization and its affiliated community-based city and suburban older worker employment centers.

Operation ABLE
180 N. Wabash Avenue
Chicago, IL
(312) 782-3335. Job Hotline: (312) 782-7700

Here is a partial list of Operation ABLE affiliations with other agencies outside Illinois. Their activities are based on the ABLE model. A service funded by the Charles Steward Mott Foundation allows the national organization based in Chicago to provide technical assistance and training to these other agencies.

Arkansas ABLE
519 E Capitol Avenue
Little Rock, AK 72202-2419
(501) 374-1318
Phyliss Haynes, executive director

Operation ABLE of Greater Boston
World Trade Center, Suite 306
Boston, MA 02210-2004
(617) 439-5580
Robin Battista, executive director

Los Angeles Council on Careers
  for Older Americans
5225 Wilshire Blvd., Suite 204
Los Angeles, CA 90036
(213) 939-0391
Sally James, executive director

Project ABLE
Crossroads Office Center
16250 Northland Drive, Suite 102
Southfield, MI 48075
(313) 433-0370
Terry Barclay, executive director

Operation ABLE of Southeast Nebraska
129 North Tenth Street
Lincoln, NE 68508-3648
1-800-422-3268 or (402) 441-7064
Jacque Haisch, program director

ABLE Senior Employment Services
NYC Dept. of Aging
2 Lafayette Street, New York, NY 10005
(212) 577-0800
Sharon Perkins, Director, Senior Employment
  Division

Vermont Associates for Training
and Development, Inc.
P.O. Box 107
St. Albans, VT 05478
(802) 524-3200
Pat Elmer, executive director

National Executive Service Corps (NESC) founded *Senior Career Planning & Placement Service,* a New York-based nonprofit organization that helps match business executives and professionals with employers looking for top people with proven management skills and extensive experience.

NESC emphasizes "quality, expertise, and experience" at affordable compensation rates: "Since most of the executives in our placement pool are people who have retired or have taken early retirement, their salary requirements are modest, and usually fringe benefits are not required."

Through its association with some 35 other Executive Service Corps operations across the nation, Senior Career has placed men and women in such top positions as CEO, executive director, controller, and in senior positions in advertising, engineering, finance, manufacturing, and marketing.

Employers pay Senior Career for locating the seasoned people they need. How much? "We charge considerably lower rates than existing executive search firms because we are a non-profit organization needing merely to cover the overhead for our service, and because the compensation requirements of the people we provide are relatively modest. Also, most of the people we provide do not require fringe benefits, so the savings may be more than our modest fee."

Senior Career boasts a blue-ribbon roster of employer clients including Campbell Soup Co., Seagram & Sons, Mutual Insurance Co., Polaroid, and many others, equally prestigious.

Senior Career Planning & Placement Service
275 Park Avenue South
New York, NY 10010-7304
(212) 529-6660

Forty Plus is a self-help network of men and women aged 40 and over who work with and for each other in finding new jobs or starting new careers. The 17 chapters of Forty Plus have a remarkable track record for placing older executives, managers, entrepreneurs, and professionals. The organization was founded in 1939 by Dr. Norman Vincent Peale, Arthur Godfrey, and the legendary IBM Chairman Tom Watson. Its slogan, "A New Beginning . . . There is no substitute for experience!" reflects the organization's positive approach to job placement.

The organization is self-supporting through dues and membership fees that are far below the cost of commercial placement services. It is staffed by volunteers—experienced, mature, and skilled individuals who are experts at matching job-seekers with employers.

I told John Pence, the executive vice president of Forty Plus of Greater Washington, that the people I was addressing in my book were older than "forty plus," and asked him how his organization relates to my readers, "Don't be misled by our name," he said. "The average age of our job-seekers is fifty-five. We have many people in their sixties, and some in their seventies."

Forty Plus offers mature job seekers fully equipped office facilities and coaching in resume-writing and interview techniques. There is a modest initial membership fee and monthly dues. If accepted, a candidate must agree to spend one day per week working for the organization in the office. Members must be unemployed or actively seeking a position or career change and earning at least $30,000 a year when employed.

In June 1989, Forty Plus received the Presidential C Flag awarded under the President's Citation Program for Private Sector Initiatives: "For outstanding strength, spirit, and effectiveness in addressing public needs."

Forty Plus Offices

CALIFORNIA

Forty Plus of Northern California
7440 Lockheed Street
P.O. Box 6639
Oakland, CA 94603-0639
(415) 430-2400
FAX (415) 430-1750

Forty Plus of Southern California
3450 Wilshire Boulevard, Suite 510
Los Angeles, CA 90010
(213) 388-2301
FAX (213) 383-7750

Orange County Division
23172 Plaza Pointe Dr., Suite 285
Laguna Hills, CA 92653
(714) 581-7990
FAX (714) 581-4257

COLORADO

Forty Plus of Colorado
393 South Harlan Street
Lakewood, CO 80226
(303) 937-6668
FAX (303) 937-6050

Northern Division
3842 South Mason Street
Fort Collins, CO 80525
(303) 223-2470 (ext. 261)
FAX (303) 223-7456

Southern Division
2555 Airport Road
Colorado Springs, CO 80910-3176
(719) 473-6220 (ext. 271)

DISTRICT OF COLUMBIA

Forty Plus of Greater Washington
1718 P Street NW
Washington, DC 20036
(202) 387-1582
FAX (202) 387-7669

HAWAII

Forty Plus of Hawaii
126 Queen Street, Suite 227
Honolulu, HI 96813
(808) 531-0896
FAX (808) 531-0896

ILLINOIS

Forty Plus of Chicago
53 East Jackson Blvd.
Chicago, IL 60604
(312) 922-0285
FAX (312) 922-4840

NEW YORK

Forty Plus of Buffalo
701 Seneca Street
Buffalo, NY 14210
(716) 856-0491
FAX (716) 852-2292

Forty Plus of New York
15 Park Row
New York, NY 10038
(212) 233-6086
FAX (212) 227-2974

OHIO

Forty Plus of Central Ohio
1700 Arlingate Lane
Columbus, OH 43228
(614) 275-0040

PENNSYLVANIA

Forty Plus of Philadelphia
1218 Chestnut Street
Philadelphia, PA 19107
(215) 923-2074

TEXAS

Forty Plus of Dallas
13601 Preston Road, Suite 301 East
Dallas, TX 75240
(214) 991-9917
FAX (214) 991-9932

Forty Plus of Houston
2909 Hillcroft
Houston, TX 77067
(713) 850-7830

UTAH

Forty Plus of Utah
5735 S. Redwood Road
Salt Lake City, UT 84123
(801) 269-4797

TORONTO, CANADA

Forty Plus of Canada
920 Yonge Street, Suite 410
Toronto, Ontario, Canada
M4W 3C7
(416) 766-1173

American Association of Retired Persons (AARP). There are few Americans 50-and-over who are not familiar with the *American Association of Retired Persons (AARP)*. With a membership of 32 million and annual revenues of about $200 million, AARP is one of the largest and most influential organizations in the U.S.

The Association was established in 1958 by Dr. Ethel Percy Andrus, "in order to better the lives of older Americans through service, advocacy, education and volunteer efforts." Currently more than 350,000 volunteers and 4,000 local chapters carry out the AARP's mission in community service; legislative and voter education efforts' health care and quality of life issues; older workers' rights and retirement planning.

Most people are familiar with AARP because of the group's lobbying activities and the discount deals, insurance, investments, pharmaceuticals, and other products and services that they offer members aged 50-and-over. Through its Worker Equity Division, the organization also maintains a program called *AARP WORKS*.

AARP WORKS includes a series of job search workshops held throughout the country for groups of 15 to 20. The workshops are led by AARP volunteer teams and community agencies.

Some of the comments of AARP workshop participants explain the benefits: " . . . helped me realize how valuable my skills are in the marketplace." "AARP WORKS gave me direction." "I now have the self-confidence to know that I can do this."

A follow-up on the experience of participants found that over a 15-month period, 35 percent have accepted new jobs. Of those actively looking for work, 71 percent were granted job interviews and 25 percent received job offers.

Call or write for more information, including time and place of upcoming workshops. The organization also publishes a number of outstanding booklets that are free to members, among them, "Working Options—How to Plan Your Job Search, Your Work Life" and "How to Stay Employable: A Guide for the Mid-life and Older Worker." Membership in AARP is a modest $8 per year. They deserve your support.

AARP WORKS
American Association of Retired Persons (AARP)
Work Force Education
Worker Equity Department
601 E Street NW
Washington DC 20049

Second Careers Program is a private, nonprofit employment service for older workers. Its two divisions, placement and corporate services, are dedicated to opening up new opportunities for older workers in both compensated employment and volunteer work.

Among the organization's concerns are the enhancement of viable work with other roles in retirement and greater acceptance and involvement of older and retired persons in the workplace. As a complement to its employment and volunteer placement programs, Second Careers offers career and retirement counseling.

Second Careers Program
2932 West 6th Street, Suite 216
Los Angeles, CA 90020
(213) 380-3166

Peace Corps' slogan says it all: "The toughest job you'll ever love." Unfortunately, many older Americans believe that the Corps is interested only in younger people. On the contrary, the Peace Corps is seeking seasoned, experienced people. It is one of the more interesting work options open to older adults.

Men and women of all ages and all walks of life are trained for service—the ideal situation for seniors seeking new experiences and adventure in exotic foreign places.

The Peace Corps makes available to interested countries Americans willing to serve abroad to meet the needs of these countries for trained manpower (and womanpower!). The phrase "trained manpower" suggests the important of skills developed over a lifetime in this important work throughout Latin America, Africa, the Near East, Asia, and the Pacific.

Peace Corps staffer Stephanie Jackson told me that most societies want more older volunteers: "They place high value on age and associate it with wisdom." Older Americans represent an enormous resource because of their experience, maturity, and demonstrated ability. Currently, 12 percent of the Peace Corps workers are 50 years old and over. The oldest is 81 and going strong. Ms. Jackson reports that "new efforts are underway to increase the number of senior volunteers by addressing their special concerns."

Serving an average of two years, seniors work primarily in the areas of agriculture and rural development, small business assistance, health, and education. Older couples experienced in farming or teaching are in particular demand.

All related expenses such as travel, medical, housing, vacation and living expenses are paid for by the Peace Corps. Volunteers receive $200 for each month of training and service. Retired individuals continue to receive their retirement benefits.

An independent federal agency with an annual budget of more than $50 million, the Peace Corps is based in Washington, D.C., and maintains three regional recruitment centers in the United States supporting 16 area offices and has overseas operations in more than 60 countries. Call or write the Washington office to locate your closest area office.

Peace Corps
806 Connecticut Avenue NW
Washington, DC 20525
(202) 254-7280 or (800) 424-8580

The National Council on the Aging (NCOA) is a large, national, non-profit organization that advocates older adults' "full participation in society."

In addition to advocacy and information dissemination, NCOA is involved in senior employment through three major programs:

1. The Senior Community Service Employment Program helps low-income workers 55 years and older to enter (or re-enter) the job market. U.S. Government funding made it possible for this program to provide work and training opportunities in 21 states to more than 10,000 older workers in a single year.

2. The National Association of Older Worker Employment Services helps workers 50 and over to find new careers. Through affiliations with local groups, the Association assists men and women 50 and over to re-enter the work force. It achieves its objectives by holding classes on job interview, skills transference, and matching skills to jobs.

3. The Senior Environmental Program provides employment opportunity for all older adults regardless of their financial status. While most of the jobs relate to the environment, there are many job opportunities that support the major work and do not require environmental skills.

In its "Public Policy Agenda, 1993–1994" NCOA recommends that Congress closely monitor enforcement of laws relating to age discrimination and that the statute of limitation to file a complaint should be lengthened past the current 180 days. The Agenda also calls for strengthening the Job Training Partnership Act and the Senior Community Service Employment Program. In addition, the Agenda recommends that incentives be available to employers that encourage the retraining and retention of older workers whose skills need upgrading.

The NCOA publishes a large number of publications—"Mature/Older Job Seeker's Guide," for example—directed at the older individual. Write or call for more information on this organization's programs and publications.

> The National Council on the Aging, Inc.
> 600 Maryland Avenue SW, West Wing 100
> Washington, DC 20024
> (202) 479-6976

The National Caucus and Center on Black Aged is a nonprofit, interracial membership organization that serves the needs of lower-income and minority elderly.

Two of its programs—New Careers Training Program for Older Workers and Title V Senior Employment Program—are particularly relevant for older job seekers.

The Caucus has published a two-volume edition of *Job Placement Systems for Older Workers.*

> The National Caucus and Center on Black Aged
> 1424 K Street NW, Suite 500
> Washington, DC 20005
> (202) 637-8400

National Association of State Units on Aging has as its goal "to provide the opportunity and benefits essential to guaranteeing the dignity of older people." In furthering its goals, the organization is concerned with a long list of aging issues; prominent among them are employment and age discrimination.

Employment/Finance is an important division of the Association.

National Association of State Units on Aging
2033 K Street NW, Suite 300
Washington, DC 20006
(202) 785-0707

The Railroad Retirement Board administers retirement and un-employment benefits programs for the nation's railroad workers and their families. In addition to its administrative responsibilities under the Social Security Act for benefits payments and Medicare, the Board maintains a placement service for unemployed railroad personnel.

The Board's placement service is operated through its field offices located in centers of railroad population that are grouped into regions.

Railroad Retirement Board
Liaison Office
2000 L Street NW
Washington, DC 20036
(202) 653-9540

The National Council of Senior Citizens has as its main areas of activity advocacy, lobbying, and information dissemination.

Among the Council's special services are Title V Senior Community Service Employment Program (SCSEP), Senior Environmental Employment (SEE), and job training.

National Council of Senior Citizens
925 15th Street NW
Washington, DC 20005
(202) 347-8800

Service Corps of Retired Executives —usually referred to as SCORE—is a nonprofit association sponsored by the U.S. Small Business Administration. SCORE's 760 nationwide offices match retired executive volunteers with budding entrepreneurs. It has a special interest in older veterans. In a single year—1991—SCORE helped more than 260 clients.

San Diego resident Bill Trueblood, 71, is a typical member of SCORE's volunteer staff. He draws on 36 years of experience as a senior executive at Proctor & Gamble. Trueblood believes that SCORE needs more minority and women volunteers.

The organization's activities involve (1) information dissemination and (2) professional education and training. SCORE members (13,000 active and retired executive volunteers in all 50 states) offer one-on-one business management counseling. Seminars and workshops on running a business are conducted periodically.

Service Corps of Retired Executives (SCORE)
1129 20th Street NW, Suite 410
Washington, DC 20036
(202) 653-6279

Opportunities for Older Americans Fund, a public foundation serving the greater Washington metropolitan area, maintains programs to open up opportunities for older persons. The organization places emphasis on volunteerism, employment, and intergenerational relations.

Among the Fund's priorities are expansion of employment options, including training, for older adults and establishing a national agenda to promote senior volunteer initiatives.

Opportunities for Older Americans Fund
1511 K Street NW, Suite 443
Washington, DC 20005
(202) 638-1007

National Executive Service Corps (NESC) finds retirees in specialties such as planning, marketing, and fund raising for nonprofit organizations.

> National Executive Service Corps
> 257 Park Avenue South
> New York, NY 10010
> (212) 529-6660

International Executive Service Corps (IESC) offers volunteer counselors for business and government in developing countries.

> International Executive Service Corps
> P.O. Box 1005
> Stamford, CT 06904-2005
> (203) 967-6000

National Hispanic Council on Aging has as its central mission to serve elderly Hispanic people by helping them to become self-sufficient. Its members in the United States, Ecuador, and Mexico do this by organizing self-help support groups and mobilizing resources on the members' behalf.

The Council provides training and educational programming for older Hispanic men and women.

> National Hispanic Council on Aging
> 2713 Ontario Road NW, Suite 200
> Washington, DC 20009
> (202) 265-20009

Elder Craftsmen, Inc. is a unique organization that encourages and advises older people in the making and selling of fine handicrafts "thereby contributing to their self-respect, financial independence, and well-being."

Despite the "men" in their name, EC is equally involved in helping older women and in professional education and training.

EC's Consignment Shop sells and markets handicrafts made by people over 60. (In New York, they receive 60 percent of the selling price.) The organization's Controlled Production Unit offers steady work to participants who produce best-selling items for the shop. A Training Studio runs a variety of crafts workshops attended by representatives and volunteers of senior groups.

Elder Craftsmen, with 16 full-time and 10 part-time employees and 90 volunteers is funded by foundation support and charitable contributions as well as by Consignment Shop sales.

(I stopped by their Lexington Avenue store on a recent visit to New York. The merchandise for sale was first rate and very affordable. It's a wonderful showcase for the outstanding talents and skills of older men and women.)

Elder Craftsmen, Inc.
135 East 65th Street
New York, NY 10021
(212) 861-5260

Following is a partial list of nationwide Elder Craftsmen shops and cooperatives. Each outlet operates independently.

If you're interested in selling quality handicrafts for extra income and in training others, contact the outlets listed here for their guidelines. Some outlets accept crafts only by people who live in designated areas. Enclose a self-addressed, stamped envelope and never send unsolicited merchandise.

Payment to consigning craftspeople varies from shop to shop, generally in the 50 to 80 percent range. The sponsoring organization retains a percentage of the retail price to cover operating expenses.

Nationwide Shops and Cooperatives

ALABAMA

\# Freedom Quilting Bee
Rt. 1, Box 72
Alberta, AL 36720
(205) 573-2225

† Prime Time Treasures
1755 Oxmoor Road
Homewood, AL 35209
(205) 870-4183

ARKANSAS

\# Arkansas Craft Guild
P.O. Box 800
Mountain View, AR 72560
(501) 269-3897

CALIFORNIA

\# Artists Collaborative Gallery
1007 Second Street
Sacramento, CA 95814
(916) 444-3764

\# Made in Mendocino Co-op
P.O. Box 510
Hopland, CA 95449
(707) 744-1300

† Golden Era Handicraft Boutique
1020 Second Street
Sacramento, CA 95814
(916) 443-7041

† The Elder Craftsman
130 "J" Street
Old Sacramento, CA 95814
(916) 449-8762

\# The Artifactory
226 Hamilton Avenue
Palo Alto, CA 94301
(415) 853-9685

\# Winkstar Luminaria Co.
c/o Rick Skalsky
824 Fremont #2
Menlo Park, CA 94025
(415) 321-8328

COLORADO

\# Mustard Seed Gallery
1932 14th Street
Boulder, CO 80302
(303) 447-8626

\# Trimble Court Artisans Co-op
118 Trimble Court Alley
Fort Collins, CO 80524
(303) 221-0051

\# Fort Collins Potters' Guild
2008 E. Lincoln
Fort Collins, CO 80524
(303) 493-9824

\# Show of Hands
2440 East Third Avenue
Denver, CO 80206
(303) 399-0201

\# Craft cooperative
* Member of the Federation of Woman's Exchanges
† Elder Craftsmen-type Shop

\#   Boulder Arts & Crafts Co-op
1421 Pearl Street
Boulder, CO 80302
(303) 443-3683

CONNECTICUT

*   Fairfield Woman's Exchange
332 Pequot Ave.
Southport, CT 06490
(203) 259-5138

*   Greenwich Exchange
for Woman's Work, Inc.
28 Sherwood Place
Greenwich, CT 06830
(203) 869-0229

*   Heritage Woman's Exchange
3 Village St.
Southbury, CT 06488
(203) 264-4884

*   Litchfield Woman's Exchange
for Woman's Work, Inc.
Cobble Court
Litchfield, CT 06759
(203) 567-8407

*   The Woman's Exchange
of Old Lyme
14 Old Lyme Shopping Center
Old Lyme, CT 06371
(203) 434-7290

*   The Woman's Exchange
of West Hartford
993A Farmington Ave.
W. Hartford, CT 06107
(203) 232-8721

DELAWARE

†   Golden Eagle Elder Craftsmen
1909 Market Street
Wilmington, DE 19802
(302) 651-3480

FLORIDA

\#   Artisan's Guild Co-op
806 W. University Ave.
Gainesville, FL 32601
(904) 378-1383

*   Women's Exchange
143 St. George St.
St. Augustine, FL 32084
(904) 829-5064

GEORGIA

†   Island Art Center
Demere Road
St. Simons Island, GA 31522
(912) 365-2868

\#   Co-op Craft Store
Box 214
Clarkesville, GA 30523
(404) 754-2244

\#   Co-op Craft Store
Box 67
Tullah Falls, GA 30573
(404) 754-6810

\#   Appalachian Studio Gallery
P.O. Box 274
Young Harris, GA 30582
(404) 379-3807

\#   Craft cooperative
*   Member of the Federation of Woman's Exchanges
†   Elder Craftsmen-type Shop

INDIANA

* Tri-State Woman's
   Exchange, Inc.
   The Hen House
   2704 Lincoln Avenue
   Evansville, IN 47714
   (812) 477-7231

* The Little Turtle Woman's
   Exchange
   6374 West Jefferson Blvd.
   Covington Plaza
   Fort Wayne, IN 46321
   (219) 432-6857

\# Creative Hands Co-op
   13730 Third Street
   Grabill, IN 46741
   (219) 627-5906

IOWA

† Chalet Gifts
   P.O. Box 4002
   Des Moines, IA 50333
   (515) 289-1933

KANSAS

† Senior Citizens Handcraft
   Shoppe
   73 S. Seventh Street
   Kansas City, KS 66101
   (913) 321-4499

KENTUCKY

\# Kentucky Hills Industry
   Pine Knot, KY 42635
   (606) 354-2813

\# Grass Roots Craftsmen
   P.O. Box 9
   Lost Creek, KY 41348
   (606) 666-7371

LOUISIANA

* YWCU Woman's Exchange
   of Baton Rouge
   201 St. Charles Street
   Baton Rouge, LA 70802
   (504) 383-7761

MAINE

\# Praxis
   136 Main Street
   Freeport, ME 04032
   (207) 865-6201

\# H.O.M.E., Inc.
   P.O. Box 10
   Orland, ME 04472
   (207) 469-7961

\# Eastern Bay Cooperative
   Gallery
   P.O. Box 126
   Main Street
   Stonington, ME 04681
   (207) 367-5006

\# The Brick Store Exchange
   105 Main Street
   Kennebunk, ME 04043
   (207) 985-3639

\#   Craft cooperative
*   Member of the Federation of Woman's Exchanges
†   Elder Craftsmen-type Shop

MARYLAND

* The Women's Industrial
  Exchange
  333 N. Charles Street
  Baltimore, MD 21218
  (301) 685-4388

MASSACHUSETTS

† Kit Clark Senior House
  1500 Dorchester Avenue
  Dorchester, MA 02122
  (617) 825-5000

The Clever Hand III
  361 Boston Post Road
  Sudbury, MA 01776
  (508) 443-8710

The Clever Hand II
  Acton Mall at Nagog Square
  Route 2A
  Acton, MA 01720
  (617) 263-9585

* Dedham Women's Exchange
  445 Washington Street
  Dedham, MA 02026
  (617) 326-0627

* The Hay Scales Exchange, Inc.
  2 Johnson Street
  N. Andover, MA 01845
  (508) 683-3691

* Old Town Hall Exchange
  Box 44
  Lincoln Center, MA 01773
  (617) 259-9876

* Port O'Call Exchange
  67 Main Street
  Gloucester, MA 01930
  (508) 283-4899

* The Wayland Depot, Inc.
  1 Cochituate Road, Box 276
  Wayland, MA 01778
  (508) 358-5386

MICHIGAN

Indian Earth Arts & Crafts
  124 W. First Street
  Flint, MI 48502
  (313) 239-6621

MINNESOTA

Northwest Econ. Dev. Inc.
  102 N. Broadway
  Crookston, MN 56716
  (218) 281-1776

Lady Slipper Design, Inc.
  Bemidji, MN 56716
  (218) 751-0763

MISSOURI

† Woman's Exchange of St. Louis
  9214 Clayton Road
  St. Louis, MO 63124
  (314) 997-4411

† Sr. Citizens Craft Shop
  Court House Square
  Independence, MO 64050
  (816) 461-0191

Craft cooperative
* Member of the Federation of Woman's Exchanges
† Elder Craftsmen-type Shop

NEBRASKA

† Heritage Craft Shop
1005 "O" Street
Lincoln, NE 68508
(402) 471-8457

NEW HAMPSHIRE

† League of N.H. Craftsmen
205 N. Main Street
Concord, NH 03301
(603) 224-3375

† Golden Age Shop
P.O. Box 578
Conway, NH 03818
(603) 447-2801

NEW JERSEY

† Golden Talents
3 Church Street
Flemington, NJ 08822
(201) 782-8989

† The Golden Ladder
12 North Dean Street
Englewood, NJ 07631
(201) 568-6517

* The Depot
22 Prospect Street
Midland Park, NJ 07432
(201) 444-6120

* The Hunterdon Exchange
155 Main Street
Flemington, NJ 08822
(201) 782-6229

* Woman's Exchange of
Monmouth Co.
32 Church Street
Little Silver, NJ 07739
(201) 741-1164

* Little Shop on the Corner
116 Elm St.
Westfield, NJ 07090
(201) 233-2210

NEW YORK

† Elder Craftstmen Shop
846 Lexington Avenue
New York, NY 10021
(212) 535-8030

† Golden Showcase for
Elder Craftsmen
Harbor Square Mall
134 Main Street
Port Jefferson, NY 11777
(516) 473-6172

† Master Crafters
42 Orchard Street
Manhasset, NY 11030
(516) 627-5484

† The Country Mouse
1138 Broadway
Elmira, NY 14904
(607) 732-1959

* The Consortium for
Children's Services
123 East Water Street
Syracuse, NY 13202
(315) 471-8331

\# Craft cooperative
* Member of the Federation of Woman's Exchanges
† Elder Craftsmen-type Shop

* N.Y. Exchange for Woman's
  Work
  1095 Third Avenue
  New York, NY 10021
  (212) 752-2330

* Scarsdale Woman's Exchange
  33 Harwood Court
  Scarsdale, NY 10583
  (914) 723-4728

* Brooklyn Woman's Exchange
  5 Pierrepont Street
  Brooklyn, NY 11201
  (718) 624-3435

Turtle Island Craftshop
  25 Rainbow Mall
  Niagara Falls, NY 14303
  (716) 284-0447

NORTH CAROLINA

* The Country Store
  University Hall
  Chapel Hill, NC 27514
  (919) 942-2855

* Sandhills Woman's Exchange
  PO Box 215
  Pinehurst, NC 28374
  (919) 942-2855

OHIO

* The Chagrin Valley
  Woman's Exchange, Inc.
  The Sassy Cat
  88 N. Main Street
  Chagrin Falls, OH 45202
  (216) 247-5033

Contemporary Art Center
  115 E. Fifth Street
  Cincinnati, OH 45202
  (513) 721-0390

PENNSYLVANIA

† Elder Craftsmen of Philadelphia
  1628 Walnut Street
  Philadelphia, PA 19103
  (215) 545-7888

† The Helping Hand
  28 York Street
  Hanover, PA 17331
  (717) 637-4688

† Vintage, Inc.
  401 N. Highland Avenue
  Pittsburgh, PA 15206
  (412) 361-5003

† Senior Craftsmen Shop
  (St. Luke's Church)
  232 Wyoming Avenue
  Scranton, PA 18503
  (717) 344-7089

Artisans Cooperative
  Box 216
  Chadds Ford, PA 19317
  (215) 388-1437

* Chestnut Hill Woman's
  Exchange
  8419 Germantown Avenue
  Philadelphia, PA 19118
  (215) 247-5911

Craft cooperative
* Member of the Federation of Woman's Exchanges
† Elder Craftsmen-type Shop

* The Old York Road Woman's
  Exchange
  429 Johnson Street
  Jenkintown, PA 19046
  (215) 885-2470

* Woman's Exchange of the
  Neighborhood League
  185 E. Lancaster Avenue
  Wayne, PA 19087
  (215) 688-1431

* The Woman's Exchange of
  Reading
  720 Penn Avenue
  West Reading, PA 19611
  (215) 373-0960

* The Woman's Exchange of
  W. Chester
  10 S. Church Street
  West Chester, PA 19382
  (215) 696-3058

* The Woman's Exchange of
  Yardley
  47 W. Afton Avenue
  Yardley, PA 19380
  (215) 493-8710

SOUTH CAROLINA

† Clown's Bazaar
  9 Broad Street
  Charleston, SC 29401
  (803) 723-9769

SOUTH DAKOTA

† Prairie People's Handicrafts
  Armour, SD 57313
  (605) 724-2404

TENNESSEE

Rugby Craft Commissary
  P.O. Box 8
  Rugby, TN 37733
  (615) 628-5166

Community Craft Co-op
  P.O. Box 608
  North, TN 37716
  (615) 494-9854

* The Woman's Exchange of
  Memphis
  88 Racine Street
  Memphis, TN 38111
  (901) 327-5681

TEXAS

† Menard Area Arts & Crafts
  P.O. Box 1135
  Menard, TX 76859
  (915) 396-2506

† Thrift & Gift Shop
  310 No. Fifth St.
  Orange, TX 77630
  (409) 886-7649

* St. Michael's Woman's Exchange
  5 Highland Park Village
  Dallas, TX 75205
  (214) 521-3862

Craft cooperative
* Member of the Federation of Woman's Exchanges
† Elder Craftsmen-type Shop

* Handcrafts Unlimited
P.O. Box 1191
Georgetown, TX 78627-1191
(512) 869-1812

UTAH

† Craft Corner
55 E. Main
Price, UT 84501
(801) 637-3164

VIRGINIA

† Norfolk Gift Shop
924 West 21st Street
Norfolk, VA 23517
(804) 625-5857

† Sr. Center Gift Shop
305 High Street
Portsmouth, VA 23704
(804) 398-3777

† Rooftop Crafts of VA
206 North Main Street
Galax, VA 24333
(703) 236-7131

† Elder Crafters Inc.
405 Cameron St.
Alexandria, VA 22314
(703) 683-4338

Cave House
279 E. Main Street
Abingdon, VA 24210
(703) 628-7721

VIRGIN ISLANDS

Craft Co-op
4 Back Street
St. Thomas, VI 00801
(809) 774-4291

WASHINGTON

† Northwest Senior Craftsmen
Pier 70—Foot of Broad Street
Seattle, WA 98121
(206) 441-2780

† Golden Crafts
105 E. Front St.
Port Angeles, WA 98362
(206) 457-0509

WEST VIRGINIA

* Cabin Creek Quilts
15085 MacCorkle Avenue
P.O. Box 383
Cabin Creek, WV 25035
(304) 595-3928

WISCONSIN

† Walworth County Sr. Center
P.O. Box 1006
Elkhorn, WI 53121
(414) 741-3169

† Craft House 55
6616 Odana Road
Madison, WI 53719
(608) 829-2455

#Craft cooperative
*Member of the Federation of Woman's Exchanges
**Elder Craftsmen-type Shop

Seniors Abroad is a nonprofit international homestay program for mature adults. The program arranges homestays among persons over 50 in the United States, Japan, Denmark, Norway, Sweden, New Zealand, and Australia.

The program promotes volunteerism, informal social supports, and community-service system development.

> Seniors Abroad
> 12533 Pacato Circle North
> San Diego, CA 92128
> (619) 485-1696

Educational Network for Older Adults is concerned with adult education, employment issues, volunteerism, and older women.

The Network assists and counsels older adults who need information about educational opportunities and programs for older adults, maintains a resource center for older adults, and holds monthly seminars and workshops. There are no fees.

> The Education Network for Older Adults
> 350 Arballo Drive, Unit 12 H
> San Francisco, CA 94132
> (415) 586-2019

Retired Senior Volunteer Program International (RSVP) was begun as a pilot project over 20 years ago and has flourished and grown. Its mission: Implementation of the Senior Volunteer Programs in the United States and several countries abroad.

RSVP is involved in information dissemination and program development as well as the training of visitors from other countries. It publishes the "RSVP International Exchange" three times a year.

Retired Senior Volunteer Program International
RSVP International
261 Madison Avenue
New York, NY 10016
(212) 687-7788

Generations Together was established to promote interaction between the young and the old and occupies a unique niche in intergenerational programming. The Center is interested "in promoting opportunities for entry or re-entry by older persons into the workplace."

Areas of activity for Generations Together include community outreach, program development, research, and information dissemination.

Generations Together
University Center for Social
  and Urban Research
University of Pittsburgh
811 William Pitt Union
Pittsburgh, PA 15260
(412) 648-7155

The Gray Panthers was founded by social activist Maggie Kuhn as a grass-roots movement to challenge and eliminate age discrimination. Targeted concerns include Social Security and pension policy and restructuring the work place to accommodate older workers.

There are almost 100 Gray Panther networks in 30 states with formal regional structures in the Northeast and Midwest as well as in California. The organization enjoys consultative status with the United Nations. Internationally, many countries have formed organizations similar to Gray Panthers.

Gray Panthers Project Fund, Inc.
311 South Juniper Street, Suite 601
Philadelphia, PA 19107
(215) 545-6555

**The American Federation of Labor and Congress of Industrial Organizations
(AFL-CIO),** through its Department of Occupation Safety,
Health and Social Security, provides guidance and information
on a broad array of programs related to its objectives.
This includes programs relating to older and retired workers.
Issues of retirement, older workers, and older women are
among the organization's concerns.

American Federation of Labor
  and Congress of Industrial Organizations
815 16th Street NW
Washington, DC 20006
(202) 637-5000

**American Federation of State, County and Municipal Employees Retiree
Program** has 115,000 union members who are government
retirees. The organization is involved in federal programs
that involve senior citizens. It publishes a newsletter, "Retiree Rights."

There are 21 chapters and 150 subchapters of the Retiree
Council nationwide.

American Federation of State, County
  and Municipal Employees Retiree Program
1525 L Street NW
Washington, DC 20036
(202) 429-1274

The Urban Institute is a private, nonprofit research and educational organization. Retirement, older women, Social Security and pension policy, and the employment of mature

adults are among the Institute's concerns in the field of aging. The Institute has a particular interest in the retirement decisions of women.

The Urban Institute
2100 M Street NW
Washington, DC 20037
(202) 833-7200

The National Urban League conducts job-training programs in more than 100 cities for workers 55 and over. The organization's main focus is on job training for the underprivileged, but it also helps mature workers seeking employment who do not qualify as "underprivileged."

National Urban League Headquarters
500 East 62nd Street
New York, NY 10021
(212) 310-9000

U.S. Department of Labor (DOL) seeks to assist all Americans who want to work, but special efforts are made to meet the unique job-market problems of older workers.

The DOL's Division of Older Workers Programs in the Employment and Training Administration administers the Senior Community Service Employment Program. This program, authorized by Title V of the Older Americans Act, makes subsidized, part-time job opportunities available in community-service activities. Low-income persons aged 55 and over are eligible for these subsidized jobs.

The Employment and Training administration has three major components that are responsible for the administration of programs relating to older workers: Office of Job Training Program (Job Training Partnership Act); Office of Special Targeted Programs; and the Division of Older Worker Programs, which is involved in formulating employment policy and for training services for persons 55 and over.

U.S. Department of Labor
Employment and Training Administration
Division of Older Worker Programs
200 Constitution Avenue NW
Washington, DC 20210
(202) 535-0521

U.S. Equal Employment Opportunity Commission (EEOC) seeks to assist older persons who believe that they have been discriminated against in employment because of age. It's the Commission's job to vigorously enforce the Age Discrimination in Employment Act, which prohibits employment discrimination against workers or job applicants over 40 years of age.

The EEOC operates through a 48-field-office structure, which integrates legal and complaint processing functions.

Publications on various aspects of age discrimination are available free of charge from the Commission.

U.S. Equal Employment Opportunity
Commission (EEOC)
2401 E Street NW
Washington, DC 20507
(202) 634-6036

The Senior Community Service Employment Program (SCSEP), funded under Title V of the Older Americans Act, is a work-training program designed to help economically disadvantaged persons aged 55 and older find jobs. The program reviews the skills and interests of job applicants in order to help local employers locate qualified employees. The specific services offered by SCSEP vary by location and sponsoring organization.

You can reach a local SCSEP program by checking your telephone directory or by contacting the Office on Aging in your state.

The Job Training Partnership Act (JTPA) focuses on job training and employment referrals for the "economically disadvantaged," with at least 3 percent of the funds allocated to each state reserved for training disadvantaged persons aged 55 and older. The program's goal is job placement with private businesses.

JTPA may also serve older workers who face employment barriers such as age discrimination even if they do not meet the program's income requirements.

A free copy of the JTPA Service Delivery Area directory is available on request.

National Association of Counties
440 First Street NW
Washington, DC 20001

For Further Reading

Allen, Jeffery G., and Jess Gorkin, *Finding the Right Job at Midlife* (New York: Simon & Schuster, 1985)

Arden, Lynie, *The Work-at-Home Sourcebook* (Boulder, CO: Live Oak Publications, 1990)

Baker, Jeremy, *Tolstoy's Bicycle* (New York: St. Martins Press, 1982)

Bloomberg, Gerri, and Margaret Holdern, *The Woman's Job Search Handbook* (Carlotte, VT: Williamson Publishing, 1991)

Bolles, Richard Nelson, *The 1992 What Color Is Your Parachute?* (Berkeley, CA: Ten Speed Press)

Broudy, Eve, *Professional Temping* (New York: Macmillan Publishing, 1989)

Carter, Jimmy, and Rosalynn Carter, *Everything to Gain: Making the Most of the Rest of Your Life* (New York: Random House, 1987)

Eyler, David R., *Starting & Operating a Home-Based Business* (New York: John Wiley & Sons, 1990)

Foster, Dennis L., *The Complete Franchise Book* (Rocklin, CA: Prima Publishing, 1988)

Fries, James F., *Aging Well* (Reading, MA: Addison-Wesley Publishing Co., 1989)

Goldstein, Harold, and Bryna Shore Fraser, *Getting a Job in the Computer Age* (Princeton, NJ: Peterson's Guides)

Hansen, Leonard J., "Life Begins at 50" (*Barron's Educational Series*, 1989)

Keefe, John and George Leute, *Exploring Careers in the Sunbelt* (New York: The Rosen Publishing Group, 1984)

Kipps, Harriet Clyde, editor, *Volunteerism: The Directory of Organizations, Training Programs and Publications* (New Providence, NJ: R. R. Bowker)

Lacey, Dan, *The Paycheck Disruption* (New York: Hippocrene Books, 1988)

Lussier, Donald E., *The Homemaker's Complete Guide to Entering the Job Market* (Englewood Cliffs, NJ: Prentice-Hall, 1984)

Maltzman, Jeffrey, *Jobs in Paradise* (New York: Harper & Row, 1990)

McDaniels, Carl, *The Changing Workplace* (San Francisco: Jossey-Bass Publishers, 1989)

Menchin, Robert S. *The Mature Market: A Strategic Marketing Guide to America's Fastest Growing Population Segment* (Chicago: Probus, 1989)

Morris, Desmond, *The Book of Ages* (New York: Viking Press, 1983)

Mowsesian, Richard, *Golden Goals, Rusted Realities* (Far Hills, NJ: New Horizon Press, 1986)

Myers, Albert, and Christopher P. Anderson, *Success over Sixty* (New York: Summit Books, 1984)

Olsen, Scott C., *250 Home-Based Jobs* (New York: Arco, 1990)

Salmon, Richard D., *The Job Hunters Guide to the Sunbelt* (Cambridge, MA: Brattle Publications, 1983)

Shank, Howard, *Managing Retirement* (Chicago: Contemporary Books, 1985)

U.S. Senate Special Committee on Aging, "Aging America: Trends and Projections," U.S. Printing Office, Washington, DC

Willing, Jules Z., *The Reality of Retirement* (New York: William Morrow & Co., 1981)

Zimmeth, Mary, *The Women's Guide to Re-entry Employment* (Mankato, MN: Gabriel Books, 1979)

The race is over,
but the work never is done
while the power to work remains
. . . It cannot be, while you still live.
For to live is to function.
That is all there is to living.

∎ ∎ ∎

—Oliver Wendell Holmes,
in a radio address on March 8, 1932,
his ninetieth birthday.

INDEX